The *Million* Dollar Car ᵃⁿᵈ *$250,000* Pizza

HOW EVERY DOLLAR YOU SAVE BUILDS YOUR FINANCIAL FUTURE

The *Million* Dollar Car and *$250,000* Pizza

Allyson Lewis, CFP

DEARBORN™
A **Kaplan Professional** Company

This publication is designed to provide accurate and authoritative information in regard to the subject matter covered. It is sold with the understanding that the publisher is not engaged in rendering legal, accounting, or other professional service. If legal advice or other expert assistance is required, the services of a competent professional person should be sought.

Associate Publisher: Cynthia A. Zigmund
Managing Editor: Jack Kiburz
Interior and Cover Design: Design Solutions
Cover Photo: Sara Trimarchi
Typesetting: the dotted i

Visual illusions at the beginning of Chapters 1 through 11 courtesy of Y&B Associates, Inc., 33 Primrose Lane, Hempstead, NY 11550.

Library of Congress Cataloging-in-Publication Data
Lewis, Allyson.
    The million dollar car and $250,000 pizza : how every dollar you save builds your financial future / Allyson Lewis.
      p.   cm.
    Includes index.
    ISBN 0-7931-3593-1 (paper)
    1. Finance, Personal. 2. Investments. 3. Saving and investment. I. Title.
HB179.L48 2000
332.024'01—dc21   99-054458

To **Mark**, **Abby**, and **J. Mark, Jr.**

• ➤

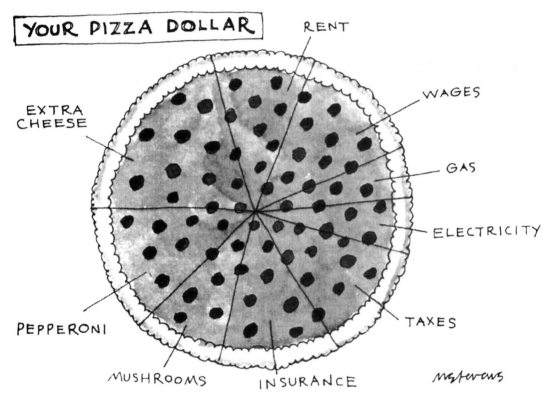

YOUR PIZZA DOLLAR

RENT

WAGES

GAS

ELECTRICITY

TAXES

EXTRA CHEESE

PEPPERONI

MUSHROOMS

INSURANCE

Contents

Preface, ix

Acknowledgments, xi

Part 1
The Seven Steps to Creating Your Financial Plan

1 First Things First: Create Your Mission Statement, 3
2 Step 2: Gather the Necessary Data, 21
3 Step 3: Establish Your Written Financial Goals, 61
4 Steps 4–7: Take Action, 79

Part 2
Understanding Your Investment Options

5 The Ten Myths of Investing, 91
6 The Ten Truths of Investing, 107
7 Your Investment Alternatives, 129
8 The Five Laws of Successful Investing, 161
9 Analyzing Your Investment Choices, 179
10 What Type of Investment Makes Sense?, 209

Part 3
Putting Your Plan Into Action

11 Choosing Your Financial Adviser, 221
12 Let's Get Real: Case Studies, 233
13 College Planning, Gift-Giving Strategies, and Estate Planning, 267
14 It's Your Turn, 283
15 Staying Motivated, 299

Appendix A The Inflation and Future Value Calculator, 303
Appendix B Monthly Savings Calculator, 307
Appendix C How Many Years Will $100,000 Last?, 309
Appendix D IRS Life Expectancy Tables, 311
Appendix E Social Security Benefits Information, 313
Appendix F How a $10,000 Investment Would Have Performed from December 31, 1988, through December 31, 1998, 315

Index, 317

Preface

In my role as a financial adviser, I often see at least one very specific monthly outflow of about $340 representing a monthly car payment.

What if we took that same $340 and every month placed it in a stock mutual fund through a 401(k) plan? Assuming an average annual rate of return of 9 percent starting at age 30, that money could grow to $1 million by age 65!

"That's great," you say, "but I already have a car. I need it to get around, and I'm stuck with the payments." Instead, let's look at something else. What if you are simply taking your family out for pizza once a week? If that meal costs you at least $20 a week, that $20 a week could be costing your family an additional $250,000!

Our financial futures all boil down to the choices we make: how you choose to spend your money today definitely impacts how you live tomorrow. Does this mean you should never buy a new car or never take your family out for pizza? Of course not! It does mean that you need a plan, a plan that helps you focus on where you are today, where you need to be in the future, and how you'll get there.

It's really that simple.

Naturally, I think *everyone* should use a professional financial adviser, whether he has $1,000 to invest or $1 million. As you'll see in Chapter 11 on choosing a financial planner, two heads can definitely achieve more than one. However, I'm also realistic enough to know that not all of you will engage a financial professional to help you achieve your goals. That's where *The Million Dollar Car and $250,000 Pizza* comes in. The book is designed for those of you who realize that money plays a significant role in your life. You know you need a financial plan, but you have never been given the tools to create that plan—until now. Even if you haven't had formal investment training, by the time you finish this book you'll have the knowledge you need to make informed—and intelligent—investment choices. So whether you're currently working with an adviser, thinking about using one, or going solo, this book can help.

In Part I, "The Seven Steps to Creating Your Financial Plan," you will answer three critical questions: Where are you today? Where do you want to be tomorrow? How will you get there? The seven steps to creating your financial plan are clearly laid out in an easy-to-follow format and include several forms to make the process even easier. By the time you finish Part I, you'll be well under way to creating your own financial plan.

In Part 2, "Understanding Your Investment Options," I'll dispel some of the common myths of investing and reinforce your knowledge with certain truths. You'll also learn about the five laws of successful investing and how to incorporate them into your own plan.

You'll also learn the lingo and the theories about the investment options open to you, including stocks, bonds, and cash—yes, cash is a critical part of any financial plan! If you are wondering how to choose between a short-term CD and an aggressive growth mutual fund, you'll find out how in Part 2. You'll come away from this section knowledgeable and confident about the financial decisions you need to make in developing and managing your financial plan.

In Part 3, "Putting Your Plan into Action," you'll learn how to choose a financial adviser to help you realize your dreams and put together all the information you've learned in previous chapters into a comprehensive financial plan.

The book is loaded with forms to help you implement your plan and make your financial dreams a reality. Also included are anecdotes and case studies to help you see how a good financial plan—and your financial goals—might be closer than you think.

Most of you want to do a good job managing money. You've worked long and hard to earn it. By the time you finish reading this book, you will have taken the time to complete the action steps at the end of each chapter and be able to say, "Now I know where I am today; I know without a doubt where I need to be in the future; and most important, I have a written plan that will get me there!"

Remember, there is no magical amount of money that will make you feel financially secure. Each person's security and happiness is rarely tied to the amount of money she has accumulated. Life is a gift that should be enjoyed. I hope that *The Million Dollar Car and $250,000 Pizza* will help you turn your dreams into reality.

Acknowledgments

Many wonderful people have worked with me to make this book a reality. I would like to begin by thanking my editor, Cynthia Zigmund, and all of the people at Dearborn for their wise counsel and guidance throughout this project, especially Sandy Holzbach, Jack Kiburz, Robin Nominelli, and Todd Schuetz.

Special thanks go to one of the true heroes of my life, Dr. Florence Krause, who served as the chair of the English department for William Woods University in Fulton, Missouri. From freshman composition through my senior year, Dr. Krause was a mentor and friend.

Some readers may wonder how a young woman could ever have learned enough about the investment world to publish a book on the subject. Well, I learned from the very best. It was one of the highest privileges to work as a junior partner with George McLeod, a financial adviser with my firm, for 5 years of my career. His 30 years of experience and incredible passion for his work made a tremendous impact on the future success of my business.

Two companies have provided me a considerable amount of technical expertise and information. Wilson Associates International (17218 Rancho St., Encino, CA 91316; 818-999-0015) has been gracious enough to allow me to use a large amount of its performance data, which you will see in Chapter 8. Wilson Associates is a leader in teaching the concepts of Modern Portfolio Theory. Wiesenberger (1455 Research Blvd., Rockville, MD 20850; 800-232-2285) publishes a very useful book entitled *Investment Performance Digest,* which is updated every year, and allowed me to present historical data and other valuable information from its pages.

Throughout this book you will find various visual illusions. Most of these pictures were compiled by Y&B Associates Inc. (33 Primrose Lane, Hempstead, NY 11550; 516-481-0256).

This book would have been impossible to finish without the help of the following people: Linda Need, for helping write the sections on insurance; David Rubinowitz for his research assistance; Susan Russenberger and Karen Berry, for the initial edits and suggestions; Melissa Powell, for some of the original graphics; Tim Barnes, for additional artwork and typesetting; Shelley Brown, for being one of the few people in the country who can actually read my handwriting and for her keyboarding skills; and Dianne Bufford, for her manuscript suggestions and marketing skills.

I also want to thank all of my friends and clients who encouraged me every step of the way.

Also, thanks to my parents, Ann and Al White of Pine Bluff, Arkansas, who have always been a source of support and encouragement to me. From the time I was old enough to search the furniture cushions for loose change to the present day, they have always believed in me. I love them with all my heart.

I want to thank my husband, Mark Lewis. God knew exactly what He was doing when He allowed us to meet. Thank you, Mark, for being the greatest father to our children and for being my best friend.

Finally, financial security and faith have a lot in common. Neither can be seen nor touched, but they both make a dramatic impact on our life. I have been very blessed to have had a personal faith in Jesus Christ since I was a teenager. Special thanks are therefore given to God.

PART ONE

The Seven Steps to Creating Your Financial Plan

First Things First
Create Your Mission Statement

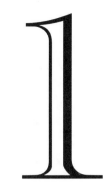

> **"**My investing has been called the 'gorilla approach.' Buy the biggest, the best, and the uncontested leader in the stock sectors you determine to be growing the fastest.**"**
> **Richard Mason,** 61
> *El Dorado, Arkansas*

> **"**If I could do it all over again, I would have invested a certain percentage of my income every month.**"**
> **Elizabeth S. Mitchell,** over 70
> *Little Rock, Arkansas*

> **"**It is never too late to start over again.**"**
> **Dennis Nordlund,** 57
> *Little Rock, Arkansas*

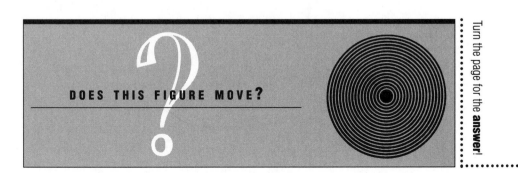

DOES THIS FIGURE MOVE?

Turn the page for the **answer!**

As a matter of fact, it doesn't. The figure is a printed set of circles, yet it creates the illusion of movement.

Investing and financial planning can be related to this illustration. The inside small solid circle could represent your personal written financial plan. All of the circles outside the solid circle can be the steps you take to implement your financial plan.

There will be times when outside forces will attempt to move you away from your written strategy. These may come in the form of stock market volatility, the birth of a new baby, or the acceptance of a new job. But you must be mentally prepared to rely on your written financial plan and realize that the outside forces are sometimes an illusion.

THREE STORIES

Story 1. Thelma Pearl Howard is a name few people know. Her story is an example of how a few people are able to create a large net worth without stopping to map out a written financial plan for themselves.

Thelma Pearl Howard was the epitome of a long-term investor. For a large portion of her adult life, Mrs. Howard worked as a housekeeper. For years she was given a small number of stock certificates in her employer's company. On various occasions these certificates would be given as gifts and over the years they began to accumulate.

The following is an excerpt from a story that was published in the *Orange County Register.*

August 4, 1996: Thelma Pearl Howard was born a poor farmer's daughter and died a millionaire thanks to Walt Disney, who hired her in the 1940s as his family's live-in housekeeper. For three decades. Howard helped raise Disney's children and grandchildren and stashed away the Disney stock she got as gifts.

When she died at 79, Howard left an estate worth $9 million.

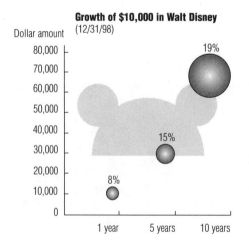

Growth of $10,000 in Walt Disney
(12/31/98)

Of course, not all of us are so blessed. Thelma Pearl Howard did not need a financial plan.

Story 2. In the early 1970s a brilliant man started a small retail company in the middle of America. If you had gone to work as a cashier in his company and made the decision to invest the maximum amount of money from your paycheck each week in his company's payroll deduction stock plan over the next 20 years, making no more than minimum wage, you would have been a millionaire.

That company was started by Sam Walton and the company stock is Wal-Mart. Literally thousands of people in northeast Arkansas have become financially independent by investing in this one company.

They did not need a financial plan.

Story 3. In 1984 a young man in Texas, with $1,000, was a student at the University of Texas. He had shown an interest in computers for some time. Not long after the semester was completed, he decided he could build higher-quality computers than IBM and sell them directly to the customer for a cheaper price.

Within 15 years, Michael Dell had turned Dell Computer Corporation into a household name. People who were able to invest in this stock during the early years have profited from being a part of the world's fastest-growing computer company. The value of Dell stock has grown so quickly that the media have coined a new word, *Dellionaires*.

These people did not need a financial plan. But these individuals are the exception rather than the rule.

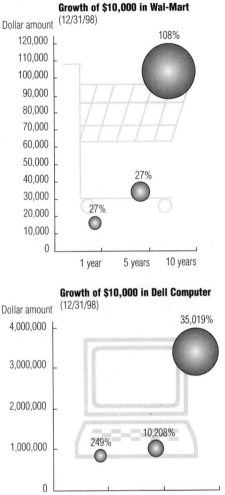

Growth of $10,000 in Wal-Mart (12/31/98)

Growth of $10,000 in Dell Computer (12/31/98)

MOST PEOPLE WORK HARD TO JUST GET BY

They will cash their paychecks and then worry about how to pay their bills. The average American has done *no* financial planning and feels trapped by money problems.

As I was researching the material for this book, I ran across an article by James Aley containing such startling information that I saved it to illustrate just how serious the problem can be if you don't take the time to create a well-defined strategy.

> In the real world, you must have a well-defined strategy if you hope to reach your future goals.

According to a study prepared for Merrill Lynch by Capital Research Associates of Chevy Chase, Maryland, the median net financial assets of U.S. households in 1993 was just $1,000. . . . Families headed by individuals 25 to 34 years old have median net financial assets of just $2 . . . [and] people between 55 and 64 had accumulated just under $7,000—an awfully meager amount considering the fact that someone retiring at the age of 65 has a life expectancy of 17 years. Americans are well aware of their savings predicament, yet they seem unwilling to do much about it. ("Skimpy Savings," *Fortune*, February 20, 1995: p. 38)

The numbers from the article in *Fortune* magazine are so shocking you may have missed their significance. The average American has financial assets of approximately $1,000, young people from 25 to 34 have a net of $2, and our soon-to-be-retiring generation has total financial savings of just under $7,000!

WHAT ABOUT YOU?

The Social Security Administration has stated that only 2 to 3 percent of Americans will be financially able to retire at the age of 65 with a comfortable standard of living. What will happen to the remaining 97 to 98 percent? They will be forced to

- reduce their standard of living;
- continue working;
- rely on other family members; and/or
- rely on outside assistance of some sort.

And beyond the lack of financial assets, as we age we should be asking where our retirement income will come from.

According to the U.S. Census Bureau, the average yearly income of Americans aged 65 and over is outlined in the chart at left.

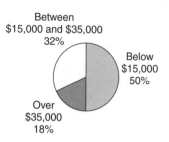

This information vividly illustrates the need for proper investment planning. It is amazing to realize that a full 50 percent of Americans aged 65 and over will attempt to live on an annual income of something less than $15,000. And that only 18 percent will have an income over $35,000. Most people want to be able to retire with an income stream of something close to what they are used to living on while they are working, yet these statistics reveal that most people haven't achieved that goal.

The first chapter of this book is devoted to increasing your odds of being among the 2 to 3 percent of Americans who have taken the appropriate steps to plan for their retirement years. The process is not a difficult one; it all boils down to asking three very simple questions:

1. **Where am I today?**
2. **Where do I need to be in the future?**
3. **How am I going to get there?**

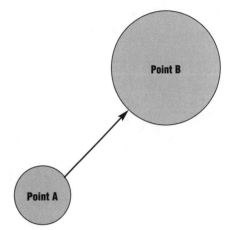

As you answer these questions thoughtfully and carefully, you will begin the path to financial independence. It's a simple path that just requires some honest evaluations and prudent choices.

Let's begin the process by briefly exploring how the answers to the three questions above can lead us down the path to financial independence.

How will you move from Point A (where you are today) to Point B (where you want to be in the future)?

Where Am I Today?

The honest answer for most investors is "I don't know" or "I'm not sure."

Most people have no idea how their financial life is currently structured. They don't know how much money they have in their checking accounts or their savings accounts. They don't know how much money they have in their IRA or 401(k) plans. They are not even sure they fully know how to read the investment statements they receive. Finally, they have absolutely no idea of how much credit card and other personal debt they currently owe.

Therefore, the very first step comes in discovering where you are today.

Where Do I Need to Be in the Future?

Again, most investors don't have a concrete answer for this question. They don't know how large their nest egg will need to be to accommodate their retirement goals.

How much will you need?

$100,000

$250,000

$500,000

$1,000,000

$2,500,000

$5,000,000

More?

Regardless of what you think you may need, it is critical that you determine a quantified amount and then answer the final question.

How Am I Going to Get There?

This is actually the simplest question. Once you know where you are today and where you need to be in the future, the answer boils down to a matter of math. A few quick financial calculations and "boom," your road map is clearly laid out for you. Then all you have to do is follow the map.

For example, if your plans says:

I am 25 years old, and I have zero financial assets and am $5,500 in debt with an interest rate of 12 percent. My plan is to get out of debt by paying $259 for 24 months and then begin to save 10 percent of every paycheck until I turn 65. By saving a fixed amount of $3,600 for 35 years (assuming a 9 percent annual rate of return), I could expect to accumulate a nest egg of approximately $776,558.71.

I will be able to save the extra $300 per month by keeping my current car and by taking my lunch to work four out of five days each week.

This may be an oversimplification of the process, but most financial plans can be created more simply than you realize. *The key to your success will be implementing the steps that are listed in the following chapters.* It is my hope that all of you reading this book will make a commitment to follow through with the steps outlined in the following pages.

This first section presents seven steps for creating your personal financial plan.

The second section provides information you need for a better understanding of various investment strategies. It also explains in detail many investment alternatives and how they can be researched and understood.

The third and final section explains how to choose your financial adviser and concludes with a recap of the information you have learned and a guide to designing your long-term strategy.

The title of this book, *The Million Dollar Car and $250,000 Pizza,* is intended to catch your attention. Lots of people imagine life without a car payment, yet they cannot imagine attempting to put a similar amount away to plan for their financial future. The thought of being required to find an extra $200 to $400 every month seems impossible to most of us, but somehow we are able to find that much to pay the minimum balances due on our credit card bills. Most of us won't hesitate to pick up the phone after a long day at work and order that $20 pizza for supper.

There is no doubt in my mind that having money and planning for your financial security are important. The problem is that most people have never been given the tools to budget their money wisely and make prudent investment decisions.

I see people every day who cash their paychecks and hope for the best. You don't have to be one of those people. There is a better way.

This book is intended to remove you from a day-to-day short-term focus on your current financial situation and help you look to your personal future. I hope you will step back, take a deep breath, and begin to believe that you are able to take control over how your retirement years will be spent. If you will take the time to carefully read this book and create your written road map, then your job becomes quite simple—all you will need to do is stay on the path you have clearly outlined.

I hope this is an exciting time for you. Imagine how you will feel five years from now, then ten years from now, and even on the day you plan to begin your retirement. Imagine being debt free. Imagine your accumulated nest egg. Imagine having your children's college education completely funded even before they graduate from high school. Imagine being able to give money away to help other people achieve their dreams.

It's simple for me to imagine your future success. Now it's time for you to be able to see that picture. But we must begin at the beginning. That means you must know what you are trying to accomplish with your money. You can only do this by implementing the seven-step process for successful financial management.

Seven-Step Process for Successful Financial Management

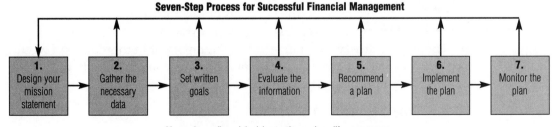

You and your financial adviser review and modify as necessary.

STEP 1: *Design Your Mission Statement*

As Stephen Covey says in his best-selling book *Seven Habits of Highly Effective People:* "The most effective way I know to begin with the end in mind is to develop a *personal mission statement* or philosophy or creed. It focuses on what you want to be (character) and to do (contributions and achievements) and on the values or principles upon which being and doing are based." (p.106, emphasis added)

Covey's thesis that we should "begin with the end in mind" is correct. We should look deep within ourselves and determine what is most important to us, and then we begin to design a lifestyle that helps us carry out and accomplish our mission.

What's important to me may not be important to you and vice versa. The action steps at the end of this chapter will prompt you to spend some time exploring the values and dreams that you consider important.

What's Important

Faith / Family / Friends / Nutrition / Exercise

Education / Vocation / Personal Wealth

Community Service / Research / Health. . .

to You?

These values and dreams will be more fully developed, but we all have dreams. We all have those moments when we sense there is something caged up inside our souls that is screaming to be let loose—those deep feelings that nag at our conscious and even our unconscious mind. Those are the ideas that need to be validated and given an opportunity to be fulfilled.

A mission statement is useful for spotlighting where we are presently. It is where we are now and the road map of the future, the direction we are headed, and the route we will take.

Our mission gives us purpose. The mission statement puts that purpose into words.

Dreams Bring Us Hope!

Yet these dreams need guidance and a clear, concise mission statement can be the foundation that moves your dreams closer to reality.

So . . . what's your mission?

There are many types of mission statements, but in this context I would like you to consider writing three separate mission statements that cover three different parts of your life experience:

1. **Personal mission statement**
2. **Vocational mission statement**
3. **Money mission statement**

The best way to tell you about mission statements is to share my own experience and how it has helped shape my attitude about my work and my money and myself.

It was only 3 years ago that I decided to create a mission statement for my business. I had been a stockbroker and financial adviser for almost 14 years. You would think in that amount of time I would have created a mission statement for my life's work. I knew what a mission statement was. I had read several of Steven Covey's books. I had even attended various conferences and seminars where people literally preached that every person needed a mission statement. I would politely nod my head, but I was not buying it.

But something inside my heart kept telling me, "Allyson, if you are just in this business to buy and sell stocks and bonds, maybe it's time you looked for another career." The truth is, selling stocks and bonds was just an occupation—that's not to say I didn't enjoy most of the work, but it was not enough, I wanted more. It was time to do some soul searching.

As I began asking myself the tougher questions and taking the time to pull away from the day-to-day busyness of my job, I began to realize there were several things I loved about my work and a few things I didn't like. Determined to make some changes, I decided to make a list of a few of the pros and cons of my business. It soon became clear that I needed to make a few changes.

Cons

- I couldn't control the movements in the stock market.
- I didn't like it when people lost money.
- There was a lot of administrative paperwork.
- The job required long hours.

Pros

- I loved meeting and working with people.
- I enjoyed the hectic pace and the new challenges.
- My personal aptitudes involve working with numbers and creative thinking.
- It was exhilarating at times.
- It was very rewarding to develop a written financial plan for new clients and watch them realize for the first time that they could attain financial independence.

- I absolutely *loved* teaching (both one-to-one and in a classroom). The happiest times were when someone's eyes lit up and I knew that person understood a new or difficult concept.
- It was fascinating to watch ordinary people begin to build sizable nest eggs for their future by implementing simple and prudent strategies into their financial plans.

All jobs have good and bad aspects, but I needed guidance and focus. So one day I grabbed a pen and a piece of paper. It was time to create my vocational mission statement. After much thought and effort, this is what emerged:

> We are all called to be stewards of our financial resources. My desire is to help my clients set written goals for their financial future and in turn help them invest wisely and prudently to reach those goals.

Let's take a closer look at this mission statement.

"We are all called to be stewards of our financial resources." This allows me to state emphatically why I try to help my clients' plan for their future. Each person has been given a certain amount of money. It doesn't matter if that amount is $1,000 or $10,000,000. It's each person's money and therefore each is called to take care of that asset. A steward is a person who carefully tends to something. It is my belief that each of my clients must tend to the resources each has been given.

The problem for many of the people who walk in my door is they don't know how to properly take care of their financial assets. They don't have any formal investment or financial planning education or simply don't have the time or the interest to manage those assets on a day-to-day basis.

"My desire is to help my clients set written goals for their financial future." You will read in more detail later in this section that very few Americans actually have written financial goals.

Again, if my clients don't have written goals, they will before they leave my office!

"And in turn help them invest wisely and prudently to reach those goals." This statement stresses the fact that I want to work within the guidelines of wise and prudent actions. It brings integrity to my work and makes me take pride in what I do for a living, but *the last three words of my statement bring life to my work.*

If I can look back in 5, 10, and 20 years and be able to say, "What a blessing that Mr. Smith was able to reach his goal to retire" or "Mrs. Jones was able to reach her goal and help put her two grandchildren through college" or, sadly, "Yes, I heard about Mr. White's accident, but because of careful planning his wife and children will be financially secure," then I will have reached my goals.

My mission statement represents my values, my hopes, and my dreams. And it truly has made my day-to-day life different. I am focused on helping my clients become better stewards of their personal resources. I am determined to help my clients set written goals, and, finally, I am committed to helping them reach their personal goals. This gives my job meaning and purpose, and it makes me excited to do what I do.

Obviously, the statement I've set down above is my *vocational* mission statement. While that is a wonderful place for you to start, you should also create other mission statements, including your *money mission statement.* This statement is the lighthouse for all the financial decisions you make for yourself and/or your family. Your money mission statement should answer many questions for you, including these:

- What purpose does money have in my life?
- What role does money play?
- Do I wrap my self-worth in the amount of money I make?
- What do I intend my money to do for me?
- What sacrifices, if any, am I willing to make today to reach future goals?
- What do I expect financial security to bring to my life?
- How important is financial planning to me at this stage in my life?
- Who will help me attain my goals?
- What am I trying to accomplish?
- What am I trying to prove?
- How does giving money away fit into my planning?
- Is making money the ultimate goal in my life?
- How much is enough?

Your money mission statement will be as individual as you are. It will establish the foundation on which everything else will be built. If you gain nothing else from this book, *designing a mission statement for how you will allow money to be a part of your life is well worth the effort.*

Here is my family's money mission statement.

> Our goal is to develop a written financial plan that will allow the Lewis family to be good financial stewards of what we have, including:
> - Setting aside at least 10 percent to be given away to our church
> - Setting aside at least 10 percent to be saved for future needs
> - Setting aside a certain portion to be put into long-term retirement plans
> - Setting aside a certain portion to be earmarked for our children's education
> - Tracking and analyzing our expenses on an annual basis and adjusting what we determine to be out of line
>
> Money is not our only security, because many things are much more important than money . . . faith, family, good health, friends. Yet we will purposefully work to plan with and enjoy the money we have been given.

The first paragraph on my family's money mission statement covers a statement of certainty.

Money is indeed a fact of life. It is how we pay our bills and buy our food and clothes. Money is a system within our culture and we must work within its rules. In reality, money does have some control over the way we live our life. It can determine the type and size of home we live in, the furniture we buy, and the cars we drive.

But with a written financial plan we can all be better stewards of the money we have been given.

The second section of my family's money mission statement presents the five priorities that my family wants to implement. These are very specific goals and by putting them in writing, we have a much better opportunity to see them come true.

The third section of my family's money mission statement links our values and money. Money can't buy happiness. Most of us would rank many things higher than wealth, but it is important to plan and then to enjoy.

Whatever form your mission statements take, they should clearly and concisely represent and reflect you. Just as a person looking at your photograph would be able to see you, your mission statements should allow you and others to more easily understand the true underlying purpose of your missions.

The most difficult mission statement for me was a personal mission statement. I was looking for some magical phrase that could provide a vision of why my life had meaning and purpose. As I reflected on who I was and why I am here, I tried to write down what I wanted my life to mean.

I wanted to be a good wife, a good mother, and a good coworker. I wanted to be respected in my chosen vocation and I wanted to play a positive role in young people's life. We all have a picture of who we want to be. As I sorted out the pictures, the image finally boiled down to this:

My personal mission is to educate, motivate, and encourage.

These goals can apply to my family, my work, and myself. They can apply to my spiritual life and to my friendships.

The beauty of a personal mission statement is that it can be as long or as short as you want it to be, but it can free you to focus on the direction you want your life to take.

Now It's Your Turn!

At the end of each section you'll find the appropriate forms for implementing the ideas you've just read about. These action steps are designed to walk you simply and methodically through the financial planning process. If you will take the time to complete these important steps, by the end of the book you'll hold in your hand a document to bring you hope!

1

Your Mission Statements

Designing your mission statements is much like going on a journey. It should produce a feeling of excitement and anticipation. These statements will come from the depths of your heart and soul. They will be the driving force of your entire future and they will carry you through the times when progress is slow and difficult.

Remember there are many different types of mission statements. You should consider taking the time to create at least three different statements:

1. Your personal mission statement
2. Your vocational mission statement
3. Your money mission statement

While all three are very closely related, they build on each other. Your personal mission is the center of your focus, what you plan to accomplish with your life. Out of this will come your vocational mission statement, what you plan to accomplish with your work. And out of this will come your money mission statement, what you plan to accomplish with your money.

It is obvious that your beliefs about life will have a continual and evolving impact on your work. The type of work you choose as a vocation will likely have an impact on the amount of money you make, and the amount of money you make will in turn affect your life, which is why it is so critical to have a vision for the big picture.

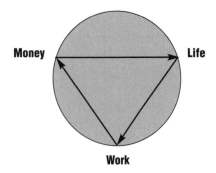

Too many people go through life without a clue about what their true purpose in life is. The truth is that money cannot buy you happiness. But that doesn't change the reality that money is a fact of life and you have been given the responsibility of doing your very best with what you have been given.

Your Personal Mission Statement

Find a quiet time and a quiet place with the following worksheets in front of you and begin to reflect on your current life. Write at least three to five positive things that you have contributed to your family, your workplace, or your community.

1. _____

2. _____

3. _____

4. _____

5. _____

What part of these positive memories do you value the most? Where do you find the most energy and strength? What do you believe is your life's mission?

_____

_____

_____

_____

Can you review this statement and shorten it or reduce it to one to three primary thoughts or objectives? Try to restate your final personal mission statement here:

_____

_____

_____

_____

Your Vocational Mission Statement

Review your personal mission statement.

Write at least three to five things that bring purpose and meaning to your work.

1. _____

2. _____

3. _____

4. _____

5. _____

Which of these aspects of your career or your life are the most important to you? Where do you find the most energy and strength? What do you believe is your work's mission?

_____

_____

_____

_____

Can you review this statement and shorten it or reduce it to one to three primary thoughts or objectives? Try to restate your final vocational mission statement here:

_____

_____

_____

_____

Your Money Mission Statement

Each mission builds on the last.

Write your personal hopes and aspirations of what your money means to you and how it controls and impacts your thoughts and actions.

1. _____

2. _____

3. _____

4. _____

5. _____

What do you believe is your money's mission?

_____

_____

_____

_____

Can you review this statement and shorten it or reduce it to one, two, or three primary thoughts or objectives? Try to restate your final money mission statement here:

_____

_____

_____

Armed with your mission statements, you will have a new vision for your life, your work, and your money. Take the time to put these mission statements on cards and post them in primary locations throughout your home and office. Carry a copy in your wallet. Let these mission statements be the road maps that guide your decisions. They will be an expression of your true values and aspirations.

Step 2: Gather the Necessary Data

> **"**Americans are hitting age 65 without adequate plans for retirement, according to a survey released by ReliaStar Financial Corp. of Minneapolis, Minnesota. The survey found that 71 percent of 65 year olds lack a written financial plan. Those folks (without a plan) are twice as likely (21 percent) to find retirement a time of financial worry as their counterparts with a plan (10 percent).**"**
>
> *Registered Investment Adviser* (November 10,1997)

> **"**A reporter once asked Albert Einstein, 'What do you consider the greatest invention of all time?' The reporter was confident that Einstein would say the wheel, the transistor, the microchip, or the printed circuit. The good doctor thought only a few seconds and then replied, 'Compound interest.' I'm sure the reporter thought himself the victim of some sort of genius humor and that he had failed to catch the punch line. However, a little thought about Einstein's answer reveals that none of the great inventions of the world would have benefited mankind without the working capital generated from compound interest. We all enjoy the benefits of compound interest every day!**"**
>
> **Bob M. Teegarden,** 61
> *Graham, Texas*

WHAT IS THIS?

Turn the page for the **answer!**

THE **ANSWER!**

When most people look at this illustration, they don't immediately realize they are looking at a color-reversed picture of the Gulf of Mexico, because they are seeing something in a new way and have no point of reference. You may feel this same frustration when attempting to gather the necessary data to create your financial plan. Your first job will be to change your point of view and, instead of focusing on the negative aspect of how much work it will be, focus on the outcome.

"Investing is not a sprint . . . it is a marathon.**"**
Stacey Harral, 32
Jonesboro, Arkansas

"In reference to what I would have done differently in my financial planning—it would be having a better way of saving. If only I had established a savings program when our children were young. Money management and setting up a budget would help all families who are just getting started. One of the best pieces of financial advice I ever received was to first ask, 'Do I really need this item and can I afford it now?' This is especially good advice for the way we live today.**"**
J.S., 70
El Dorado, Arkansas

GATHERING THE NECESSARY DATA

One of the best medical experiences I ever had was in November 1996 during a visit to the Mayo Clinic in Rochester, Minnesota. It was a terrible winter and I vividly remember walking out of the Rochester airport in subfreezing weather at 10:00 PM wondering why in the world I had decided to travel several hundred miles to have doctors I had never met review my case.

I had been told to appear on a certain floor of the main building at 8:00 AM the next morning. I walked into a waiting room with no fewer than 250 chairs lined up row by row, side by side. I checked in and sat down. By 10:00 AM the wait was growing wearisome. I had not been allowed to eat or drink since 10:00 PM the night before. They finally called my name and I was put into a private room. The doctor arrived, and for the next 45 minutes he did nothing but listen to my medical background. He had brought with him the lengthiest medical health history questionnaire I had every seen. Patiently he went through the questions one at a time. His concern was obvious. I felt as though he had no other patients to treat for the rest of the day. He was unhurried, which made the two-hour wait seem worth every minute.

Next, he left the room and I was asked to change into an examination gown. When he returned with his nurse, he again took the necessary time and paid very close attention to what I was telling him.

Only after listening carefully to my history and examining my current physical condition did he begin to schedule my tests for that day. Next came the blood work, the X-rays and the CAT scan. I felt the information necessary to make an appropriate diagnosis and prescribe treatment had been gathered.

All of the test results were in by the next day; it was determined that I had rheumatoid arthritis. Once the doctors knew what my ailment was, they were confident in their recommendations for treating the illness. The good news is they were right and I am fine.

This experience illustrates the importance of gathering data.

Even skilled doctors need to ask many questions and complete a thorough examination before they can identify a problem and recommend a plan of action.

What does this have to do with financial planning? Everything. You can't begin to develop your own financial plan unless you first have all the facts. *Good data is the key.* You must be honest and the data must be current. Gathering data is one of the most difficult steps in financial planning. It is time consuming and requires a great deal of effort on your part. Most of us have our financial records scattered in various places, and budgeting is a joke. We say we know how much we spend, but basically we spend until the checking account runs dry and we begin to run for cover.

Consider that now for the very first time you are going to make a commitment to organize your finances. That involves answering many difficult questions and then analyzing the information and determining a course of action.

What Data Will You Need?

To gather the proper data you will need to find the following documents:

1. **Assets**
   - Current bank statements—checking, savings, IRAs, and the like
   - Brokerage or insurance IRA statements
   - Current personal brokerage statements

- Current mutual fund statements
- A listing of all stock and bond certificates held in a lockbox or at home
- Annuities
- Life insurance policies
- Business ownership valuations
- Retirement benefit statements—401(k), pension, deferred compensation, and so on
- A listing of any tangible investments—land, precious metals, collectibles, art, antiques, and the like
- A listing of ownership of any income-producing investments— rental houses, farmland, commercial property, mineral rights, oil and gas leases, and so on
- Any additional financial information

2. **Income**
   - Where does your primary income come from?
   - How stable is your income?
   - Will your income be increasing or decreasing—at what rate?
   - Do your receive commissions or bonuses?
   - Do you rely on alimony or other supplemental income?

3. **Debt**
   - What is the dollar amount of your total debt?
   - What is the dollar amount of your mortgage?
   - What is the dollar amount of your car loan(s)?
   - What is the dollar amount of your student loan(s)?
   - What is the dollar amount of your credit card debt?
   - What is the dollar amount of your other debt?
   - What interest rate corresponds with each loan?
   - What are the minimum payments and how much are you paying?
   - When do you anticipate paying off each loan?

4. **Budget**

After you have gathered the critical information, you'll need to take a long, hard look at your personal expenses.

Among the keys to achieving your future financial success are the choices you make with the money you're earning today. As the title of this book implies, too many people won't blink an eye at stretching their budget to the limit to buy a house they can't really afford or push their paycheck to the brink to buy a too-expensive car. Or they may have smaller recurring expenses they may want to reconsider.

Would you rather drive a "million-dollar car" and eat a "$250,000 pizza" or begin to plan for your financial future? How you choose to budget your money today will affect your future financial security. Doesn't it make sense that you would rather choose a more affordable home or a less expensive car today and find the extra $100 or $500 or $1,000 you know you will need to save for your future?

It's time to get excited about reviewing your budget and gaining control of your spending!

Reviewing Your Personal Spending

Budgeting is a simple mathematical process, but according to Larry Burkett of Christian Financial Concepts, only 45 percent of American families have taken the time to develop and implement a written monthly budget. Even fewer people put these numbers in writing and commit to reviewing them on a regular basis.

In an online survey on Larry Burkett's Web site *(www.cfcministry.org)*, Burkett collected the following information:

What Type of Budget Plan Do You Use?	
I have a written budget plan.	45%
I have a general idea of where my money goes.	33%
I try not to overdraw my checking account.	11%
I've never been on a budget.	9%
Budgeting doesn't work for me.	2%
(Total votes as of June 7, 1999: 493)	

Without a written budget, you're unable to know exactly how and where you're currently spending your money. It's no wonder that so many people feel unable to save for their future when they are so totally out of control with their spending. Most investors believe saving and investing are the first steps toward financial independence, but you must first gain control of your spending habits to be able to make room in your budget for savings.

If you will step back and reflect on the day-to-day frustrations you relate to money, the feeling of chaos will rank at the top of the list for most people. If you will take the time to bring some order to your spending, you will find more security in your day-to-day living.

HOW CAN YOU BEGIN THE BUDGETING PROCESS?

My family uses the Checkbook Method: at the end of the year we go through our checkbook and credit card statements to fit every transaction into the appropriate budget category. This was fairly easy to do because of the type of checking account we use, but we will highlight the various tools needed in Chapter 11. Once we had every transaction listed in the computer spreadsheet, it was easy to see where we were currently spending our money and to create a 12-month forward projecting budget for the next year.

Once we knew what we had actually spent the year before, we simply designed a budget worksheet and input the actual figures from last year and goals for the new year. Beside the goals was a blank line to let us track our actual spending on a month-by-month basis. Our goal was to stay within last year's amounts or even reduce the amounts in some areas.

This process is something my husband and I do together. It allows us to understand the current choices we are making with our income. And it further allows us to make decisions about how we hope to plan for the future.

Here is a story that may help you understand this freedom.

> A budget is not a restriction; it actually gives you more freedom.

An elementary school playground was surrounded by an old fence inside of which was a dirt path where the grass had been worn away by the feet of small children. One day the fence was torn down, and the teachers noticed how the young students had begun to congregate and play within a much smaller area toward the center of the playground. Once their "boundary" was removed, the children were no longer sure of the safe areas, so rather than having their freedom expanded, they actually gave up their freedom. The same is true with your money. A well-constructed budget will allow you to spend more freely. It will clearly define your boundaries and allow you to walk as close to the fence as you are willing. Without the boundaries that a budget provides, you are likely to find more frustration.

In office visits with many of my clients, I find that very few people really know where their money is actually going. They will comment, "We have an *idea* of how we spend it." But when I ask them to take the Checkbook Test, many people are surprised by the amount of money they spend on unbudgeted items.

The budget in Figure 2.1 is an example of using the Checkbook Method to find out exactly how you spent last year's money and how you can set specific goals for this year's budget. The family shown in this example has a combined income of $120,000 per year.

Notice in the example that this family wanted to increase savings and had worked hard to completely pay off the balance on their credit cards. The key to your success here is putting your budget in writing and monitoring your spending on a regular basis. You must be realistic when preparing your personal budget goals. If you are attempting to increase your savings, then increase it slowly. If you are attempting to reduce your overall spending, then try to look at the numbers and create a budget that is attainable.

If you are looking for places to reduce your monthly outflows, you may want to review some of the expenditures I call Money Magnets. Many purchases are Money Magnets—the little payments so subtle that you swear you will never miss the money. But at the end of the month you might be surprised if you add up all these expenses.

The Small Money Magnets

1.	Eating out at lunch	$5.00 × 20 days = $100
2.	Snacks at work	$1.00 × 20 days = $ 20
3.	Soft drinks at work	$2.00 × 20 days = $ 40
4.	Yogurt/ice cream for family	$4.00 × 5 days = $ 20
5.	Gum	$0.50 × 10 days = $ 5
6.	Internet connection	$ 25
7.	Extra phone line for Internet	$ 24
8.	Call waiting	$ 5
9.	Caller ID	$ 5
10.	Pager service	$ 20
11.	Subscriptions—magazines/papers	$ 20
12.	CDs (one per month)	$ 14
13.	Movie rentals (one per week)	$3.00 × 4 = $ 12
14.	Impulse purchases at the grocery store	$ 25
15.	Recreation—golf/tennis/aerobics	$ 50
16.	Pets—food/ grooming	$ 30

FIGURE 2.1   *The Checkbook Method*

Month	Last Year's Actual	This Year's Goal	This Year's Actual
Personal Savings/Investments	250	350	
Retirement Investments	833	833	
Mortgage/Rent	1200	1200	
Electric Utility	200	200	
Gas Utility	50	50	
Telephone/Other Phone Costs	75	75	
Cell Phone	50	50	
Pager	20	20	
Water	25	25	
Cable TV	33	33	
Home Maintenance	150	150	
Lawn Maintenance	50	50	
Real Estate Taxes			
Car Payment	340	340	
Car Insurance	200	200	
Gasoline	125	125	
Car Maintenance	20	20	
Food/Groceries	700	700	
Tolietries			
Eating Out	400	400	
Entertainment	100	100	
Clothing	200	200	
Vacations	200	200	
Childcare/Dependent Care	300	300	
Tuition			
Visa	250	0	
MasterCard			
Discover	75	0	
Other Consumer Debt			
Student Loans			
Homeowners Insurance			
Health Insurance			
Life Insurance	100	100	
Disability Insurance	50	50	
Doctors - Copay	35	35	
Dentists	15	15	
Eyeglasses	15	15	
Prescription Drugs	25	25	
Household Help	175	175	
Dry Cleaning	125	125	
Beauty Salon/Barber	41	41	
Pets/Vet			
Subscriptions	20	20	
Florists	20	20	
Gifts	300	300	
Church Donations	1000	1000	
Community Donations	50	50	
Art/Dance/Misc. Personal	30	30	
CPA	30	30	
Professional Dues			
Club Dues	45	45	
Miscellaneous	200	200	
Other			
Totals	**$8,122**	**$7,897**	

This list of Money Magnets alone adds up to a whopping $415 per month. The items are like little magnets. They pull money out of your budget, but because each is such a small amount, you are unaware of the overall impact. If you are a smoker, cigarettes can be very expensive—$2 per pack × 30 days can add an additional $60 per month to your expenses.

Assuming you are willing to review the small money magnets in your budget, would saving and investing this amount of money make any difference in your financial future?

If you have a budget problem, should you sell your house? That is a very difficult question and can only be answered by you. But I've

Monthly	5 Years	10 Years	15 Years	20 Years	25 Years
$ 50	$ 3,678	$ 9,208	$ 17,417	$ 29,647	$ 47,868
100	7,397	18,417	34,835	59,295	95,737
250	18,492	46,041	87,086	148,237	239,342
500	36,983	92,083	174,173	296,474	478,683
1,000	73,966	184,165	348,345	592,947	957,366

Assumes an annual investment return of 8% compounded monthly but does not reflect the impact of taxes.

had more than one couple in my office who have found themselves in very difficult financial straits. After going through the necessary budgeting process, they realize the primary culprits are their home, their cars, and their consumer debts.

Some of these people won't be able to continue meeting their monthly expenses, much less begin to save for their financial goals, without making drastic cuts in some of their large outgoing expenses. The good news is that most investors will be just fine.

Regardless, it is important to have a clear understanding of where your money is going. You may want to review your big money magnets before moving on.

> A well-defined family budget is one of the keys to your financial success.

In Figure 2.2, you will find a budget worksheet. Why not take the Checkbook Test to see how you are *really* spending your money.

The Big Money Magnets
1.   A large house
2.   Large car payments
3.   Too much personal debt
4.   Large cell phone bills
5.   Clothes
6.   Dining out
7.   Overspending on Christmas and birthday presents

FIGURE 2.2   *Budget Worksheet*

	MONTH 1	MONTH 2	YEARLY AVERAGE
Personal Savings/Investments			
Retirement Investments			
Mortgage			
Electric Utility			
Gas Utility			
Telephone			
Water			
Cable TV			
Home Maintenance			
Lawn Maintenance			
Real Estate Taxes			
Personal Property Taxes			
Car Payment			
Car Insurance			
Gasoline			
Car Maintenance			
Food			
Toiletries			
Clothing			
Entertainment			
Visa/Amex/MasterCard/Loans			
Vacations			
Childcare/Dependent Care			
Tuition			

	MONTH 1	**MONTH 2**	**YEARLY AVERAGE**
Homeowners Insurance			
Health Insurance			
Life Insurance			
Disability Insurance			
Doctors			
Dentists			
Eyeglasses			
Drugs			
Household Help			
Dry Cleaning			
Beauty Salon/Barber			
Pets/Vets			
Subscriptions			
Florists			
Gifts			
Church Donations			
Community Donations			
Art and Dance			
CPA			
Professional Dues			
Miscellaneous			
Other Club Dues/Car Phones			
Other			
MONTHLY TOTAL			

Armed with the information uncovered in Figure 2.2, you can review your income and your expenses. If you are like many people, you may be wondering how you are currently making ends meet even though you are committed to making your money begin to work for you.

There are three typical scenarios: (1) your current expenses are exceeding your current income; (2) your current expenses meet your current income but are more than you would like; or (3) your current income exceeds your expenses.

Scenario #1: Your current expenses are exceeding your current income.

This is the time for an honest evaluation of exactly how you are spending your money. Have you purchased a home or a car that has put a strain on your ability to pay your monthly bills? Have you built up sizable balances on various credit cards and are now unable to keep up?

If you have found yourself in such a situation, please don't despair, but you must realize that difficult situations sometimes require difficult solutions.

Here are some ideas for consideration:

- Create a series of concrete steps to correct the problem.
- Put your current budget in writing.
- Review your current budget and highlight the areas of spending that could be reduced or eliminated.
- Make a list of every fixed expense—especially consumer debt. List each balance, to whom the debt is owed, what the minimum payment is, how much you are paying, and when you can expect to pay off each debt.
- Create a timeline for reducing your debt.
- Commit to not creating additional debt regardless of the situation.
- Consider using a cash budget for one or two months—you place the necessary amount of money for each budget category into an appropriately labeled envelope budgeted for that month and the spending for that category stops until the next budget cycle when the envelope is empty.

LET'S TALK ABOUT DEBT

Consumer debt is one of the biggest problems most people face. Credit allows you to buy something today by committing dollars you hope to earn in the future. By using credit you are immediately reducing the amount of available money you will have next week, next month, and/or next year. Doesn't this strike you as implementing exactly the opposite strategy of the one you'd like? Don't you actually want to have *more* money available next week, next month, and next year? Of course you do.

It's a lot easier to explain debt by comparing real-life scenarios. Assume your family wants to buy a new dining room table and chairs. The set costs $1,650. For this example, I called a local discount furniture company and asked about their current financing plans. The employee put me in touch with the out-of-state bank that currently handles all of the company's work. The interest rate as of April 4, 1999, was a whopping 20.65 percent. On a $1,650 purchase, the buyer would be required to pay back at least 3 percent of the loan each month for a minimum payment of approximately $50 per month.

Let's compare buying the set on credit and saving for the purchase. (See Figure 2.3.)

Notice the difference in the number of months it takes to pay for the furniture under each scenario. Using credit, it will take just over 47 months to pay off the loan. But saving takes only 32 months. And the overall cost of the dining room suite is $2,338.57 after you pay all of the interest charges, whereas the total cost would be only $1,600 if you saved for the purchase because you would earn an additional $62.95 in interest. This illustration assumes that the purchase price doesn't increase over the 32 months. If the price increased 10 percent as a result of inflation, you might have to save for an additional 3 months. The benefits are still clear.

It quickly becomes apparent that buying on credit is a poor choice. All of us want it now, but the reality check comes at the end of the month when we are sitting at a desk full of bills and receiving a paycheck that never quite seems to be enough. Is that really how you want to live for the rest of your adult life? No.

None of us really wants to live on the financial edge, but so many of us do and don't know what to do about it. Let's be specific. Stop reading right now and gather up every single bill you have, including fixed expenses, extra expenses, and all of your consumer debt (including credit card bills).

Line up the credit card bills and other consumer debt obligations and make a list. Include the names of the payers, the current amounts owed, the interest rates, and the minimum payments.

FIGURE 2.3   *Buying on Credit (20.65%) with a Purchase Price of $1,650 versus Saving (3.00%) and Paying Cash*

	Date	Payment	Interest	Balance		Date	Deposit	Interest	Balance
1	04/01/99	50		1650	1	04/01/99	50		50
2	05/01/99	50		1600	2	05/01/99	50		100
3	06/01/99	50		1550	3	06/01/99	50		150
4	07/01/99	50		1500	4	07/01/99	50		200
5	08/01/99	50		1450	5	08/01/99	50		250
6	09/01/99	50		1400	6	09/01/99	50		300
7	10/01/99	50		1350	7	10/01/99	50		350
8	11/01/99	50		1300	8	11/01/99	50		400
9	12/01/99	50		1250	9	12/01/99	50		450
10	01/01/00	50		1200	10	01/01/00	50		500
11	02/01/00	50		1150	11	02/01/00	50		550
12	03/01/00	50		1100	12	03/01/00	50		600
13	04/01/00	50	283.94	1333.94	13	04/01/00	50	9.75	659.75
14	05/01/00	50		1283.94	14	05/01/00	50		709.75
15	06/01/00	50		1233.94	15	06/01/00	50		759.75
16	07/01/00	50		1183.94	16	07/01/00	50		809.75
17	08/01/00	50		1133.94	17	08/01/00	50		859.75
18	09/01/00	50		1083.94	18	09/01/00	50		909.75
19	10/01/00	50		1033.94	19	10/01/00	50		959.75
20	11/01/00	50		983.94	20	11/01/00	50		1009.75
21	12/01/00	50		933.94	21	12/01/00	50		1059.75
22	01/01/01	50		883.94	22	01/01/01	50		1109.75
23	02/01/01	50		833.94	23	02/01/01	50		1159.75
24	03/01/01	50		783.94	24	03/01/01	50		1209.75
25	04/01/01	50	218.67	952.61	25	04/01/01	50	28.04	1287.79
26	05/01/01	50		902.61	26	05/01/01	50		1337.79
27	06/01/01	50		852.61	27	06/01/01	50		1387.79
28	07/01/01	50		802.61	28	07/01/01	50		1437.79
29	08/01/01	50		752.61	29	08/01/01	50		1487.79
30	09/01/01	50		702.61	30	09/01/01	50		1537.79
31	10/01/01	50		652.61	31	10/01/01	50		1587.79
32	11/01/01	50		602.61	32	11/01/01	50	25.16	1662.95
33	12/01/01	50		552.61		Totals	1600	62.95	1662.95
34	01/01/02	50		502.61					
35	02/01/02	50		452.61					
36	03/01/02	50		402.61					
37	04/01/02	50	139.93	492.53					
38	05/01/02	50		442.53					
39	06/01/02	50		392.53					
40	07/01/02	50		342.53					
41	08/01/02	50		292.53					
42	09/01/02	50		242.53					
43	10/01/02	50		192.53					
44	11/01/02	50		142.53					
45	12/01/02	50		92.53					
46	01/01/03	50		42.53					
47	02/01/03	88.57	46.04	0					
	Totals	2338.57	688.57						

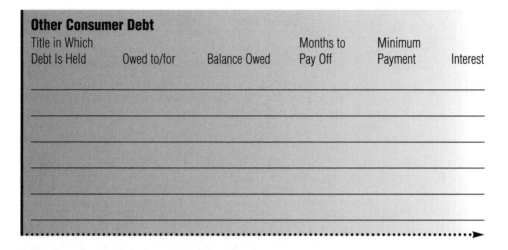

Other Consumer Debt

Title in Which Debt Is Held	Owed to/for	Balance Owed	Months to Pay Off	Minimum Payment	Interest

Next, we'll create a written plan of action. Here are some hypothetical numbers and how you might be able to implement a debt reduction strategy into your overall investment plan.

Assume someone has the following credit card and consumer debt. I have listed the balances left to pay, the interest rates, the amounts the consumer has chosen to pay each month, and the remaining amount of time it will take that person to pay off each of these debts.

	Balance	Interest Rate	Monthly Payment	Time Left
Credit Card #1	$ 3,000	11%	$ 77	4 years
Credit Card #2	1,500	14	125	13 months
Car	9,000	9	224	4 years
Gas Card	300	12	50	6 months
Retail Store Card	600	16	100	6 months
Home	90,000	7	598	30 years

Several authors, including Larry Burkett and Dave Ramsey, have discussed the following strategy—a debt reduction strategy they call "the snowball effect." It works like this: You first organize all your bills in reverse order, listing those with the smallest balances first and moving down the list to the largest bill. Don't concern yourself with interest rates or minimum payments. The new list would be rearranged as follows:

	Balance	Interest Rate	Monthly Payment	Time Left
Gas Card	$ 300	12%	$ 50	6 months
Retail Store Card	600	16	100	6 months
Credit Card #2	1,500	14	125	13 months
Credit Card #1	3,000	11	77	4 years
Car	9,000	9	224	4 years
Home	90,000	7	598	30 years

Now that you have organized your bills, it's time to take control of them. First, you must begin to get ahead of the payments. And to do that you'll need a strategy that pays off the smallest balance in full. You must be able to generate some extra cash quickly, which may mean looking through your house to find something to sell. How much money could you raise in a garage sale? Or, could you work one day a week at a second job? Could you work some overtime? What could you do to earn enough money to pay off your smallest credit card bill? In our example, we need $300 to pay off the smaller balance. Whatever you choose to do to raise the first amount of money will set off a snowball effect that will bring you great pride if you are willing to stick to your plan.

After you pay off the $300 gas card in full, you have $50 of additional money to begin to increase your payments on the retail store card. By paying $150 a month you'll pay off that bill in 4 months rather than 6 months. Then take the extra $150 a month and use that money to pay on credit card #2, which you would then pay off in 8 months instead of 13 months. You are now able to take the extra $275 a month and add it to the $77 for a total of $352 a month, and credit card #1 will be paid off in a total of 6 months.

You next work to pay off the car. Adding the $352 to the current payment of $224 will give you a whopping $576 a month to begin to carve away that debt. If you are able to stick to this plan, the car will be paid off in 12 additional months.

	Current	1 Month	4 Months	8 Months	16 Months	28 Months
Gas Card	50	0	0	0	0	0
Retail Store Card	100	150	0	0	0	0
Credit Card #2	125	125	275	0	0	0
Credit Card #1	77	77	77	352	0	0
Car	224	224	224	224	576	0
Home	598	598	598	598	598	598
Totals	1,174	1,174	1,174	1,174	1,174	598

This means you have paid off a total of $14,400 of original debt in approximately 28 months rather than over a four-year period. At the end of the 28 months, you have freed up a total of $576 a month, which can now be used to make additional principal payments on your home or to save for a new car or for your retirement.

How would an additional $576 of free cash flow a month make you feel? Probably great! Debt reduction should be a priority goal. In our example, it would take just over two years to accomplish. But it will require commitment, persistence, and discipline. For 28 months you might feel as though you were not making progress because you were choosing to take the savings and increase the payments on your remaining debt. Debt is a choice. . . .

You must make a determination not to use tomorrow's money to purchase today's pleasures.

Scenario #2: Your current expenses meet your current income but more closely than you would like.

This is a common situation known as living from paycheck to paycheck. It is how most Americans live. They can usually meet their monthly obligations, but they don't have an investment plan for their future, and they have little or no money in a savings account should any unexpected expenses arise. This scenario is not a desperate situation, but almost all people want to have greater financial security. How we *feel* on an emotional level is very important. If a feeling of panic arises when the car breaks down (and at some point it probably will) and you are wondering where you would find the money to pay for the repairs, then it is important to consider taking some of the steps listed above.

Most people who live from paycheck to paycheck plan to keep the house they are living in and continue driving the same car, but they are likely to be burdened with several credit card payments that are infringing on their ability to build up a savings account. Therefore, it could be wise, if this is your situation, to focus on reducing consumer debt and other small expenses to free up the additional money necessary to begin to fund your financial plan.

Scenario #3: Your current income exceeds your expenses.

Bliss! *This is the goal.* And the beauty of it is that your success is not entirely dependent on your income. Rather, success is mainly a function of choices and simple math.

Matthew and Esther (a true story but the names have been changed) are a wonderful example of how one family has chosen to live within their means. This is a story of effort and encouragement. Matthew is 35 and has two associates degrees and a BA in printing management from Arkansas State University. His wife, Esther, is 30 and has a BS in education from the same university. They have been married five years and have one daughter, Hannah, who is two. When Matthew and Esther married, they decided that Esther would stay home, and so they began creating a livable budget that would allow them to exercise their choice.

As a customer service representative at a well-known Jonesboro company, Matthew has an annual income of $42,536 per year, which breaks down to a gross pay check of $1,636.01 every two weeks.

One of Matthew's recent pay stubs is reprinted in Figure 2.4.

You can see that he and Esther are using an automatic savings plan to accumulate personal savings and retirement assets. They request that $60 be withheld from each paycheck for a Christmas Club savings account, and $114.52 is withheld for their 401(k) contributions. After all of the other withholdings for life insurance, disability insurance, medical insurance, dental insurance, and taxes, Matthew and Esther have a take-home pay of $918.86 every two weeks, plus 401(k) of $114.52 and a Christmas club contribution of $60.00, totalling $2,186.76 per month.

In the budget in Figure 2.5, you will see how they have allocated their money.

Let's examine some of the items in Matthew and Esther's budget.

1. They set savings as a priority.
2. They chose to buy a $48,000 home, which resulted in a mortgage payment within their budget. The mortgage is on a 15-year payoff schedule.
3. With a small child they both felt they needed one nice car. Esther drives a 1996 Dodge Caravan, which will be paid off in one year and six months. When Matthew needed a new car, he bought a 1986 Volkswagen Golf for $800. It has 130,000 miles on it, but it is in very good mechanical shape and he was able to pay cash.
4. A loan was made against Matthew's 401(k) to refinance the couple's house. It will be paid off in four years and is currently their only consumer debt.
5. Charitable giving was one of the most important budget choices for both. They both believe strongly in tithing, and even though

FIGURE 2.4   *Matthew's Pay Stub*

EMPLOYEE ID	EMPLOYEE INFORMATION		S.S. #	CHECK NO.	PERIOD ENDING	PAYMENT DATE
				11037064	3/28/99	3/25/99

EARNINGS				TAXES AND DEDUCTIONS					
DESC	HOURS	CURRENT	YTD	DESC	CURRENT	YTD	DESC	CURRENT	YTD
REGULAR	80.00	1,636.01	9,816.06	AR W/H	78.36	470.16			
				IXMAS CU	60.00	360.00			
				DENTAL	9.90	59.40			
				FIT W/H	264.74	1,588.44			
				401(K)	114.52	687.12			
				401 LOAN	23.12	138.72			
				LIFE 5X	16.71	80.62			
				DEP LIFE	.69	4.14			
				AD&D 5X	1.57	9.42			
				DEPADD5X	.98	5.88			
				MEDICAL	24.00	144.00			
				MEDICARE	23.23	139.38			
				SS-EE	99.33	595.98			

TOTAL HOURS	BASE RATE	CURRENT GROSS	CURRENT TAXABLE GROSS	CURRENT TAXES & DEDUCTIONS	CURRENT NET PAY
80.00		$1,636.01	$1,487.59	$717.15	$918.86

W-4 FILING STATUS FEDERAL	WORK STATE	YTD CURRENT GROSS	YTD TAXABLE GROSS	YTD TAXES & DEDUCTIONS	YTD NET PAY
S-00	S-00	$9,816.06	$8,925.54	$4,283.26	$5,532.80

STATEMENT OF EARNINGS AND DEDUCTIONS—DETACH AND KEEP THIS STUB FOR YOUR RECORDS

they are working within a strict budget, this outflow brings them more joy and sense of well-being than any of the other expenses.

6.   The hospital bill from their daughter's birth will be paid off in one year and four months.

After all of these bills are paid, the couple has a planned surplus of approximately $23 per month. For many people this budget would create too much stress, yet Matthew and Esther view it as a challenge. Here are some of their secrets:

- They plan ahead and shop in bulk for all food.

- Esther steers clear of "budget busters," such as brand-name soft drinks, candy, prepackaged foods and other snacks. (If you review your grocery receipts, I think you'll be amazed at how much money you spend on these items.)

FIGURE 2.5   *Matthew and Esther's Budget*

1	Christmas Club	120.00	Homeowners Insurance		43.15
	Retirement Savings/401(k)	229.04	Health Insurance		0
			Life Insurance		0
2	Mortgage	409.51	Disability		0
	Electric Utilities	60.00			
	Gas Utility	60.00	Doctors		0
	Telephone	60.00	Dentists		0
	Water	30.00	Eyeglasses		0
	Cable	0	Drugs		0
	Home Maintenance	0	Household Help		0
	Lawn Maintenance	0	Dry Cleaning		0
	Real Estate Taxes	0	Beauty Salon/Barber		0
	Personal Property Taxes	5.00	Pets/Vets		0
			Subscriptions		8.50
3	Car Payment	280.01	Florists		0
	Car Insurance	67.05	Gifts		0
	Gasoline	58.00			
	Car Maintenance	0	5	Church Donations	355.33
				Community Donations	0
	Food	240.00		Art and Dance	0
	Tolietries	0			
	Clothing	0		CPA	0
	Entertainment	0		Professional Dues	0
4	Visa/Amex/MasterCard/Loans	46.24		Miscellaneous/Termite Control	6.25
	Vacations	0		Other-Club Dues/Car Phone	60.00
	Childcare/Dependent Care	0	6	Other/Hospital	25.00
	Tuition	0			
				Monthly Total	2,163.08

- Esther has been very creative and has learned how to make her own kitchen and bathroom cleaning products.
- They enjoy shopping at garage sales and auctions.

I realize that Matthew and Esther are the exception rather than the rule. Oh, there are many people who have the same income, but a very different picture would likely unfold if we could look at their budgets. In most cases, there would be no $120 Christmas Club monthly savings account, no commitment to funding a 401(k), and most likely an assortment of credit card balances that would stretch already tight budgets.

The above example is encouraging, which doesn't mean there aren't occasions when Matthew and Esther feel the crunch of an unexpected repair cost, but their experience proves that material things are not the most important. More importantly, theirs is a great example of commitment and financial success. *Your current level of income is not the key to your financial success. It's how you choose to spend your income.*

Many of you may be living on a two-person income, and both of you may be highly paid professionals. Yet I see many people in my office every week with high incomes but even higher expenses. It has become the American way. Big cars and bigger houses. That's great, if you can truly afford it.

Before you commit to such large expenses, wouldn't it be nice to have a specific dollar amount etched into your monthly budget that you set for your short-term savings and an amount for your long-term savings? Matthew and Esther have been able to accomplish this with an annual income of $42,536. Can you do the same working within your income?

Granted, I live in a small rural community in Arkansas, and prices here are extremely attractive to people living on a budget. But even here, a family still has to make prudent choices to live within its means . . . and still have money left over to save and invest for its future. This would entail the following actions:

- Eating at home
- Not having caller ID, call waiting, cable TV, or similar monthly fees
- Working hard to eliminate the small Money Magnets
- Planning meals at least two weeks in advance and buying in bulk
- Planning and budgeting ahead for recreational activities and using public zoos and parks rather than more expensive attractions.

Many people could do these things regardless of their income, but it will take time to pay off their consumer debt and a commitment to living within their means.

Whatever scenario fits you, only so much money is coming in after taxes, and there are definite limits on how far that money can be stretched. It is critical that all of you reading this book commit to a plan for your future. It boils down to *choices* and *simple math*. If you make $50,000 after taxes, you must plan to spend less than $50,000. If you make $100,000 after taxes, you must plan to spend less than $100,000. The ability to succeed rests on the choices you make for spending your money.

What's the point? Budgeting is one of the few areas of financial planning over which you have total control. If your budget is out of line, you can start taking steps today to bring it back in line—a matter of choices and simple math. The goal:

$$\text{Expenses} <\!/\!= \text{Income}$$

Today is the day to begin.

CONCLUSION . . .

Although gathering data is the starting point, it is also probably the most difficult of all tasks. Some people feel inadequate to even answer the questions. Some people don't know where to look for the data; and some people wouldn't know what the correct information was even if they found it, and they certainly have never attempted to create or live by a budget!

If you fall into this category, don't despair! The simplest thing you can do is take it one step at a time. Set aside some time on a quiet evening or a Saturday morning to find all the documents you need. Then begin to place the information into the appropriate categories and I believe you'll be surprised by how much better you feel by just taking this action.

A detailed questionnaire is reprinted on page 44 to help you. While this information is fresh in your mind, it might be good to pull together as many of your financial records as you can find. Make a list of what you don't find and attempt to locate all of the information within a specific time.

Finding this information is the first step in bringing your financial future into focus. Even the process of going through the filing cabinets and desk drawers to locate statements and folders will give you a sense of accomplishment. You will begin to control the financial planning process. You will probably begin to feel good about the steps you are currently taking to reach your future goals.

Once you have completed this step, it's time to set your goals for the future.

ACTION STEP

Gather Data

Whether you are able to fill out the necessary information or you choose to have a professional adviser help you, it is still essential to have the following items from which you will find most of the data:

1. **Assets**
   - Current bank statements—checking, savings, IRAs, and the like
   - Additional IRA statements
   - Current brokerage statements
   - Current mutual fund statements
   - A list of all stocks and bond certificates held in a lockbox or at home
   - Annuities
   - Life insurance policies
   - Business ownership valuations
   - Retirement benefit statements—401(k), pension, deferred compensation, and so on
   - A list of any tangible investments—land, precious metals, collectibles, art, antiques, and so forth
   - A list of ownership of any income-producing investments—rental houses, farmland, commercial property, mineral rights, oil and gas leases, etc.
   - Any additional financial information

2. **Income**
   - Where does your primary income come from?
   - How stable is your income?
   - Will your income be increasing or decreasing—at what rate?
   - Do your receive commissions or bonuses?
   - Do you rely on alimony or other supplemental income?
   - What steps could you take to increase your income?

3. **Debt**
   - What is the dollar amount of your total debt?

- What is the dollar amount of your mortgage?
- What is the dollar amount of your car loans?
- What is the dollar amount of your student loans?
- What is the dollar amount of your credit car debt?
- What is the dollar amount of your other debt?
- What interest rate corresponds with each loan?
- What are the minimum payments and how much are you paying?
- When do you anticipate paying off each loan?
- How do you feel about the debt you are carrying?

4. **Expenses**
- You will need a copy of your most current budget.

Investment Profile Worksheet

Name: _____   Spouse/Joint holder name: _____
Client Social Security   Spouse/Joint holder Social Security
   number:_____ - _____ - _____   number:_____ - _____ - _____
Date of birth: _____ Age:____   Date of birth: _____ Age:____
Plans to retire at age _____   Plans to retire at age _____
Occupation: _____   Occupation: _____
Employer: _____   Employer: _____
Income: _____   Income: _____

Address: _____

City:_____   State:_____   Zip: _____

Primary phone: _____   Pager:_____
Home phone: _____   Fax: _____
Mobile phone: _____   E-mail: _____

U.S. citizen? ___ yes ___ no

Name of primary bank: _____

Emergency contact's name: _____   Phone: _____
Emergency contact's address: _____

Risk Tolerance (check one):
_____ Ultraconservative
_____ Fairly conservative
_____ Moderate
_____ Fairly aggressive
_____ Ultra-aggressive

Client objective: Rank in order of priority 1–4
_____ Income
_____ Aggressive income
_____ Capital appreciation
_____ Speculation

What was the first year you purchased:
Stocks?   _____
Mutual funds?   _____
Bonds?   _____
Options?   _____

Total income: _____
Net worth: _____
Liquid assets: _____

Current Bank Accounts

Title in Which Asset Held	Name of Bank	Number	Account Number	Balance	Yield

Current CDs

Title in Which Asset Held	Name of Bank	Number	Account Number	Balance	Yield

Holdings in Bonds

Title in Which Asset Held	Name of Bonds	Type of Bond Gov./Muni/Corp.	Face Value	Current Value

Mutual Funds

Title in Which Asset Held	Name of Fund	Account Number	Number of Shares	Cost	Current Value

Common Stocks

Title in Which Asset Held	Name of Stock	Cost per Share	Current Price/Share	Number of Shares	Current Value

Annuities

Title in Which Asset Held	Name of Annuity	Beneficiary	Original Cost	Current Balance

Real Estate Holdings

Title in Which Asset Held	Name of Property	Mortgage/Rate?	Income	Current Value

Life Insurance Policies

Title in Which Asset Held	Name of Company/ Policy Number	Beneficiary	Death Benefit	Cash Value

Other Privately Held Businesses

Title in Which Asset Held	Name of Business	Cost	Income	Current Value

Other Investment Holdings

Title in Which Asset Held	Name of Asset	Cost	Income	Current Value

Important Contacts

Primary attorney:
Company:
Address:
Phone:

Other legal contacts:
Company:
Address:
Phone:

Primary CPA:
Company:
Address:
Phone:

Primary financial adviser:
Company:
Address:
Phone:

Investment Expectations

Risk-Return Profile
Your anticipated investment time horizon:
Ten years or more   Five to ten years   Three to five years
My expected rates of return: 1 year ___%   3 years ___%   5 years ___%
Your tolerance for risk can be described as: (select one)
___ Can tolerate losing money for more than one year through difficult periods in a market cycle
___ Can tolerate losing money for six to nine months through difficult periods in a market cycle
___ Can tolerate losing very little money

Tax Information
Income tax rate _____%   Capital gains tax rate _____%

Inflation Expectations
Inflation rate _____%
(In today's environment I use a 3% inflation rate for retirement planning and an 8% inflation rate for college education costs.)

General Information
Annual retirement income goal:
Income needed if death occurs at ____
Present time:
Income needed if disability occurs at ____

Current Net Worth
Cash
Securities
Real estate
Other (specify)
Total Net Worth

Investment Experience
Number of years _____
Type of experience (be specific):

Inheritance
Lump-sum inheritance amount _____
Age expected _____

Anticipated Retirement Income

Pension:	Monthly benefit _____	Annual benefit _____
Social Security:	Monthly benefit _____	Annual benefit _____
Joint Social Security:	Monthly benefit _____	Annual benefit _____
Rental income:	Monthly benefit _____	Annual benefit _____
Other income:	Monthly benefit _____	Annual benefit _____
Total Income:	Monthly benefit _____	Annual benefit _____

Mortgage Information
Value of property: $_____ Mortgage amount: $_____
Interest rate: _____% Monthly payments: $_____
Expected to be paid off by _____.

Other Consumer Debt

Title in Which Debt Held	Owed to/for	Balance Owed	Minimum Interest Payment	Rate

Your Personal Feelings toward Money

How would you feel if you had three months of expenses in an emergency fund?

_____

_____

_____

_____

How would you feel if you had a working and realistic budget? Would the budget be a burden or a liberating guide?

_____

_____

_____

_____

_____

How do you feel about owning stocks? Nervous? Excited? No feelings?

_____

_____

_____

_____

_____

What other personal feelings regarding your money and your personal planning will be helpful for you and/or your financial adviser to understand? Have you had any past experiences (good or bad) that will influence your future decisions?

_____

_____

_____

_____

_____

What are your expectations from your financial adviser?

_____

_____

_____

_____

Design and Implement a Realistic Budget

There is no reason that you shouldn't be able to design a workable and useful budget for your family. While this process, if done correctly, will take a bit of time, it will prove to be one of the most eye-opening experiences of the entire planning process.

Remember that good data are the key to your success. Many people have a mental picture of where their money is being spent, but until you take the Checkbook Test, you will never have a complete budget.

Your job is to go through every check and every credit card transaction for at least a three-month period. It's more useful if you take time to record every single transaction.

You'll probably be surprised at how different your *actual* spending habits are from those you *thought* you had. Feel free to copy the following pages and begin to chart your actual spending habits.

Once you have finished the calculations for each month, use the annual spreadsheet on the following page to come up with a ledger of what your expenses have actually been.

Money Magnets: Adjust Your Budget

Now that you possess the actual numbers, you can begin to modify them to create a family budget. The actual data allow you to see where you are currently spending your money and where you might be able to find some areas of improvement.

For many people, it will come back to the small and large Money Magnets. In the case of my family, we were spending an extraordinary amount of our budget at a local discount grocery store, so we took the process one step farther and began to keep the actual receipts from every grocery store visit. And in much the same fashion, we began to monitor how we were spending our food budget.

You can monitor your receipts by using the type of worksheet found on page 55.

Checkbook Spreadsheet

Month of _____							Monthly Subtotal
Personal Savings/Investments							
Retirement Investments							
Mortgage/Rent							
Electric Utility							
Gas Utility							
Telephone/Other Phone Costs							
Cell Phone							
Pager							
Water							
Cable TV							
Home Maintenance							
Lawn Maintenance							
Real Estate Taxes							
Car Payment							
Car Insurance							
Gasoline							
Car Maintenance							
Food/Groceries							
Tolietries							
Eating Out							
Entertainment							
Clothing							
Vacations							
Childcare/Dependent Care							
Tuition							
Visa							
MasterCard							
Discover							
Other Consumer Debt							
Student Loans							
Homeowners Insurance							
Health Insurance							
Life Insurance							
Disability Insurance							
Doctors - Copay							
Dentists							
Eyeglasses							
Prescription Drugs							
Household Help							
Dry Cleaning							
Beauty Salon/Barber							
Pets/Vet							
Subscriptions							
Florists							
Gifts							
Church Donations							
Community Donations							
Art/Dance/Misc. Personal							
CPA							
Professional Dues							
Club Dues							
Miscellaneous							
Other							
Monthly Total							

Last 12 Months' Total Budget

Year _____	Past Annual Subtotals
Personal Savings/Investments	
Retirement Investments	
Mortgage/Rent	
Electric Utility	
Gas Utility	
Telephone/Other Phone Costs	
Cell Phone	
Pager	
Water	
Cable TV	
Home Maintenance	
Lawn Maintenance	
Real Estate Taxes	
Car Payment	
Car Insurance	
Gasoline	
Car Maintenance	
Food/Groceries	
Tolietries	
Eating Out	
Entertainment	
Clothing	
Vacations	
Childcare/Dependent Care	
Tuition	
Visa	
MasterCard	
Discover	

Year _____	Past Annual Subtotals
Other Consumer Debt	
Student Loans	
Homeowners Insurance	
Health Insurance	
Life Insurance	
Disability Insurance	
Doctors - Copay	
Dentists	
Eyeglasses	
Prescription Drugs	
Household Help	
Dry Cleaning	
Beauty Salon/Barber	
Pets/Vet	
Subscriptions	
Florists	
Gifts	
Church Donations	
Community Donations	
Art/Dance/Misc. Personal	
CPA	
Profesionnal Dues	
Club Dues	
Miscellaneous	
Other	
Annual Total	

	Month of	Month of	Bimonthly Subtotal
Regular food items			
Special dinner items			
Soft drinks			
Milk			
Food			
Baby food			
Laundry items			
Paper goods/Trash bags			
Snacks/Candy/Crackers			
Cereal			
Sandwich meat			
Baby formula			
Juice			
Soap			
Toys			
Film			
Diapers			
Miscellaneous			
Other			
Other			
Other			
Other			
Monthly Total			

Completing this worksheet helped us understand exactly how we were spending our money. Once we knew where the grocery money was being spent, we made a few adjustments to our spending habits:

- We shopped after publication of the Wednesday paper showing all the sale prices for food, and we made a list of the items that were on sale that we used on a regular basis. One of the local grocery stores matches any advertised price, so we made a list and began to buy things matching those on sale.
- We looked for coupons in the Sunday paper.
- We made a complete grocery list and tried to stick with it.
- Instead of buying premade foods, we began to cook.

The difference was amazing—we were able to reduce our family's average grocery bill by 10 to 12 percent. In addition, rather than reducing our ability to buy what we want, our family turned our saving steps into a game to see how much money we could save.

As Benjamin Franklin said. "A penny saved is a penny earned."

Then the question becomes: What are your personal Money Magnets?

Ask yourself the following questions:

The Big Money Magnets	Too Much	Needs Work	Just Right
House	_____	_____	_____
Cars	_____	_____	_____
Personal debt	_____	_____	_____
Cell phones	_____	_____	_____
Clothes	_____	_____	_____
Eating out	_____	_____	_____
Presents	_____	_____	_____

The Small Money Magnets	Too Much	Needs Work	Just Right
Lunch	_____	_____	_____
Snacks	_____	_____	_____
Soft drinks	_____	_____	_____
Yogurt/Ice cream	_____	_____	_____
Gum	_____	_____	_____
Internet	_____	_____	_____
Extra phone lines for Internet	_____	_____	_____
Call waiting	_____	_____	_____
Caller ID	_____	_____	_____
Pager	_____	_____	_____
Subscriptions	_____	_____	_____
Music CDs	_____	_____	_____
Movie rentals	_____	_____	_____
Impulse purchases	_____	_____	_____
Recreation	_____	_____	_____
Pets	_____	_____	_____

You are trying to find money by changing your current spending habits. Going through this process for our family allowed us to save money by:

- reducing our usage of cell phones;

- shopping and changing long-distance providers;

- reevaluating our insurance coverage and switching some of it to reduce costs;

- reducing the number of our bank accounts;

- paying off all consumer debt (we still have a mortgage) to reduce the amount of interest;

- drastically reducing our average grocery bill; and

- changing our Internet services to reduce our monthly costs.

Overall, these changes gave us such a tremendous feeling of accomplishment. It wasn't that any single item would have provided us with a huge amount of money, but, added together, we were able to free up a significant sum of cash each month.

How did that feel? It felt *great!* Now it's your turn. Where can you find a little extra money in your budget? Then what will you do with that extra money?

Pay off debt? Invest for your child's future? Put it aside for an emergency fund? Begin to save for your next car, so you will be able to pay cash? Fund your 401(k)?

The budgeting process puts you ahead of the game instead of behind. It allows you to make decisions ahead of time rather than reacting to unforeseen circumstances.

Your New Budget

Year _____	Past Annual Subtotals	Goals For This Year	Actual For This Year
Personal Savings/Investments			
Retirement Investments			
Mortgage/Rent			
Electric Utility			
Gas Utility			
Telephone/Other Phone Costs			
Cell Phone			
Pager			
Water			
Cable TV			
Home Maintenance			
Lawn Maintenance			
Real Estate Taxes			
Car Payment			
Car Insurance			
Gasoline			
Car Maintenance			
Food/Groceries			
Tolietries			
Eating Out			
Entertainment			
Clothing			
Vacations			
Childcare/Dependent Care			
Tuition			
Visa			
MasterCard			
Discover			
Other Consumer Debt			
Student Loans			
Homeowners Insurance			
Health Insurance			
Life Insurance			
Disability Insurance			
Doctors—Copay			
Dentists			
Eyeglasses			
Prescription Drugs			
Household Help			
Dry Cleaning			
Beauty Salon/Barber			
Pets/Vet			
Subscriptions			
Florists			
Gifts			
Church Donations			
Community Donations			
Art/Dance/Misc. Personal			
CPA			
Professional Dues			
Club Dues			
Miscellaneous			
Other			
Annual Total			

Create Your Debt Reduction Strategy

To take control of your debt, you must first know and understand how much your monthly spending is affected by your current debt load.

Line up your credit card bills and other consumer debt obligations, such as car loans and student loans, and make a list. Include the name of the payer, the current amount owed, the interest rate, and the minimum payment. You will want to list these debts from the smallest to the largest balance.

Title in Which Debt Held	Owed to/for	Balance Owed	Months to Pay Off	Minimum Payment	Interest

Listing your debts allows you to begin implementing the "snowball effect" described on page 35.

If you don't have some of the information, such as the current balance or the number of months left to pay off a loan, you may wish to call the credit card company or the lending institution that is carrying your loan.

Next, you must determine a way to quickly pay off in full the first debt. What will you do? Is there a part-time position you could take to help you earn the extra money? If debt has become a problem area, it may take some serious planning and commitments to conquer this most important financial planning priority.

Finally, you will want to use loan calculation software or call the loan companies to find out how long it will take to pay off your loans by adding in the extra principal repayments. You may be amazed at how much you can shorten your payoff periods with a little diligence.

Step 3: Establish Your Written Financial Goals

> "When we met in the first grade, most of our friends played with Barbie dolls. Allyson White Lewis and I compared and analyzed our coin collections. Today, in our late thirties, we compare our stocks and bonds."
>
> **Bea Cheesman,** 39
> *Pine Bluff, Arkansas*

> "It is essential to save a little . . . all your life and invest in quality companies only."
>
> **Ann R. White,** 64
> *Pine Bluff, Arkansas*

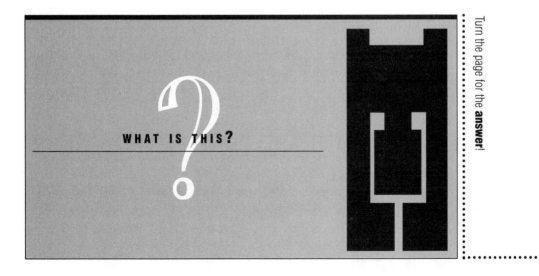

WHAT IS THIS?

Turn the page for the **answer!**

THE **ANSWER!**

Many people who look at this illustration see a goalpost. And because we are talking about setting written goals, I thought this picture made my point. In football, you don't score a touchdown unless you cross the goal line. If you land on the one-yard line, you don't receive the six points. If you land even one inch away from the goal line, you don't score any points.

The same is true with financial goals. Mental goals count for zero points but written goals are a touchdown. *Please don't finish this book without taking the time to establish written financial goals.*

P.S. If you rotate the page a quarter turn, you will see this is not really an example of a goalpost. It is a very large E!

"I simply wish I had started saving years earlier.**"**
Aaron F. Barling, 70
Barling, Arkansas

"A survey of mutual fund investors conducted by Montgomery Asset Management, a San Francisco-based management firm, revealed that investors are more concerned about their vacation plans than their mutual fund investments, taking 28 days to plan a vacation and 9 days to research a fund investment.**"**
Financial Planning Online (July 14, 1997)
www.fponline.com/news/montgomerysurvey/html

SETTING WRITTEN GOALS

Before you begin the process of writing your financial goals, it is important that you understand your ultimate goals. It's easy to get lost in the num-

POLICY OBJECTIVES
SET YOUR OBJECTIVES
　　Lifestyle • College Education • Retirement Goals
INVESTMENT PARAMETERS
　　How Much Risk Can You Tolerate? • What Return Do You Expect? • What Assets Are Permitted in the Portfolio? • What Investment Constraints Are Appropriate?
TIME HORIZON
　　How Long Is Your Investment Horizon?

bers if you don't know exactly what you are trying to accomplish. You must know what your ultimate objectives are.

Are they to increase your current standard of living?
To save for your children's education?
To enjoy a secure retirement?

Sit down and decide what you want and need from your financial plan. Your mission statement will serve as a guide.

Set Your Objectives

With the vision of your ultimate objectives firmly planted in your mind, use the data you have gathered to lay out written objectives and goals for your plan. These objectives and goals act as guidelines for the plan.

The more definite you can be in setting your objectives and goals, the more likely you can create a realistic and satisfactory plan for your financial future.

Your policy statement might include phrases like these:

- I am 50 years old.
- I plan to retire in 15 years
- To supplement my pension income I need to accumulate an additional $400,000. I currently have accumulated $175,000, so I need to invest to fill the shortfall.
- I expect to invest in a balanced blend of cash, stocks, and bonds. By using a balanced approach to my asset allocation, I expect to reduce the overall volatility of my portfolio.
- I expect to earn an annualized return of 6.5 percent to 8.0 percent on my total investment portfolio.
- I consider myself a relatively conservative investor.
- My overall objective is conservative income with some growth.
- My minimum rate or expected return is –2 percent.
- I do wish to hold a portion of my investments in international securities.

Percentage of investors who do not know that the top long-term capital gains rate is 20 percent is 82 percent.
Source: Dreyfus Corporation

- I do not wish to hold more than 40 percent of my assets in any one security.
- My federal income tax bracket is 31 percent.
- My long-term capital gains tax bracket is 20 percent.

As you can see, these written objectives and goals are designed to be very specific. They paint a very clear picture for both you and your financial adviser (if you have one). If you were planning to drive to a distant destination, especially if you were unfamiliar with the area, you would likely create a detailed and specific itinerary. Your written goals should be equally planned.

Determine Your Parameters

Next you must determine your investment parameters. No one knows your investment profile better than you do. Do you want low-risk, medium-risk, or high-risk investments? What type of assets do you want to hold—long-term or short-term?

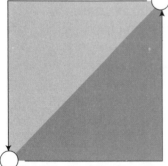

Low Risk = Potential for lower returns

High Risk = Potential for higher returns

Risk is an unusual concept. It is the hinge that drives most investment decisions. Will you put your money in the stock market or will you sleep better at night with all of your money in the bank?

Risk is the one ingredient that makes determining your investment parameters so fascinating. We all understand that risk is what gives investors the potential for higher returns. The skill lies in creating a blend of investments that will allow you to achieve the overall rate of return on your portfolio without exposing yourself to unnecessary risks.

I don't mean people dislike losing money. I mean they hate it. Looking at the stock market from 1995 through the first six and one-half months of 1998, you might begin to believe it was impossible to lose money in the market. It seemed if you bought a stock—it would go up!

Then came July 18, 1998, and the Dow Jones Industrial Average started on one of its roller-coaster rides. After having climbed to an intraday high

> If I have learned anything about people over the past 17 years, it is this: PEOPLE HATE TO LOSE MONEY!

of 9,412 on July 17, the market fell to an intraday low of 7,379 by September 1—a loss of 2,033 points, or 21.60 percent, in less than six weeks!

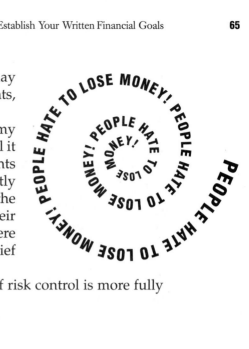

WOW! Risk had reared its ugly head. In my nice little financial planners' circle, we might call it market volatility, but the truth is that my clients were losing money. They were standing by silently and watching their net worth shrink. They saw the value of their IRA money go down. They saw their mutual funds drop in value. Many people were shocked when they realized the impact this brief decline had made on their 401(k) plans.

So how can you control risk? The concept of risk control is more fully explored in the last part of Chapter 8.

Establish Your Time Span

What is your time span for reaching your goals? Do you have 40 years to save or only 5 years?

It is very important that you plan for the appropriate time horizon. You'll want to develop a timeline for your financial plan. Again, this timeline needs to be fairly specific and include all those short-term and long-term goals and dreams.

My timeline looks like this:

1998	
1999	
2000	Abby starts school
2001	J. Mark starts school
2002	
2003	
2004	
2005	
2006	
2007	
2008	
2009	

2010		
2011		
2012		
2013		
2014	Allyson will have 30 years with her firm/Abby starts college	Amount needed _____
2015	Abby and J. Mark in college	Amount needed _____
2016	Abby and J. Mark in college	Amount needed _____
2017	Abby and J. Mark in college	Amount needed _____
2018	J. Mark in college	Amount needed _____
2019	Mark and Allyson begin retirement	Amount needed _____
2020		
2021	Mark's Social Security can start	
2022	Allyson's Social Security can start	
2023		
2024		
2025		
2026		
2027		
2028	thru life expectancy	
Death		
Estate Phase		

Tom McDonald, Jonesboro, Arkansas

Your timeline will be as individual as you are; it must be specific and it must include specific amounts of money that you expect to need to accomplish each goal.

QUANTIFYING YOUR SPECIFIC GOALS

Once you have determined when you will need money to fund a specific goal, you must then quantify that goal. Being able to quantify your personal financial goals could prove to be one of the most gratifying aspects of this entire book. So much of the mystery of financial planning stems from not having a true understanding of how much money you actually need to accumulate to accomplish your goals. Once you quantify that number and come up with something concrete, the mystery vanishes and you become more confident about your future.

We will quantify goals using a five-step process:

The Five-Step Process for Quantifying Goals

1. Find out the goal's cost in today's dollars.
2. Determine the number of years you will have to fund the goal.
3. Using the inflation tables in Appendix A, inflate the cost of the goal to see what it will be in the year you'll need the money.
4. Determine an assumed annual rate of return.
5. Use the tables in Appendix B to determine exactly how much money per thousand dollars you will need to save on a monthly basis to fund the goal within the designated time frame.

Let's review the five-step process:

1. Assume you have a child you would like to put through college. You look in Chapter 13 and see that the average cost for one year in an in-state public university is currently $9,959. Now you know the cost of one year in today's dollars.
2. To determine the number of years you will have to fund this goal, you simply subtract your child's age from 18. (If you were using the five-step process to plan for your retirement, subtract your current age from the age at which you are planning to retire.) For this illustration we use a four-year-old child, so 18 minus 4 leaves 14 years to fund the goal.
3. Next, turn to the inflation table in Appendix A. Assuming an 8 percent inflation rate for the future cost of higher education, round the cost to $10,000. For every $1,000 needed in today's dollars, you can assume you will need $2,937.19 ($2,937.19 is the 14th year cost for an 8 percent inflation rate). Next, multiply that number by 10 because you need a total of $10,000 and the $2,937.19 is per $1,000 needed. So $2,937.19 × 10 = $29,371.90. This calculation gives you the inflated cost of one year of an average in-state public education.
4. Then you will be asked to determine an assumed annual rate of return. This is the loaded question. No one can possibly know what the future holds for any specific investment that you choose. But history can at least serve as a guide and you can then raise or lower your expectations from that number.

   Over the last 70 years:

   - Cash and other short-term investments have averaged   3.75%

- Longer-term bonds and fixed income investments
  have averaged   5.25%
- Stocks have averaged   11.00%

For this college example, assume you use some blend of stocks and bonds and expect to earn an average of 8 percent.

5. Using the Monthly Savings Calculator table in Appendix B, you can calculate approximately how much you will need to save monthly to fund your goal within the designated time frame. The table shows that you will need to save $3.225 per $1,000 per month. Since you need roughly $30,000 in future dollars, you will need to multiply $3.225 by 30 for a total of $96.75 per month. However, this example just covers the cost of one child's first year of college. It would cost $96.75 per month times 4, or $387.00 per month, to cover all four years. If you cannot afford that amount, save what you can. It will still put you ahead of most people.

It is amazing how much power this five-step process has to put each of your financial goals into perspective. Just this simple example proves that you can plan to reach your goals:

1. The cost of an in-state public education is $9,958 per year today.

2. My daughter is 3 and will start college in 15 years.

3. Considering that higher education costs have been increasing at 8 percent per year, I'll adjust that figure by 8 percent for 15 years. The inflation calculator in Appendix A indicates that $1,000 will cost $3,172.17 in 15 years. If the cost is roughly $10,000 today, we will need $31,721.70 to cover her first year of college (10 × $3,172.17).

4. Assume an 8 percent rate of return.

5. Using the table in Appendix B, we would need to save and invest $2.871 per $1,000 every month to fully fund our daughter's college education within the designated time frame. $2.871 times 32 = $91.87 per month times four years of college = $367.48. (Remember to calculate the cost for each of your children.)

You can quickly and easily begin to quantify every financial goal—from family vacations and college education to your retirement. However, you must understand these calculations are simply hypothetical illustra-

QUANTIFY . . . QUANTIFY . . . QUANTIFY
What types of goals can be quantified?

- College education costs
- Buying a new home or car
- Providing for aging parents

- Retirement costs
- Covering future health care costs
- Buying any specific big-ticket item

tions of what might happen. *It is impossible to know what rate of return you will actually earn or what the inflation rate will actually be.* But that should not keep you from being truly excited about attempting to quantify the dreams you have for yourself and your family.

Just as my own mission statement says, "We are all called to be stewards to what we have been given," quantifying your personal goals and putting them on a specific timeline can bring great freedom to your saving and spending habits. Some people are not saving enough and some people could actually be saving too much. Wouldn't it be nice to know if you were on track? For many investors this step is where budgeting decisions have to be made:

- If we need to be saving $100 a month for our child's education, how are we going to be able to do that?

- Now we know we need to be investing at least $2,000 a year into each of our IRAs and funding our 401(k) plans.

- Where can we find the $225 a month for the money to replace our car in four years?

While everyone's questions will be different, now is the time to review your monthly budget and establish priorities for how you are going to spend your income.

Some of you may complete the budgeting process and realize that you simply do not have enough income to cover your regular monthly bills and any additional savings needed for a child's education or an IRA contribution. If this describes your current situation, then you may need to go back and review the section on budgeting that begins on page 24. I know this can be one of the most challenging areas of financial planning, but if you begin to gain some control over your personal spending and shift that money into personal savings, I believe you will feel a tremendous sense of accomplishment.

MENTAL GOALS VERSUS WRITTEN GOALS

In his book *Success,* Glen Bland refers to a study on goals that indicates 87 percent of all people have not taken the time to set goals for themselves; 10 percent have goals but have not yet written them down; and only 3 percent have written goals. The same study concluded that the 3 percent who actually take the time and effort to put their goals in writing accomplish 50 to 100 times more than people who have not established written goals and objectives.

Mental goals = 0
Written goals = 100

Why is this true? There is something deep inside the human mind, a subconscious, and a place where thoughts and inspiration begin. It is here that you must go to find the personal knowledge of what your goals will be. Some unexplainable experience happens when we take the time to visit that place. When you are willing to slow down and think and put your thoughts on paper, that very action of mapping out a written strategy will draw you closer to achieving your goals. This is not meant to be some humanistic experience. It is a crucial step toward securing your financial future.

Conclusion.   Written goals can be viewed as a turning point for your personal financial plan.

If you have created a mission statement, gathered the information, and taken the time to write down your goals . . . then the rest of the plan is merely an execution of the obvious. The first three steps discussed here allow you to march deliberately down a predetermined path toward success.

Establish Your Written Goals and Objectives

I've created a short list of common financial goals; check the ones you hope to accomplish, and include a start date and a finish date beside each goal.

Investment Goals	Start	Finish
Plan for retirement	_____	_____
Educate children or grandchildren	_____	_____
Accumulate a nest egg	_____	_____
Increase income	_____	_____
Reduce debt	_____	_____
Plan for a second home	_____	_____
Reduce taxes	_____	_____
Increase monthly investment amount	_____	_____

Personal Financial Goals	Start	Finish
Increase financial knowledge	_____	_____
Create a family budget	_____	_____
Learn how to read newspaper financial quotes	_____	_____
Learn how to read statements	_____	_____
Read more	_____	_____
Join or start an investment club	_____	_____

Circle your two goals in each category. Write some or all of your goals on a card and keep them with your mission statements. Look at your goals often; they should serve as a reminder that you need to be committed to doing the day-to-day activities that will help you to reach your goals.

Break the goals into manageable parts. Set timelines to review your progress. Share your goals with your spouse or with a friend and ask him or her to help you to be accountable for your progress.

Design Your Timeline

Quantifying your goals is incredibly important, but it's also necessary to create a realistic timeline. Your timeline allows you to visually lay out your financial future and then simply choose the goals you plan to fund. To create your timeline, choose the goals you wish to fund and use the five-step process in Action Step 7 to calculate the future value needed and your monthly savings goal. Then plot your goals on the timeline.

Your Timeline

	Name of Goal	Future Value Needed	Monthly Savings Goal
2000			
2001			
2002			
2003			
2004			
2005			
2006			
2007			
2008			
2009			
2010			
2011			
2012			
2013			
2014			
2015			
2016			

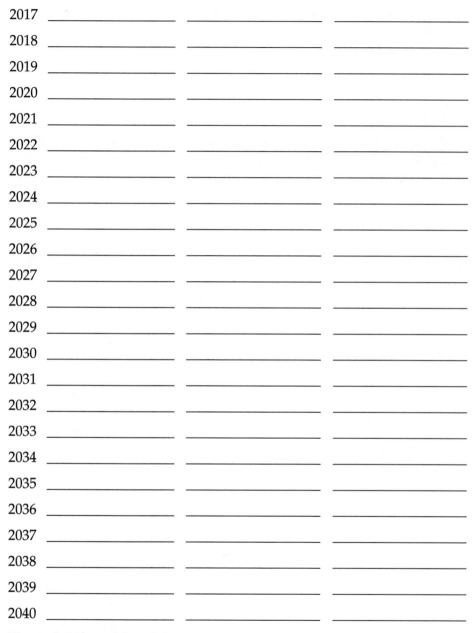

2017 _____   _____   _____

2018 _____   _____   _____

2019 _____   _____   _____

2020 _____   _____   _____

2021 _____   _____   _____

2022 _____   _____   _____

2023 _____   _____   _____

2024 _____   _____   _____

2025 _____   _____   _____

2026 _____   _____   _____

2027 _____   _____   _____

2028 _____   _____   _____

2029 _____   _____   _____

2030 _____   _____   _____

2031 _____   _____   _____

2032 _____   _____   _____

2033 _____   _____   _____

2034 _____   _____   _____

2035 _____   _____   _____

2036 _____   _____   _____

2037 _____   _____   _____

2038 _____   _____   _____

2039 _____   _____   _____

2040 _____   _____   _____

Through Life and Death

Your timeline and your quantified goal sheet will allow you to calculate the total amount of money you will need to accumulate in order to fulfill your future financial plan. It will further allow you to rank your priorities and fund them accordingly.

For example:

- College education—$120,000—by 2014
- Retirement planning—$750,000—by 2019
- Vacation home—$200,000—by 2006

These totals may seem daunting but when they are broken down into manageable pieces and you start to fund them on a regular basis, you should be amazed at just how many goals you can reach.

Quantify Your Goals: The Five-Step Process

The five-step process is fully explained on page 67. The calculation tables are found in Appendixes A and B.

1. Find out the goal's cost in today's dollars.
2. Multiply that figure by the number of years you need to fund the goal.
3. Inflate the cost to see what the cost will be in the year you need the money.
4. Determine an annual rate-of-return assumption.
5. Use the tables in Appendix B to determine exactly how much money you will need to save on an annual or monthly basis to fund the goal within the designated time frame.

Choose the first financial goal you need to quantify _____.
Then apply the five-step process:

1. Cost in today's dollars _____
2. Number of years _____
3. Inflate _____
4. Annual rate of return _____
5. Tables _____

Choose the second financial goal you need to quantify _____.
Then apply the five-step process:

1. Cost in today's dollars _____
2. Number of years _____
3. Inflate _____
4. Annual rate of return _____
5. Tables _____

Choose the third financial goal you need to quantify _____.
Then apply the five-step process:

1. Cost in today's dollars _____

2. Number of years _____

3. Inflate _____

4. Annual rate of return _____

5. Tables _____

The value of quantifying your goals is that it will allow you to set realistic expectations of what you can and should plan on achieving.

You can quantify everything from the largest to the smallest financial goal. It doesn't matter if you hope to fund your retirement or if you are simply saving for a new dining-room table. The process allows you to set specific financial targets and illustrates precisely how much money you should be saving on a regular basis to reach your various goals.

What Types of Goals Can Be Quantified?

- College education costs
- Retirement costs
- Buying a new home or car
- Covering future health care costs
- Providing for aging parents
- Buying any specific item (e.g., diamonds, boats, computers, etc.)

All of your financial goals should be quantified. Once you see the amount each goal will require, you can prioritize your goals and fund them as you are financially able.

8

Develop Your Monthly Investing Strategy

Very few investors are able to place a large sum of money on my desk when they are 35 or 40 years old and say, "Here is $50,000; take good care of it and I will be back in 25 or 30 years to use it for my retirement."

If you could provide your financial adviser with a $50,000 lump sum that could grow in a tax-deferred vehicle for 25 years with an average 8 percent rate of return, it could prove to be a good thing. While this is a terrific strategy, it only works if you have an extra $50,000 lying around. For most people, a monthly investment strategy will help them accomplish the same goal.

A $360.05 monthly investment strategy earning the same 8 percent return in some type of tax-deferred investment vehicle would grow to the same $342,423.75 in 25 years. But what if you don't have $360.05 to invest each month?

$342,423.75

Lump sum investment of $50,000 at 8% for 25 years

$50,000

Option One: Plan to work five additional years because over a 30-year period you would need to invest $229.76 at 8 percent.

Option Two: Invest in more aggressive vehicles and hope to make a 10 percent return over a 25-year period. If you use this criterion, a $258.08 monthly savings will accomplish the same goal.

You *must* begin to save for your future. Some people are amazed at the actual amount of money required to fund their future financial goals while, at the same time, they don't hesitate to take on a huge monthly mortgage or a large seven-year car payment. Many people can't imagine saving $200, or $300, or $500 a month to meet their future obligations.

It all comes back to your choices. How are you going to spend your money now?

These numbers simply reinforce the Social Security Administration's contention that approximately 2 to 3 percent of the American population can afford to retire at age 65 without any additional outside assistance.

The choice is yours . . . pay yourself first and plan to invest 10 percent of every paycheck. This no doubt may mean making some changes in the way you currently spend your income. But the question remains: Do you want to be in the 3 percent or the 97 percent category?

Steps 4–7:
Take Action

❝I am so glad I joined the Million-Dollar Investment Club ten years ago. I feel I have gained knowledge (and wealth!) in making sensible decisions in my own financial affairs. After seeing widows and divorcees absolutely in a panic about their financial situation, I have used the knowledge I have gained to encourage the women I come in contact with to do whatever it takes to be on top of their family finances. I go into orbit when a woman says, 'Oh, I'm not interested in business, I leave that up to my husband (or my broker).' I want to tell them, 'Get real, this concerns *you;* you are walking in a minefield if you don't know about your own money affairs.'

"I spend time every day on the Internet, reading publications, and watching TV business channels. I even write a detailed investment newsletter every month that I distribute to my investment group. It has become a fascinating hobby for me and has enriched my life and my pocketbook!**❞**

Sunny Steed, 60something
Pine Bluff, Arkansas

WHICH CIRCLE ISN'T PERFECTLY ROUND?

Turn the page for the **answer!**

Both circles are perfectly round in fact, but the clutter of additional lines can make the small circle seem to be an odd shape.

Steps 4–7 evaluate information, recommend a plan, and then implement and monitor the plan. These steps in the financial planning process can help you remove the clutter and enable you to come full circle in managing your money.

> **"**If you sacrifice a small amount now, you can gain a secure tomorrow.**"**
> **Frankie Roberts,** 52
> *Little Rock, Arkansas*

> **"**When I was 18 years old, I started my first job as a personnel secretary in an industrial plant. I worked for $.75 per hour. I opened a savings account and consistently saved a part of each check on a weekly basis. This one act started me on a lifestyle of saving a portion of my earnings that continues to this day.**"**
> **D. W.,** 64
> *Jonesboro, Arkansas*

STEP 4: *Evaluate the Information*

There comes a time in the planning process—after you have designed a mission statement, after you have gathered the necessary data, after you have set written goals—when you must find someone to evaluate the information. This step should not be underestimated. Having someone evaluate the data and begin to explore where you need to take your personal financial plan is a crucial step to designing a well-balanced, well-thought-out plan.

Who Is Qualified
Certified Financial Planner / Financial Adviser / Stockbroker / Tax Adviser / CPA
to Evaluate This Information?

Many people may be qualified to help you evaluate your financial situation. Now is the time to learn how to determine which type of adviser will most closely suit your personal needs.

Certified Financial Planner

A certified financial planner is a person who has taken several training courses to gain the knowledge and expertise to design written financial plans for clients.

These courses include:

- Financial planning and insurance
- Investment planning
- Income tax planning
- Retirement planning and employee benefits
- Estate planning

Each of these courses teaches certified financial planners both skills and ethics. A certified financial planner carries the designation CFP, which assures clients that the planner has fulfilled the necessary requirements and has kept up sufficiently with his or her continuing education to be able to offer clients a high level of service and professionalism. According to the Board of Standards for Certified Financial Planners, there were 34,102 CFPs as of May 31, 1999.

For these services, a customer may pay a fee or may pay commissions. Before you agree to the services offered by a certified financial planner, you should have the CFP fully outline all fees and costs.

Financial Adviser or Stockbroker

An adviser or broker may also be a fully licensed and trained financial executive. He or she may work for a major national or regional company, or for an independent investment company. While working for one of these companies, most financial advisers are given ongoing training, having already passed the Series 7 examination. This training and testing should mean that your stockbroker can help you create and maintain a financial plan for your family. However, because different financial advisers often focus on different aspects of investing, you may wish to see samples of financial plans and ask how fees are determined. By seeing the type of work different brokers/advisers perform, you should be better equipped to make an informed decision. Your job is to find a financial adviser whose long-term strategies and values conform with yours.

Tax Adviser or CPA

A tax adviser or CPA may also be an excellent source of information for your financial planning process. In many cases, it is advisable to take a team approach. You may wish to hire a financial adviser and a CPA or tax attorney to work together as a team to prepare and/or review the working financial plan.

Remember that taxes play a role in your financial planning process, and while they should not be the only factor in your financial decisions, it is good to study their impact.

The chart below illustrates some of the differences and similarities between the various advisers:

Certified Financial Planner	Financial Adviser/ Stockbroker	Tax Adviser/CPA
Fee Based and/or Commissioned Based	*Fee Based and/or Commissioned Based*	*Fee Based*
Gathers data and establishes goals	Should gather data; establishes goals	Should gather data; establishes goals
Evaluates information and recommends a plan	Evaluates information and recommends a plan	Evaluates information
		Depends on qualifications and licenses of the person
Implements the plan	Implements the plan	
Monitors the plan	Monitors the plan	Monitors the plan
		May consider tax impact/ prepare returns

Whether you choose a fee-based financial planner, a financial adviser, or a CPA, you may wish to interview several of these professionals to compare and contrast their strengths. It is also important to compare and contrast the costs associated with each type of planner. The bottom line: Will they get you where you need to go?

How will your adviser evaluate the information?   Many financial advisers in today's environment are aided by a wide assortment of computer software. Therefore, it is quite likely that the adviser of your choosing will input the data that you have gathered into a computer for analysis.

The plan generated from a computer analysis will probably include some or all of the following:

- A written policy statement outlining the parameters of your goals and objectives
- A clear statement of your risk tolerance level
- A review of your budget
- A list of your current financial assets and current asset allocation
- Help in quantifying your specific goals and guidance on how to reach those goals
- A review of your estate plan and insurance
- Specific recommendations regarding how much money you should be investing on a regular basis to reach your written goals
- Recommendations for any changes in your current holdings and for specific investments to match your risk tolerance level while allowing you to maximize your rates of return within your risk constraints

Conclusion. Evaluating the information you've gathered is as important as the first three steps. A skilled adviser may uncover pitfalls in your current financial plan that can be quickly corrected simply because they were identified.

However, just as a medical doctor has machines available to run lab tests and other tools to evaluate certain types of information, it is the doctor's advice and judgment that you count on for a correct diagnosis and treatment.

In the same way, many investors have found that while they may be able to gather the correct data, they don't have the expertise to go to the next step.

STEP 5: *Develop a Plan*

Once you have chosen a certified financial planner or financial adviser who has taken you through the necessary paperwork to create a written financial plan or you have evaluated the information on your own, the next step is to develop the actual financial plan itself.

The plan may be broken into several sections:

- A review of your current financial data
- An outline of your goals and objectives
- A review of your current asset allocation

- An explanation of your risk tolerance levels
- Specific recommendations
- A method and timetable for implementation
- A schedule to monitor recommendations

Your written financial plan should allow you to see a vision of your future. This single document is a treasure. I can't begin to tell you what a difference a plan will make.

Almost every person who walks into my office anticipates to some degree that they will be OK if they save a certain amount of money and make the right investments. Their hope is that the day they turn 65 and walk out of their workplace after a lovely retirement party, they will have good health, a long life, and financial security.

Won't it be a great feeling to take the mystery out of your planning? Well, *by designing a money mission statement, setting quantified goals, and laying out a plan of action to reach those goals, you'll be well on your way to your financial freedom.*

The best plans are very simple. You should be able to understand your adviser's recommendations and, in the best of all worlds, you should still be able to understand the recommendations after you get home!

This is your plan. These recommendations are there to accomplish your goals. If you have any questions or hesitations about the plan, now's the time to voice your concerns.

Of course, you do have options:

1. You may choose to pay an ongoing fee to a fee-based financial planner for developing your initial plan and managing the investments.

2. You may choose to pay a one-time fee to a fee-based financial planner for developing your initial plan and hire someone else to manage the investments.

3. With all the information available in books and on the Internet, you may wish to create your own financial plan and manage your investments yourself.

4. However, many of you will still choose to hire a professional adviser to recommend a plan of action.

Conclusion.   Regardless of who prepares your financial plan, you should slowly and methodically walk through this new document. The document is a powerful tool, and you will be one of the very few people in America who have taken the time to commit to putting their current financial situation in writing. By taking the time to determine where you are today, where you want to go in the future, and how you plan to get there, you have dramatically increased your odds of accomplishing your goals.

You cannot begin to estimate the power of a financial plan. Writing your financial goals and committing them to paper will put you in the "three percent club." Why do so few Americans take time to properly plan their financial future when the process can be so simple? Possibly because many people feel they have waited too late to begin planning or they feel there's no money available to implement a financial plan. Whatever the reason, those individuals should rethink their position.

Now is the time to take control of your financial future!

STEP 6: *Implementing the Plan*

Once a financial adviser (for those of you using one) has recommended a specific plan of action, it is your responsibility to implement the various aspects of the plan. This can be one of the most difficult steps of the financial planning process for one basic reason—the fear of losing your money.

Most people have worked their entire life to accumulate their money, and any type of change to their current way of investing can feel uncomfortable. Fear of losing money is one of the biggest objections to investing for the longer term, and it should be recognized as a valid objection.

People can and will lose money in various types of investments. Yet these very same people know they must implement a plan of action that will allow them to achieve their future personal financial goals. Therefore, one of the roles of advisers should be to educate clients about every individual investment alternative until the clients fully understand the underlying risk-return relationship of each portion of their financial plan.

DALBAR conducted a study of what people expected from their advisers. The 1997 study found that "making money does not top the investor's list of priorities; rather, most people seek to be educated (83%). . . ." The study also found that
- 80% want a financial adviser to minimize their tax bill;
- 70% want their financial adviser to provide the highest returns for their portfolio;
- 64% want . . . a financial plan; and
- 58% want their financial adviser to change their investments.

Source: Quantitative Analysis of Investor Behavior Study (1997); DALBAR, Inc., Boston.

If risk could be more adequately understood, investors should be able to increase their comfort level. In actuality, using modern portfolio theories and some computer screening tools, your financial adviser should be able to more fully quantify the actual amount of risk you are willing to assume and build a plan around your risk tolerance level. The concept of risk will be explored in greater detail in Chapter 8.

The fear quotient should nonetheless not be underestimated. Most people will tell you that the expected rate of return will never be high enough if they cannot sleep well at night.

Consider Taking the Sleep Test

Before you implement your proposed investment plan, you may want to sleep on the recommendations for a couple of days and see how you feel. As simple as this test is, it can save you a lot of future trouble.

At times, the various stock markets go down, which usually cause individual stocks and stock mutual funds to drop in value. At other times, interest rates go up, which typically cause individual bonds and bond funds to drop in value. The point is that there are no perfect investments. But there should be a way to blend together a portfolio of assets that will allow you to reach your personal financial goals while still allowing you to sleep at night. If you don't think you will be comfortable with the recommended plan, talk to your financial adviser about your concerns and work together until you reach a comfort zone.

The final decision is yours. Don't feel rushed or pressured into a decision. It *is* your money and the adviser is acting as a facilitator only. Trust your personal judgment—it's a very trustworthy gauge.

Nonetheless, the day will come when it's time for that crucial meeting with your financial adviser. The checkbook will come out, money will be handed over to the firm of your choosing, and you'll direct the financial adviser to place the orders that implement your investment strategy. This will most likely not be a one-time event. It is quite common for the implementation phase of the financial planning process to stretch over the entire life expectancy of the client. Your financial adviser will probably establish one or several systematic investment plans to help you accumulate the necessary capital to reach your future goals.

You may have financial assets scattered in many different physical locations. For many investors, keeping up with the sheer amount of mail has become an impossible task. One of the best parts of implementing a financial plan with a trained planner is that the planner will work with you to organize your finances and make your life simpler.

Part of the implementation process may include helping you physically organize your investments. The advantage of having one financial adviser is that he or she will have all the information relating to your personal situation and will be much more likely to help you make wise and prudent decisions on an ongoing basis.

Feeling organized is a wonderful encouragement alone to many people. Before they had a plan, many of my clients felt they had a "shoebox strategy" because they kept all of their financial information in a shoebox. Now they have a consolidated plan that is moving them closer and closer to their personal destination. Financial disorganization is like trying to steer a large cruise ship whose propellers are pointing in different directions. But

You and Your

Money Markets / Bonds / Stock Certificates
Annuities / Savings / Checking / Visa

Financial Adviser

with the propellers in exactly the right position and a trained captain guiding the crew, a ship can chart the course of its choosing.

The same is true with the implementation of your financial plan.

Conclusion.   Implementing the plan is a lot like rappelling off a cliff for the first time. It is critically important to have completed all of the necessary training and "gear checks." But there comes a time when you are required, and even encouraged, to take that first step over the edge to the side of the mountain. A solid financial plan will be your rope and your financial adviser will be your guide.

STEP 7: *Monitoring the Plan*

It is an amazing fact that many investors will finally turn their hard-earned money over to their financial adviser and will commit to implementing a financial plan, but they won't devise a structured method of monitoring the performance of their money.

To properly monitor your investments you should do the following:

- Learn to read all sections of your investment statements.
- Schedule regular performance reviews with your financial adviser or, if you are managing you own investments, schedule specific times to review all of your holdings.
- Attend classes to increase your personal knowledge.
- Read to understand investment terms and definitions.
- Understand how various indexes act as a benchmark for performance.
- Realize that monitoring performance is partly *your* responsibility.

Reviewing the Financial Planning Process

Each step of the financial planning process builds on the step before. Very few people become rich by accident. Therefore, the rest of us need a financial plan. Only a small percentage of Americans take the time to develop a written financial plan. You want to be a part of that percentage. The investors who take the time to develop a written financial plan have a much better opportunity to accomplish their future goals.

These are the seven steps to creating your written financial plan:

1. Design your mission statement
2. Gather the necessary data
3. Set written goals
4. Evaluate the information
5. Recommend a plan
6. Implement the plan
7. Monitor the plan

PART TWO

Understanding Your Investment Options

The Ten Myths
of Investing

> "My only regret is that I did not begin a regular plan of investing every month when I received my first paycheck. I wasted at least 15 years."
>
> **Beverly Bowman,** 69
> *Cherokee Village, Arkansas*

> "The best investment we ever made was General Electric stock. I have learned to buy quality."
>
> **Mary S. East,** 70
> *Little Rock, Arkansas*

> "Hindsight is always better than foresight."
>
> **Wallace Cummings,** 69
> *North Little Rock, Arkansas*

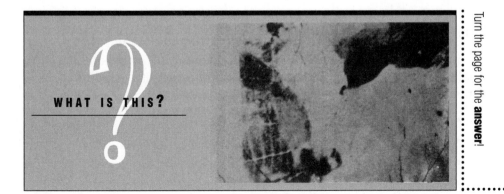

WHAT IS THIS?

Turn the page for the **answer!**

It's a cow! Go back and look at the shadows and you'll see the head of a cow. When I first saw this picture, I couldn't see anything; it looked like a lot of spots to me. Then someone told me that it was the head of a cow and she began to point at the cow's eyes. Once I saw the eyes, I saw the cow. Just as someone pointed out the highlights that allowed me to see the cow, Part 2 will increase your knowledge of some of the highlights of the investment process. Chapter 5 is intended to dispel a few myths.

Having finished Part 1, you should now have an understanding of the seven steps to creating your financial plan. Now imagine this:

You are sitting at a drafting table with a large, blank sheet of drafting paper in front of you. Your pencil is resting comfortably in your hand and your mind is alert. Suddenly and with enormous patience and care, you begin to draw blueprints of a building. The lines of the drawing are crisp and clear. The underlying engineering has been well thought out, and as the drawing takes shape, the beauty and functionality amaze even you. This is not just any building. It is the outline of your financial future.

And as blueprints go, your blueprint is a work of art.

Unfortunately, it is still just a blueprint. Your next step will be gaining knowledge and therefore increasing your confidence to the level necessary to accomplish your goals. This is a very exciting part of the process because it gives you the power to dream and moves you a little further toward financial independence.

Many myths and a few startling truths surround the process of financial planning and wealth building. Revealing the ins and outs of the misconceptions should help you move closer to financial security. This chapter will highlight ten of the most common myths of investing.

MYTH 1: *All Investors Are Created Equal*

All investors are *not* created equal. Each person has unique and varied qualities that make up his or her ability to invest and save. Some of these differences include:

- Age
- Income
- Current net worth
- Current debt load

- Number and age of children
- Personal risk tolerance
- Current level of investment knowledge
- Current interest in investing.

These factors indicate that we are all different and subsequently the way we approach our finances will be different. Some people have no plan; they "shoot from the hip." Others carefully and methodically plan for their future.

The point: One Size Does Not Fit All. Each investor is different.

MYTH 2: *Men and Women Want Different Things from Their Money*

While I will agree that men and women will differ in the ways they are willing to invest their money, both are working toward the same goal. Most investors are hoping to achieve one thing: *financial security.*

Even though the amount of money it takes to achieve financial security differs from person to person, almost every investor says the same thing: "Help me plan to accumulate a large enough sum of money to provide a replacement income for our retirement years."

MYTH 3: *CDs Are Safe*

CDs are insured by the Federal Deposit Insurance Corporation (FDIC) up to $100,000 for principal and interest. But *safe* may not be the proper word to describe them. Let me illustrate with a brief pop quiz.

Quickly scan the paragraph below and count the number of "Fs."

FINISHED FILES ARE THE RESULT
OF YEARS OF SCIENTIFIC STUDY
COMBINED WITH THE EXPERIENCE
OF MANY YEARS.

How many "Fs" did you count? There are six!

FINISHED FILES ARE THE RESULT
OF YEARS OF SCIENTIFIC STUDY
COMBINED WITH THE EXPERIENCE
OF MANY YEARS.

Now that you see the paragraph in this format, it's easy to see there are actually six "Fs." Many people see only three "Fs." They look at the "Ofs" and read them as "Vs" from the sound and skip over the letter. I find this to be a fascinating brainteaser with an excellent application to investing.

What you think you see may not be what you *really* see!

I would like to illustrate my theory that I call "The Three 'Ofs' of Safety" by showing you a table of the actual rates of return for six-month CDs from 1969 through 1997 as provided by the Federal Reserve Board. They represent the average annual return an investor would have received by owning six-month CDs and rolling them over into a new six-month CD each time they matured.

6-Month CDs					
Year	**Return**	**Year**	**Return**	**Year**	**Return**
1969	7.91%	1979	11.44%	1989	9.08%
1970	7.65	1980	12.99	1990	8.17
1971	5.21	1981	15.77	1991	5.91
1972	5.02	1982	12.57	1992	3.76
1973	8.31	1983	9.27	1993	3.28
1974	9.98	1984	10.68	1994	4.96
1975	6.89	1985	8.25	1995	5.98
1976	5.62	1986	6.50	1996	5.47
1977	5.92	1987	7.01	1997	5.73
1978	8.61	1988	7.85		

Source: Federal Reserve Board.

For purposes of illustration, let's assume that a 60-year-old man named Harry walked into his financial adviser's office in 1969 and told him, "I am 60 years old. I have accumulated $100,000 in savings and I want you to invest this money to provide me with a supplemental income. And, by the way, I *want no risk!* So please invest this $100,000 into six-month CDs and mail me the interest once a year."

The financial adviser followed Harry's instructions and at the end of 1969 mailed Harry a check for $7,910 ($100,000 × 7.91% = $7,910). Harry was very pleased with his strategy. In 1969 Harry could have purchased a luxury car for $7,910 or lived very comfortably.

But two years passed and at the end of 1971 the financial adviser mailed Harry a check for $5,210, explaining, "Harry, interest rates have declined and the amount of interest has been reduced." Harry wasn't pleased that his supplemental retirement income had dropped from $7,910 to $5,210 in just two years, and he began to wonder what would happen if interest rates continued to fall.

But by 1981 Harry was feeling like a genius. His $100,000 principal was FDIC-insured, and he had just received a check for $15,770. His strategy was working again.

However, by 1983 Harry was not so thrilled. That year he received a check for $9,270, a cut from his 1981 check of $15,770. And if we fast-forward to 1997, we find a very unhappy Harry. In 1997 he received a check for $5,730.

As Harry began to reflect on his no-risk strategy of putting all of his retirement savings into six-month CDs, he realized he had a few misconceptions about safety and risk.

The Three "Of's" of Safety are outlined below:

1. Safety of principal.   CDs do offer safety of principal. As previously mentioned, they are federally insured by the FDIC for up to $100,000. Harry's money was protected from any risk against principal.

2. Safety of income.   CDs didn't offer Harry a guaranteed stream of income. In fact, the volatility and unpredictably of interest rates have been a constant source of worry for investors who are living on the interest checks they receive from their investments. These investors, like Harry, are forced to accept whatever amount of interest they receive as their income, and they are expected to adjust their standard of living around the movements in interest rates. The only thing that is certain in our economy is that it will change constantly.

3. Safety of purchasing power.   CDs didn't offer Harry any protection against inflation. In fact, while Harry emphatically stated that he wanted not risk, he unwittingly opted for the most certain risk of all: inflation.

Inflation was a horrendous problem for Harry. He started his investment strategy in 1969 with $100,000. And in 1969 his principal of $100,000 would actually buy $100,000 worth of goods and services. His principal in 1969 would have almost allowed him to buy a mansion. It would have certainly purchased a very large home with plenty of land.

But as sure as the sun rises, inflation began to eat away Harry's purchasing power. Let's just assume that inflation was 3 percent from 1969 to 1997. At a 3 percent inflation rate, Harry's principal would now spend like $43,707. I feel pretty confident that no investor would intentionally invest $100,000 with the expectation that 28 years later that investment would be worth $43,707.

Further, inflation not only affected the purchasing power of Harry's principal, it also affected the purchasing power of the annual interest checks he was expected to live on. If he received a check for $7,910 in 1969, Harry would need to be receiving $18,907, using the same 3 percent inflation rate, to maintain the same standard of living, but as you know, he was actually receiving only $5,730.

If this were a true story, Harry would now be 88 years old with a supplemental income that wouldn't keep him above the poverty level.

This does not mean you should not own CDs. I often use CDs to provide safety of principal and a current income to certain portfolios. But, I believe you should be aware of how to properly place CDs into your portfolio.

MYTH 4: *It Takes a Lot of Money to Work with a Financial Adviser*

Many people think you must have already accumulated a large sum of money before you can seek the advice and expertise of a financial adviser. Everyone needs a plan. It doesn't matter if you have millions of dollars or if you live on $450 a month.

Your job is to find the adviser or planner that specializes in helping people just like you.

MYTH 5: *You Better Wait Until the Market Is Low Before Investing Your Money*

This is one of my favorite myths. Of course, I would love to be able to time the stock market perfectly and know when buying is low and selling high. But it is virtually impossible to time the stock market. People have tried for years to pick the market's best entry and exit points. And while a few have succeeded for short periods of time, few, if any, have been able to profit from the strategy over the long term.

Investors are always afraid of buying at the wrong time. In rebuttal to this misconception, one of my favorite advertisements is the hypothetical Louie the Loser, reprinted in Figure 5.1.

FIGURE 5.1   *Louie the Loser*

Because Louie knows time is more important than timing when investing.

Louie the Loser invested $10,000 a year in The Investment Company of America over the past 20 years. Because Louie's timing is terrible, it's no surprise that each year he somehow picked the worst possible day to invest – the day the unmanaged Dow Jones Industrial Average peaked.

How has Louie done?

In spite of his bad timing, he still managed to turn his total investment of $200,000 into more than $1 million, growing at an average rate of 15.7% a year.

What's truly telling, however, is that even if Louie had picked the *best* days to invest, he wouldn't have done that much better – 17.2% a year.

What Louie learned is that while there are good times and bad times, over the long haul any day is a good day to invest. As a result, he fared much better than if he had waited for the "perfect" time to invest.

Louie's story offers proof that *time is more important than timing when investing.* That's one thing we know for sure.

Here are The Investment Company of America's total return and average annual compound returns with all distributions reinvested for periods ended 12/31/97 (the most recent calendar quarter), assuming payment of the 5.75% maximum sales charge at the beginning of the stated periods: 10 years, +15.60; 5 years, +16.35; 12 months, +22.34.

The figures shown reflect past results which are not predictive of future results. Share price and return will vary, so investors may lose money by investing in the fund. The shorter the time period of the investment, the greater the possibility of loss. Fund shares are not deposits or obligations of, or insured or guaranteed by, the U.S. government, any financial institution, the Federal Deposit Insurance Corporation, or any other agency, entity or person.

Investments on the Worst Possible Days (Market Highs)

Date of Market High	Cumulative Investment	Account Value on 12/31
9/8/78	$ 10,000	$ 8,323
10/5/97	20,000	19,212
11/20/80	30,000	32,496
4/27/81	40,000	41,689
12/27/82	50,000	65,247
11/29/83	60,000	87,809
1/6/84	70,000	103,628
12/16/85	80,000	147,920
12/2/86	90,000	189,462
8/25/87	100,000	207,428
10/21/88	110,000	244,658
10/9/89	120,000	326,136
7/16/90	130,000	337,556
12/31/91	140,000	436,902
6/1/92	150,000	477,729
12/29/93	160,000	542,994
1/31/94	170,000	553,346
12/13/95	180,000	732,608
12/27/96	190,000	884,008
8/6/97	200,000	**1,157,701**

Average annual return: +15.7%

A program of regular investing neither ensures a profit nor protects against a loss, and investors should consider their willingness to keep investing when share prices are declining.

MYTH 6: *You Can Believe Everything You See on TV or Read in a Publication*

More than one client has called me after watching a television report warning that the stock market is about to collapse. These clients then ask if they should sell everything in their account.

Or they read an investment magazine that is reviewing mutual funds for the past year, and they don't see their mutual fund listed in the report. Even worse, they see in a publication that their mutual fund has received a neutral or a negative rating. Or they see in the latest research report on one of their stock holdings that the rating has been reduced.

Reading and staying informed is an important part of investing. Unfortunately, newspapers are written daily and magazines are published monthly. Therefore, you will often see your personal investment holdings in the press on a fairly regular basis. The problem is that sometimes the articles are favorable and sometimes they're negative, but they can make a real impact on the way you feel about your investment strategies.

Sometimes the negative press takes precedence over the good news that abounds, and you're forced to decide whom and what you are to believe. Yet you must decide whether you are going to be a long-term investor or someone who reacts to every article. The sheer amount of information available is incredible.

Here are a few things that may help you overcome the day-to-day jitters:

- Buy quality.
- Invest for the long term.
- Diversify your investments.
- Consider investing on a regular basis.
- Review the long-term track records of a stock or mutual fund before investing.
- Increase your personal understanding of how risk works.

MYTH 7: *Rates of Return Remain Fairly Constant*

The seventh myth is that you can always count on the same rates of return that you have enjoyed over the past five years. The various markets are living, constantly changing vehicles. Although you want to choose investments that have had good long-term track records with above-average performances, you can't simply rely on past performance, as shown in Figure 5.2, to predict which investment alternatives will do well in the future.

FIGURE 5.2   *Historical Investment Returns from 1990 through 1998*

Master Review Table™—1990s									
Year	**1998**	**1997**	**1996**	**1995**	**1994**	**1993**	**1992**	**1991**	**1990**
Inflation	1.6	1.7	3.3	2.5	2.8	2.7	2.9	3.1	6.1
FHA Mortgage Rate	7	7.9	8.2	8.2	8.7	7.5	8.5	9.3	10.2
Prime Rate	8.4	8.4	8.3	8.8	7.2	6	6.3	8.4	10
Dow Jones 30 Ind. Avg. with div.	18.1	24.9	28.9	36.9	5	16.9	7.4	24.2	−0.6
S&P Comp Index with div.	28.6	33.4	23	37.6	1.3	10	7.6	30.4	−3.3
NASDAQ Index	39.6	21.6	22.7	39.9	−3.2	14.8	15.5	56.8	−17.8
Wiesenberger Growth Mutual Fund Avg with div.	19.2	24.7	19.3	31.2	−1.4	11.9	8.7	36.6	−4.5
Wiesenberger Income Mutual Fund Avg with div.	9.6	19.2	12.2	23.7	−2	11.7	8.9	22.1	−0.8
Nelson U.S. Equity Peer Universe Index	15.1	26.4	21.4	32.9	0.8	16	12.2	39.3	−3.2
Morgan Stanley Europe with div.	28.9	24.2	21.6	22.1	2.7	29.8	−4.3	13.7	−3.4
Morgan Stanley EAFE with div.	20.3	2.1	6.4	11.6	8.1	32.9	−11.9	12.5	−23.2
Morgan Stanley Pacific Index with div.	2.7	−25.3	−8.4	3	13	36	−18.2	11.5	−34.3
US Single Family House Price	1.6	3.4	1.9	2.8	4.8	4.3	1.3	1.3	1.9
Farmland	5.8	6.2	7	6.4	6.3	3.2	1.4	2.9	2.3
REITs	−18.8	18.9	35.8	18.3	0.8	18.6	12.2	35.7	−17.4
Moody's Corp. Bond Yield, Aaa	6.5	7.3	7.6	7.6	8	7.5	8.1	8.8	9.3
Lehman Bros. Corp. Long Term Index	9	13.5	2.2	27.9	−5.8	13.6	9.3	21	6.5
Lehman Bros. Trsy. Long Term Index	13.5	15.1	−0.9	30.7	−7.6	17.3	8	18.5	6.3
Lehman Bros. Muni. Long Term Index	6.9	11.3	4.4	23.3	−9.1	14.8	10.2	13.6	7.2
US Treasury 10-Year Bond Yield	5.3	6.4	6.4	6.6	7.1	5.9	7	7.9	8.6
Salomon US Treasury 10-Yr. Bond Index	12.9	11.3	0.1	23.7	−7.8	11.9	6.5	17.2	6.8
US Treasury 3-Year Bond Yield	5.1	6.1	6	6.3	6.3	4.4	5.3	6.8	8.3
US Treasury 3-Month Bill Yield	4.9	5.2	5.1	5.6	4.4	3.1	3.5	5.5	7.8
Certificates of Deposit Yield 3-Month	5.5	5.6	5.4	5.9	4.6	3.2	3.7	5.8	8.2
Taxable Money Market Average	5.1	5.1	4.9	5.5	3.8	2.7	3.4	5.7	7.8
US Savings Bonds	5.1	5.4	4.6	4.6	4	5.2	6	6	6
Gold	0.6	−22.2	−4.6	1.2	−2.4	17.5	−5.6	−10.1	−2.5
Silver	−15.1	25.7	−7.4	4.9	−4.1	38.4	−4.7	−7.8	−19.4
Rapaport Diamond Index	−1.1	2.6	6.6	1.4	0.7	1.3	−0.4	−0.6	0.3
Wiesenberger Equity Variable Annuity Index	12.7	17.4	16.8	25.5	−1.6	17.5	4.6	30.5	−6.6
Wiesenberger Fixed Inc. Variable Annuity Index	4	6.8	4.7	12.8	−2.6	8	5.6	13.8	4.3

Source: Wiesenberger Investment Performance Digest, 1999 Edition, Wiesenberger, a Thomson Financial Company, 1455 Research Blvd., Rockville, MD 20850; 800-232-2285.

It's apparent that the same investment can have a wide range of actual year-to-year returns. Most investors tend to focus on the averages, and the volatility of many investment alternatives can smooth out over time, but the difficult periods are real and can impact your ability to make prudent decisions.

Take a few minutes to review Figure 5.2. Look at Standard & Poor's composite index (S&P 500). The S&P 500 is an index of 500 widely held common stocks. By reviewing this index, you can track the overall trends of the stock market.

From 1990 through 1998, the S&P 500 had one negative year (–3.3% in 1990), one lackluster year (+1.3% in 1994), two decent years (+7.6% in 1992 and + 10% in 1993) and five truly outstanding years of growth (+30.4% in 1991, +37.6% in 1995, +33.4% in 1997, and +28.6% in 1998). Looking back over these returns, investing in the stock market appears to be as easy as picking up money off the ground.

But let me illustrate the emotions of many investors, using Aunt Jane as an example. Aunt Jane decided to invest in the stock market for the very first time on December 31, 1989. She was thrilled at the prospect of increasing her potential for higher returns by investing in an S&P 500 Index fund.

As usually happens with first-time investors, Jane invested just before a difficult year and by the end of 1990 had lost 3.3 percent. (Of course, the press was all over the fact that the stock market was in a difficult period that could get much worse.) Jane became very concerned and decided she was not cut out for the stock market, so on December 1990 she sold all of her holdings for a loss.

Now that Jane was out of the market, the S&P 500 Index rallied sharply in 1991 and was up 30.4 percent (the press was really excited!) and Jane thought she was the only person in the country not making money. So on January 2, 1992, she put her money back in and by year's end made 7.6 percent. In 1993 she made 10 percent, but in 1994 only 1.3 percent. The market had become quite volatile and the nightly news was filled with contradicting projections. On December 31, 1994, Jane sold everything and, as fate would have it, the next four years provided the best performance the S&P 500 Index had ever shown, but Jane was on the sidelines; she never got back in because the market was always "too high."

Human nature is just like that—sell a holding if it is performing poorly over a short time and buy it after it has gone up. But the difficulty of the stock market is that you are often called to take action against what human nature tells you because bad periods are often followed by good returns and good periods are often followed by bad returns.

So what are you going to do? Try to stop worrying about what the stock market is going to do over the next quarter or even over the next year or two and focus on the long-term growth potential of some of the greatest companies in the world.

MYTH 8: *Move All of Your Money to Your Best-Performing Investment in the Past Year*

This myth advises the opposite of what you probably should be doing. The famous investor Warren Buffett has created a fortune for himself and for the shareholders in his company, Berkshire Hathaway, by implementing the exact opposite investment strategy. He looks for stocks that are currently out of favor and buys them while their share prices are low. He is often quoted as saying, "The time to buy straw hats is in the wintertime." His point should be well taken.

As a mother of two children under three, I, with my husband, often shop the end-of-the-season sales. We bought my son's winter coat at the end of last winter for 40 percent off. Temperatures were rising and the store realized that not many people would buy the coats at full price. We bought the coat at almost half price last year, and as fall approached, the same coats were selling at full price again.

Investing is the same. You have to reverse your thinking. If the stock of a quality company is down because of a temporary slowdown, that may be the time to buy. Or if the stock market has taken a drop from some unforeseen news, use that as an opportunity to add to your quality holdings at lower prices.

It's human nature to want to stick with the winners in your portfolio, and I believe that good performance often leads to more good performance. Yet a very interesting study has clearly illustrated that the best-performing investment vehicles of one year often become the worst-performing the next year.

Notice that over the past five years, only one of the ten investment alternatives repeated as the top-performing asset. In fact, often the top performers of one year become poor performers the next and sometimes the reverse is true. If you looked at the Nasdaq returns of –3.20 percent in 1994, you might have been inclined to sell your holdings or you might have been hesitant to invest any new money into such a poorly performing asset category. Yet the next year the Nasdaq index was the number one per-

FIGURE 5.3   *Investment Vehicle Rankings, 1994–1998*

Year-to-Year Rankings 1994–1998									
1998		**1997**		**1996**		**1995**		**1994**	
1. NASDAQ	39.63	1. S&P 500	33.40	1. REIT	35.75	1. NASDAQ	39.90	1. Dow Jones 30	5.00
2. S&P 500	28.58	2. Silver	25.70	2. Dow Jones 30	28.91	2. S&P 500	37.60	2. One-Family House	4.80
3. Dow Jones 30	18.13	3. Dow Jones 30	24.90	3. S&P 500	22.96	3. Dow Jones 30	36.90	3. S&P 500	1.30
4. Leh Brs LT Treas	13.52	4. NASDAQ	21.60	4. NASDAQ	22.71	4. Leh Brs LT Treas	30.70	4. REIT	0.80
5. Weis VA Eq	12.73	5. REIT	18.90	5. Weis VA Eq	16.80	5. Weis VA Eq	25.50	5. Rapaport Diamond	0.70
6. One-Family House	1.60	6. Weis VA Eq	17.40	6. Rapaport Diamonds	6.60	6. REIT	18.30	6. Weis VA Eq	(1.60)
7. Gold	0.57	7. Leh Brs LT Treas	15.10	7. One-Family House	1.84	7. Silver	4.90	7. Gold	(2.40)
8. Rapaport Diamond	(1.10)	8. One-Family House	3.40	8. Leh Brs LT Treas	(0.87)	8. One-Family House	2.80	8. NASDAQ	(3.20)
9. Silver	(15.05)	9. Rapaport Diamonds	2.60	9. Gold	(4.64)	9. Rapaport Diamond	1.40	9. Silver	(4.10)
10. REIT	(18.82)	10. Gold	(22.20)	10. Silver	(7.44)	10. Gold	1.20	10. Leh Brs LT Treas	(7.60)

Source: Wiesenberger Investment Performance Digest, 1999 Edition, Wiesenberger, a Thomson Financial Company, 1455 Research Blvd., Rockville, MD 20850; 800-232-2285.

forming class with a total return of 39.90 percent. Then look at silver in 1996—ranking number ten with a –7.44 percent return only to move to the number two spot in 1997 with a 25.70 percent return and then falling back to number nine in 1998 with a –15.05 percent return.

The swings from year to year can be confounding. So what are you going to do? It all goes back to selecting the proper mix of investments. As you read further in this book, you'll learn about *asset allocation,* which is the technical term for choosing the right blend of cash, bonds, and stocks to help you meet your personal goals while allowing you to invest within your risk tolerance levels.

Myths 7 and 8 are all about trying to catch the latest investment wave. All of us want to be in the right place at the right time, but the problem is that none of us knows when or what the next big move will be. Far too many people find themselves jumping from investment to investment just after all the money has been made. Then they turn right around and sell just before more money is going to be made.

MYTH 9: *The Specific Mutual Fund You Choose Is the Most Important Factor in Your Investment Success*

So many people are so overwhelmed by the sheer number of mutual fund choices that they are never able to implement their investment plan. For this research I used Morningstar Principia data dated March 31, 1999. Chicago-based Morningstar, Inc., is a leading provider of investment information, research, and analysis. Its extensive line of Internet software and print products provide unbiased data and commentary on mutual funds, U.S. and international equities, closed-end funds, and variable annuities. Established in 1984, Morningstar continues to be the industry's most trusted source of key investment issues. For more information about Morningstar, visit www.morningstar.com or call 800-735-0700.

I searched for all growth and income mutual funds with a ten-year track record and found 143 funds that met the criteria. I next attempted to split the 143 funds into quintiles (20 percent) so you could see the variance in performance. Over this ten-year period the top individual fund averaged 22.83 percent and the worst individual fund averaged –8.80 percent.

The top 28 funds averaged:	18.40%
Funds 29–56 averaged:	16.31%
Funds 57–84 averaged:	15.23%
Funds 85–112 averaged:	14.20%
Funds 113–143 averaged:	10.28%

While all of us would have liked to have picked funds in the top quintile, which could have generated an 18.40 percent average return, the real question is, "Which ten-year average would you have been terribly disappointed in earning?" Even 10.28 percent is an outstanding average historically. Your money would compound very nicely at that rate.

What this research tells us is that it doesn't necessarily matter which specific mutual fund you are in but rather you should choose a mutual fund with a long-term track record, whose objectives and risk factors most closely align with your goals. And remember, the longer your investment outlook, the better your chances for higher returns.

MYTH 10: *Investing in the Stock Market Is Not for Everyone*

If you're going to constantly worry about your money, investing in the market is not worth the risk. This may seem like a trick comment because this same statement appears in the myth section and in the truth section. While some people don't tolerate risk very well, they should know that a portfolio of "safe" investments like CDs, Treasuries, passbook savings, money markets, or fixed annuities may not allow them to make an annual rate of return high enough to reach their future retirement goals. For some people, not accumulating a large enough nest egg could be the biggest risk of all.

If we talk about not sleeping at night, it's easy to calculate the anticipated rate of return that your plan will require. If a portfolio of "guaranteed" investment vehicles won't help you reach your goal—then you are guaranteed to fail.

FIGURE 5.4   *Average Percentage Returns of 143 Mutual Funds over the Ten-Year Period, March 31, 1989–March 31, 1999*

Top 28 Funds	Funds 29–56	Funds 57–84	Funds 85–112	Funds 113–143
22.83%	17.33%	15.67%	14.68%	13.40%
20.54	17.20	15.66	14.62	13.39
19.54	17.18	15.62	14.60	13.38
19.35	16.97	15.60	14.55	13.34
19.28	16.96	15.58	14.53	13.31
19.27	16.91	15.56	14.50	13.20
18.81	16.85	15.55	14.50	12.98
18.72	16.78	15.48	14.47	12.97
18.69	16.67	15.46	14.43	12.66
18.66	16.51	15.46	14.41	12.59
18.57	16.34	15.41	14.38	12.34
18.56	16.33	15.37	14.30	12.15
18.49	16.26	15.26	14.29	11.99
18.37	16.24	15.21	14.26	11.86
18.32	16.20	15.20	14.25	11.86
18.15	16.09	15.20	14.23	11.74
18.13	16.08	15.15	14.16	11.18
18.08	16.07	15.13	14.13	10.99
18.07	15.99	15.13	14.12	10.94
18.00	15.95	15.06	14.04	10.76
17.83	15.94	15.02	13.99	10.64
17.82	15.90	14.99	13.98	10.45
17.78	15.88	14.98	13.91	9.93
17.68	15.87	14.85	13.89	9.71
17.59	15.83	14.85	13.82	9.03
17.53	15.82	14.85	13.78	8.98
17.51	15.76	14.81	13.68	8.22
17.37	15.73	14.71	13.67	7.76
				7.31
				1.45
				−8.80
Average Return **18.40%**	**16.31%**	**15.23%**	**14.20%**	**10.28%**

Source: Morningstar, Inc.

So what are you to do if you can't stomach the risk of the stock market but your financial projections uncover a need for a higher rate of return? Consider these ideas:

- You can lower the income you think you'll need at retirement age.
- You can reduce your current outgoing expense level so you'll be able to invest a large portion of your current income.
- You can work with your financial adviser to increase your personal understanding of how stock and stock mutual funds investments work.

Knowledge is the key: While hundreds of banks around the country were failing during the Great Depression, many companies, such as Coca Cola, kept on selling their products. In fact, these are companies that made it safely through one of the worst periods in our recent economic history and are still in business today: Chrysler (merged recently with Daimler-Benz), Coca-Cola, Eastman Kodak, General Electric, General Foods, Goodyear Tire and Rubber, International Business Machines, Proctor & Gamble, and U.S. Steel.

The ten myths just described are merely some of my favorites. Part of what makes investing your money so difficult is that many correct decisions run contrary to human nature. We are creatures of emotion, and we have a hard time separating emotion from strategy.

The Ten Truths
of Investing

> **"**You've always heard that money talks; all it ever said to me was 'Goodbye!'**"**
> **Madelene Clark,** 81
> *Jonesboro, Arkansas*

> **"**I wish I had taken an interest in investments and studying stocks, mutual funds, and the like and started financial planning at an early age. I still know very little about investing and am learning. The best financial advice I ever received? Putting all my resources together. The worst advice? Going into business with relatives. Last, it is never too late to learn how to invest.**"**
> **S.S.,** 66
> *Jonesboro, Arkansas*

HILL OR CRATER?

Turn the page for the **answer!**

It depends on the direction from which you view the picture. If you look at it upright, you see a crater. If you turn the picture over, you see a hill. The truths of investing are often the same. Your perspective will make an impact on how you choose to view investing.

   This chapter is filled with some favorite investment truths that should give you some insight into how the professionals attempt to manage their money.

> **❝** Get a good financial planner, buy good stocks and investments, and sit back and let them work for you. Don't look at your investments every day, but do review them at least once a year. Don't panic when the market dips. **❞**
> **Geraldine Milam,** 64
> *Graham, Texas*

> **❝** Make sure you have a sense of direction. Find an investing formula that works for you. . . . The best piece of advice I ever received was to have a regular monthly investment plan and stick with it. **❞**
> **Mike Stovall,** 40
> *Graham, Texas*

Just as there are common misconceptions about investing, there are also many truths. These truths should be the building blocks of your personal knowledge for understanding your investment strategies. The ten truths listed in this chapter are by no means exclusive, but they are offered to answer some of the most common questions and concerns that you may have.

TRUTH 1: *No One Should Know More About Your Money Than You!*

Here is a conversation you might hear during the initial meeting with a new customer in my office:

   Allyson: It's a pleasure to meet with you this morning, and I look forward to working with you. Let's get right down to business and talk about your financial goals and objectives.
   Client: *I want to be able to retire and put my children through college.*

Allyson: Do you know when you plan to retire or how much income you will need to be able to retire comfortably?

Client: *I haven't thought about that.*

Allyson: Have you tried to quantify your future financial needs to determine how much money you will need to accumulate before you retire?

Client: *No, I don't even understand the question.*

Allyson: Financial planning will allow us to find out where you are today, determine a specific amount of money that you will need to accumulate for your future, and then design a written plan that will outline how much money you will need to begin to save now to reach those future goals. How does that sound?

Client: *That sounds great. I would love to have a plan.*

Allyson: Let's begin by looking at your monthly budget.

Client: *What budget? (Customer says this with a slightly embarrassed laugh.)*

Allyson: We will need to work on that, but let's go on and we will begin to take an inventory of where you are today. (I take out a detailed questionnaire and walk the customer through each category.) Approximately how much money do you keep for emergencies? Say in checking, savings, and money market accounts.

Client: *I don't know the exact balances, but there is a ballpark figure.*

Allyson: What rate of return are you earning on those investments?

Client: *I'm not sure.*

Allyson: Approximately how much money do you have in stock and mutual funds?

Client: *I've got three mutual funds and a 401(k).*

Allyson: And how much money is in each fund and what are the stated objectives of the funds?

Client: *I'm not sure, but I will bring you the statements?*

Allyson: (After receiving the same type of responses from each investment category, I begin to wind the conversation down.) Mr. Client, as your financial adviser, I have three goals for our relationship.

1. I want you to spend some time really thinking about why you are saving and investing the money. I would like you to create a money mission statement for yourself. This will allow me to design a written financial plan that is closely aligned with your personal dreams and values.

2. Then I will create your plan and come back to you with a detailed financial review that will allow you to gain control of your finances. This will include a budget , a detailed inventory of your current financial assets, a discussion of your current and proposed asset allocations, and a plan for how much additional money you will need to save and invest to attempt to reach your stated goals.

3. My third goal is for you to be my partner in the responsibility of properly managing your money. This is your money. I want you to clearly understand the investments you are buying, why we are buying them, and the risks and potential benefits of each item. Further, I want to help you learn how to read your investment statements, the newspapers, and research reports, so you will be able to be involved in the management of your assets. How does that sound?

Client: *That sounds exactly like what I was hoping you would say.*

Allyson: If I am properly doing my job, my clients will become educated (or more educated) about managing their money.

TRUTH 2: *Fear Paralyzes*

This is the "Chicken Little" syndrome and it is very real. Many people wake up in the morning and expect the sky to fall. I hear it all the time, and outside economic indications may indeed be real.

There will always be some outside event that can hurt the stock market. Figure 6.1 lists a few of the reasons that you should not invest in the stock market.

There will always be some economic event, nightly news item, or uncertainty on the political horizon that will cause you to have concern about the short-term performance of the stock market. Some of these events, like the record-setting market decline in 1987 or the Gulf War in 1990, do cause stock market losses. Yet, the beauty of being a long-term investor is that you don't have to worry about short-term swings in the markets. This volatility is a part of investing and should not disrupt your overall investment strategies.

TRUTH 3: *It Is Time in the Market, Not Timing the Market*

Very few days go by without my hearing the comment, "Allyson, the stock market still seems awfully high to me. Should we wait until it drops before we make these purchases?" The obvious answer is that we should wait if we know exactly when the stock market is going to drop and how far and how long it is going to stay down. But we *don't* know the answers to those questions, so my response is usually, "No, we should most likely go ahead and purchase the investments today and trust that our longer-term systematic investment strategy will help smooth out the volatility in our entry points."

FIGURE 6.1 *Reasons for Not Investing in the Stock Market*

If you are waiting for the right time to invest, the time is now.

1934	Depression	1967	Newark race riots
1935	Spanish Civil War	1968	USS Pueblo seized
1936	Economy still struggling	1969	Money tightens—markets fall
1937	Recession	1970	Cambodia invaded—Vietnam War spreads
1938	War clouds gather	1971	Wage-price freeze
1939	War in Europe	1972	Largest U.S. trade deficit ever
1940	France falls	1973	Energy crisis
1941	Pearl Harbor	1974	Steepest market drop in four decades
1942	Wartime price controls	1975	Clouded economic prospects
1943	Industry mobilizes	1976	Economic recovery slows
1944	Shortages of consumer goods	1977	Market slumps
1945	Postwar recession predicted	1978	Interest rates rise
1946	Dow tops 200—market too high	1979	Oil prices skyrocket
1947	Cold war begins	1980	Interest rates at all-time high
1948	Berlin blockade	1981	Steep recession begins
1949	Russia explodes A-bomb	1982	Worst recession in 40 years
1950	Korean War	1983	Market hits new highs
1951	Excess profits tax	1984	Record federal deficits
1952	U.S. seizes steel mills	1985	Economic growth slows
1953	Russia explodes H-bomb	1986	Dow nears 2000
1954	Dow tops 300—market too high	1987	Record-setting market decline
1955	Eisenhower illness	1988	Election year
1956	Suez crisis	1989	October "Minicrash"
1957	Russia launches Sputnik	1990	Persian Gulf crisis
1958	Recession	1991	Soviet Union collapses
1959	Castro seizes power in Cuba	1992	Congress passes NAFTA
1960	Russia downs U-2 plane	1993	1st Democrat in White House in 12 Years
1961	Berlin Wall erected	1994	One of the worst years on record for bonds
1962	Cuban Missile Crisis	1995	Dow breaks 5000, market "too high"
1963	Kennedy assassinated	1996	1st Democrat re-elected to White House since FDR
1964	Gulf of Tonkin	1997	Asian turmoil
1965	Civil rights marches	1998	500-point drop in July
1966	Vietnam War escalates	1999	Worries about Y2K

Source: Reprinted by permission, MFS Investment Management.

In other words, I have *no* idea if today is a good day or a bad day, but I do not believe saving one or two points in the purchase price of a stock or a mutual fund will make a tremendous difference in the long run. And even if you were lucky enough to pick one low entry point, you would likely miss several others.

The Price of Procrastination

Suppose you made a hypothetical $10,000 investment in the unmanaged Standard & Poor's 500 Index for the five-year period ending March 31, 1999. Your $10,000 would have grown to $31,998. Now let's say you tried to time the market and ended up missing its ten best days (the ten best single-day performances for the S&P 500 during the period). Your $31,998 would have shrunk to $22,461.

It's time, not timing, that counts when it comes to your investment return.

Conclusion: No matter how long you've put off investing for retirement, it's never too late to start. Your financial consultant can help you establish a savings program that fits your needs, as well as your budget. (© 1999, 2000 AIM Management Group Inc. All rights reserved. Used by permission of AIM Management Group Inc.)

Hypothetical $10,000 Investment in the Unmanaged S&P 500, March 31, 1994–March 31, 1999

Period of Investment	Average Annual Total Return	Growth of $10,000
Fully Invested	26.19%	$31,998
Miss the 10 Best Days	17.57	22,461
Miss the 20 Best Days	12.21	17,792
Miss the 40 Best Days	3.85	12,078
Miss the 60 Best Days	−2.72	8,713

Source: Information provided by Towers Data, Bethesda, MD.

TRUTH 4: *Investing in the Stock Market Is Not for Every One*

If you are going to constantly worry about your money, it's not worth the risk.

Things you need to know:

- Stocks are very volatile.
- Volatility is what makes risk so hard to live with.
- Dividends reduce the losses in bad years and exaggerate the gains in good years.
- In the past 31 years, there have been 6 years of negative total returns, including dividends, and 25 positive years.
- In the past 31 years, there have been 19 years of double-digit total returns, including dividends and 2 negative double-digit years.

- Several good years are often followed by one or two difficult years, which are often followed by excellent years.

The following chart shows the total return of the S&P 500 from 1968 through 1998:

As the chart clearly illustrates, stocks can and do at times lose money. You must be willing to tolerate the periods of negative returns. In 1973 and1974 the Standard & Poors 500 Index dropped by more than 40%. That meant if you had $10,000 invested in that stock index, two years later that investment was worth $6,000.

$$\$10,000 - 40\% \ (\$4,000) = \$6,000$$

It is very easy to look at the historical returns that common stocks have offered over the last twenty five years and say, "Yes, the market fell sharply in 1973 and 1974, but look at the incredible returns of 1975 and 1976 of 37.19 percent and 23.57 percent, respectively." Hindsight makes the difficult periods seem bearable, but I assure you, if you were the investor receiving those monthly statements reflecting a 40% loss in value—it would be a very unpleasant experience.

Investing in stocks may not be for everyone. But you must find a place to invest the growth portion of your portfolio to help you reach your future financial goals, so if it is not going to be stocks, what will it be?

S&P 500 Total Return			
1968	10.98	1984	6.10
1969	−8.43	1985	31.57
1970	3.93	1986	18.56
1971	14.25	1987	5.10
1972	18.90	1988	16.33
1973	−14.77	1989	31.37
1974	−26.39	1990	−3.27
1975	37.16	1991	30.41
1976	23.57	1992	7.61
1977	−7.41	1993	10.02
1978	6.39	1994	1.32
1979	18.20	1995	37.58
1980	32.27	1996	22.96
1981	−5.01	1997	33.36
1982	21.44	1998	28.58
1983	22.39		

Source: Wiesenberger Investment Performance Digest, 1999 Edition, Wiesenberger, a Thomson Financial Company, 1455 Research Blvd., Rockville, MD 20850; 800-232-2285.

TRUTH 5: *There Is a Big Difference between Trading and Investing*

Investors all too often become caught up in the game of wanting to be in the highest-performing stock or mutual fund each year—in investment jargon known as chasing the "hot dot."

Chasing the Hot Dot

In a study conducted over several years, Dalbar found that mutual fund investors earned far less than reported returns as a result of their investing behavior.

This gap of 10 percent is explained by the behavior of equity fund investors. In their attempt to cash in on the impressive stock market gains,

Index vs. Investor Returns

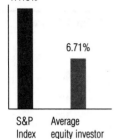

17.18%

6.71%

S&P   Average
Index   equity investor

Source: Quantitative Analysis of
Investor Behavior Study (1997);
DALBAR, Inc., Boston.

investors jump on the bandwagon too late and switch in and out of funds to time the market.

The problem is that most people are not willing to structure a strategy and then stick with their plan. They tend to sell when the stock market goes down and they wait until it has retraced all or most of its losses before they are willing to buy back into the stock market. Simply put, investors are not willing to be investors!

Dalbar's Web site *(www.dalbar.com)* continues this thought by stating, "Even with all the data that are currently available, the average investor holds his mutual funds for a total of only 30 months."

That datum astounds me! If history tells us that jumping from sector to sector and fund to fund is not a viable strategy, why do people still try to time the markets?

If you were going to invest some of your capital into a privately held small business, you would look at the business plan, check the management team, scrutinize the product, monitor the customer service, and definitely look at the future forecasted projections for profit.

If you then decided to invest in the company, you would probably not be investing for a few months or even a few years. Most people who invest in privately held businesses hold on to those investments for years and years. One reason is that privately held investments are harder to sell and another is that most small business owners take great pride in their business and believe in the future of their success. They are not going to let one bad quarter or an economic slowdown shake them from their business plan.

Unfortunately, the actions of public shareholders are quite the opposite:

- They don't try to understand the business of the company they are investing in.
- They don't know the business plan.
- They haven't researched the management of the company.
- They often can't explain the product.
- They have no idea about the company's customer service.
- And they cannot read profit projections.

These people are not investors. They are traders. They have no loyalty to the companies they own. They don't understand or believe in the corporation's future and they don't view themselves as owners. In fact, I view them as speculators.

These people are hoping to invest in something that will give them the fastest ride to financial security and will jump from investment to investment to investment, hoping that one or two of their choices will pay off.

TRUTH 6: *People Do Lose Money in Stocks*

People lose money in stocks. It is just that simple. If you buy a stock at $50 and it drops to $30 and you need to sell, then you have just realized a capital loss of $20 a share.

What kinds of things can make the markets drop?

- A change in the economic forecast
- Increasing inflation (almost always a bad sign for the short-term market)
- Along with rising inflation, rising interest rates that can create uncertainty
- A drop in anticipated corporate profits
- Foreign currency problems
- War
- Political uncertainty

This list can go on and on. As an investor you must realize there will be periods when stocks will drop in value. And the truth is, we don't know if or when they will ever come back, so your job is to allocate your assets to match your level of risk tolerance and then ride out the volatility.

TRUTH 7: *A Systematic Investment Plan May Help Some Investors Reach Their Future Financial Goals*

This is one of my favorite strategies because it can be put into place regardless of your current financial status.

A systematic investment plan allows you to select a predetermined amount of money that you are willing to invest on a systematic—or regular—basis into a defined investment vehicle, such as saving a $100 a month to put into the XYZ stock mutual fund.

Then let's say we enter a period of extreme volatility with the following results:

	Price per Share*	Amount Invested	Number of Shares*
Month 1	$10.00	$ 100	10.00
Month 2	9.25	100	10.81
Month 3	8.50	100	11.77
Month 4	12.00	100	8.33
Month 5	11.38	100	8.79
Month 6	10.00	100	10.00
Month 7	7.00	100	14.28
Month 8	8.75	100	11.43
Month 9	9.63	100	10.39
Month 10	10.13	100	9.88
Month 11	10.50	100	9.52
Month 12	10.00	100	10.00
Average	$ 9.76	1,200	125.20
			× $10 per share closing price
Total Value			**$1,252.00**

*Amounts rounded to nearest cent.

You notice from this table that the price volatility actually worked to your advantage. In the seventh month, when the price dropped to $7 per share, your $100 bought 14.28 shares, which is several more shares than you were typically able to acquire with your monthly $100 investment. By using a systematic investment plan, you are able to take most of the emotion out of your decisions: You'll be able to buy more shares when the market drifts lower, and you'll buy fewer shares when the market goes higher.

I can see several benefits to this strategy:

- It is a strategy that most people can afford to implement.
- You can begin with low initial investments; some plans begin with a $25 minimum.
- You can set the plan on automatic draft, so the money will be automatically sent from your checking or savings account to the investment of your choosing.
- You can implement this strategy using a wide variety of investment vehicles: money market funds, stock mutual funds, bond mutual funds, variable annuities, individual stocks, or unit trusts.
- This strategy automatically employs dollar cost averaging as illustrated in the table shown above.

I have personally used systematic withdrawal plans since 1984. Of the many advantages in working as a financial adviser, one is knowing to invest the maximum amount of money into our retirement plan on a monthly basis. I also have 8 percent of my paycheck placed in our company stock purchase plan (this plan is subject to a cap). In addition, I have money taken from my paycheck every two weeks and automatically invested in a money market account.

These three systematic plans are helping me plan for three of my personal financial goals:

1.   The 401(k) contributions are working to meet my family's future retirement planning needs. I'll keep this money tied up until I'm 59½. If I need it before then, I may be assessed a 10 percent penalty.

2.   The company stock purchase plan allows my family to build a personal net worth available to me after a 13-month holding period. This company stock purchase plan allows me to build a portion of my nest egg while allowing me to have access to the funds without penalty before I'm 59½.

3.   The money market deposits serve as our emergency fund and provide the working reserves for avoiding worry if we need a new set of tires for the car or if the air conditioner needs repair.

These personal systematic investment plans have been the easiest and the most profitable investments for my family.

Implement these strategies as soon as possible.

TRUTH 8: *Men and Women May Approach Investing Differently*

I believe men and women want many of the same results from their money. They both want to accumulate enough assets to give them a sense of financial security. They obviously want to deal with a financial adviser who treats them with honesty and respect. And they want to feel they are being given sound advice. However, how male and female investors arrive at these goals often differ considerably.

I am not a psychologist nor do I have training in that field, but I do have more than 17 years of experience in helping people manage their investments, and I'd like to share some of my observations with you.

Men

I find that men want a straight answer. They want the big picture and very few, if any, of the details. Most often, they believe they are capable of making sound financial decisions if they are given some coaching. Men relate well to visual explanations and pictures. They like charts and graphs. They rely on the numbers to tell the story.

When they are ready to make investment decisions, they line up their options and make an educated choice based on the facts presented. They are often ready to decide the same day recommendations are made, and they gain a sense of accomplishment at completing the task at hand at which time they are ready to move on to their next responsibility.

Women

Women also want the answers, but my female clients often want to explore the details and the definitions. They will involve themselves in the decision-making process. Women relate well to stories. They certainly understand charts, graphs, and numbers, but they often want more than that—a deeper understanding of what they are getting into.

Even if a woman is ready to make an investment decision, she will often ask for a little more time before committing any money. She wants to take that time to discuss the idea with a friend or financial mentor or a spouse. Women often may take a little time to let the recommendations sink in so as to become more comfortable. When she does make the decision, she will have all the facts, all the details, and, as a result, will make a very well-thought-out choice.

Both women and men need to believe they can trust their financial adviser.

TRUTH 9: *You Can Learn from Active Investors*

You can learn a lot by talking to people who have been active investors for a long time.

It was 1982 and I had just received my license to buy and sell stocks and bonds. I had celebrated my 22d birthday and I was ready to manage money—other people's money.

Three years earlier in 1979, my maternal grandmother, Martha Rowell, died. She had left my mother an inheritance, and at that point my mother had to decide who was going to manage her money. She decided to take the initiative in understanding the various stocks, bonds, and real estate that she had recently inherited. After some deliberation, she took over the management of her portfolio.

Here are some of the lessons I learned from my mother:

Success.   Mom inherited a few shares of AT&T stock in 1980. AT&T had been known as a quality company with quality products and services, and through the years my mother had added to her position in AT&T until she had acquired a total of 1,000 shares. But in 1984 AT&T was the defendant in an antitrust trial and was forced to split into seven additional companies.

In February 1984 my mother now owned shares of stock in eight separate companies: 1,000 shares of AT&T and 100 shares each of Ameritech, Bell Atlantic, BellSouth, NYNEX, Pacific Telesis, Southwestern Bell, and U.S. West. While the exact returns have varied from company to company, the percentage returns have exceeded my mother's expectations:

	Dates to:	Total Return (%)	Total Annual Equiv. (%)
Ameritech	2/84–1/99	2,392.13%	24.04%
Bell Atlantic	2/84–1/99	1,389.35	19.83
BellSouth	2/84–1/99	1,697.33	21.35
NYNEX	2/84–7/97*	711.15	16.87
Pacific Telesis	2/84–3/97*	1,402.45	22.99
Southwestern Bell	2/84–1/99	1,987.43	22.57
U.S. West	2/84–1/99	2,594.62	24.69

*Pacific Telesis was acquired by SBC Communications and NYNEX was acquired by Bell Atlantic. In addition, in October 1996 my mother received an additional spin-off of a company called Lucent Technologies. She received 324 shares of this stock and this is its performance:

Lucent Technologies	10/96–2/99	379.69%	93.35%

Source: © Bloomberg LP. All rights reserved.

The most interesting part of this research is that it reinforces one of my favorite investment concepts: Buy the stocks of the companies you know and use every day. Everyone knows you will continue to use the telephone, and with the potential of the Internet and the telephone companies joining their technology with other ventures, AT&T has been a good investment for my mother. Anytime you can say the *worst-performing* stock made an annual total return of 16.87 percent and was able to average that over a 15-year period, you are doing a pretty good job of managing your money. And even though my mother began with 100 shares of each spinoff, she has accumulated several more shares through stock splits.

Success.   In 1981 or 1982 my mother decided to buy shares of Exxon stock because she used gasoline and felt we always would. As of December 31, 1981, Exxon was trading at $7.81 per share and closed June 16, 1999, at $81.25 per share. My mother has bought and sold that stock at various times, but you can clearly see that this was one of her better purchases.

Mistake.   Don't sell a quality stock just because it's in a slump. My mother owned approximately 2,000 shares of a quality utility company that was invested in several nuclear plants. Short-term research indicated that this type of investment could impact the quality of future earnings and could cause a reduction in the company's quarterly dividend. As a new stockbroker, I alerted my mother and on April 10, 1985, we sold the 2,000 shares of stock at $10 per share for roughly $20,000. At that time the stock was paying $0.975 per share in dividends, or $1,950 a year in income. Here is the history of the stock from the day we sold it:

Date	Closing Price*	Annual Dividends*	Annual Income
04–10–1985	$10.00	$0.98	$1,950
04–10–1986	11.88	1.03	2,050
04–10–1987	11.81	1.07	2,140
04–10–1988	11.69	1.07	2,140
04–10–1989	11.69	1.07	2,140
04–10–1990	12.88	1.07	2,140
04–10–1991	14.00	1.07	2,140
04–10–1992	16.00	1.10	2,200
04–10–1993	21.63	1.14	2,280
04–10–1994	18.75	1.18	2,360
04–10–1995	20.75	1.22	2,440
04–10–1996	22.75	1.26	2,520
04–10–1997	21.25	1.30	2,600
04–10–1998	27.50	1.34	2,680

*All numbers rounded to nearest cent.

If my mother had ignored the advice of her young daughter, she would now have 2,000 shares of this utility stock worth $55,000; as you can see, her dividends would now be paying her $2,680 a year from the dividends. She should have continued to be an investor. This was a very large utility company. People in its area of the country still need electricity. We simply let a short-term problem overshadow long-term objectives.

Could the utility have gotten into a bad long-term situation? Absolutely! All companies have risk.

Mistake. To make the utility story even more unsettling, my mother took the proceeds from the sale of her utility company and bought shares in an oil company. On April 12, 1985, my mother bought 1,100 shares of stock at $19.88 each for a total investment (including commissions) of $22,213.92. Eighteen months later she sold those shares at $11.63 each and received a check for $12,627.00 for a realized capital loss of $9,586.92.

Mistake. In the early to mid-1980s many people were looking for ways to shelter income. A number of limited partnerships which could be invested in many things, began to spring up all over the country. Some of the common investments were in shopping centers, apartment complexes, airplane and computer equipment leases, oil and gas properties, and some exotic ventures.

Like many other people at this time, my mother and father were persuaded to borrow the necessary money to fund their purchases; the tax benefits along with the cash flow would be wonderful long-term investments. It was anticipated that these would be five-year to seven-year holdings and everyone involved would benefit.

Unfortunately, that's not what happened. In 1986 Congress enacted a number of sweeping tax law changes that overnight took away many of the tax advantages of these limited partnerships. My parents were left with a bank note to pay off investments that carried little or no economic value.

We all learned several lessons:

- Think long and hard before you invest in concepts that are not economically driven but rely on creative tax advantages for their merit.

- These investments were highly illiquid. Even had an investor been wise enough to want out before the tax reform came along, there was little or no secondary market.

- Make sure that you personally understand the economic concept of your investments. How will you make money? What are the projections? What is your downside risk? What is the upside potential? What will the duration of the investment be?

- Who is the management team? Do you know its track record? Does it specialize in this area of investing?

- Finally, could you easily explain the benefits of these investments to your fifth-grade child? If it doesn't make sense to you, don't invest the money.

My father, who came from a family of bankers, was born in 1928, just one year before the stock market suffered its most famous decline in October 1929.

When my father was about six years old and the Depression was still in full swing, he found a crate of Palmolive soap. Being the industrious young boy that he was, during his next bath he went to work carefully taking off the wrapper of each bar of soap and sticking them to the bathroom tile like wallpaper. You can imagine how proud he was of the work, and you can probably also image how his mother felt when she saw his handiwork.

As an investor during the Depression, my dad's family should have been looking into the maker of Palmolive soap—Colgate-Palmolive. And had you been astute enough (and had the money) to purchase 100 shares of Colgate-Palmolive in 1934, through stock splits you would now have 8,205 shares, which as of June 15, 1999, were worth $100.25 per share for a total value of $822,551!

When most people knew the worst of the Depression was over, they knew people would need soap. Yet they had lost money in the market before and were afraid. I can't blame them. Even the most patient investors had to wait almost ten years for the Dow Jones Industrial Average to reach predepression levels.

My paternal grandmother, Mary Nell Wortham, had also been interested in stocks for years. She has made some marvelous investments and below are a few of her success stories.

Success.   Buy what you know and use. My grandmother's best investments have been high-quality companies whose products she used every day.

For example:

- She talked on an **AT&T** telephone.
- She had local and long-distance service provided by **SBC Communications.**
- She blew her nose on **Kimberly-Clark** Kleenex tissues.
- She filled their car with **Exxon** gasoline.
- She shopped at **Wal-Mart.**
- She cooked on a **General Electric** stove.
- She drank **Coca-Cola** products.
- She banked at **Simmons First National Bank.**

She knew and understood these companies and she became an investor in them. She believed in their products and she believed in the value of being a shareholder of the companies.

Success.   One of my favorite stories is the Coke story.

In 1982 or 83 my grandmother already owned 300 shares of Coca-Cola stock. She had some extra money and decided to buy an additional 200 shares of Coke stock for a total of 500 shares. The stock split as follows:

From an investment of approximately $36,000 that my grandmother purchased when she was 79, her money grew to over $750,000 in 16 years. She no longer owns all of her shares. She has used that stock for her living expenses and charitable gifts. This is one investment that has truly paid off for our family.

July 1986: 3 for 1	1,500 shares
May 1990: 2 for 1	3,000 shares
May 1992: 2 for 1	6,000 shares
May 1996: 2 for 1	12,000 shares

My grandmother held the Coke stock through good and bad periods of investment performance. She didn't sell on April 23, 1985, when Coca-Cola changed the product's recipe. She didn't sell in 1987 when the stock fell from a high of 52.248 on August 26, 1987, to a low of 26.849 on October 19, 1987. In less than two months, the value of her Coke stock dropped in half. She didn't sell in the summer of 1998 when the stock again moved from a high of almost 81.50 on August 25, 1998, to a low of 53.63 one month later on September 25, 1998. On paper she watched the dollar value of her remaining 7,000 shares of stock drop from $570,062 to $375,375 for an unrealized loss of $194,687. The question had to be asked, "Had anything happened to the underlying value of the company?" "Was it really selling that many fewer soft drinks?"

The short-term swings would drive most investors crazy, but my grandmother plods along holding quality companies for a lifetime. Will she ever sell all of her Coke stock? Who knows . . . but when I asked her why she bought the stock in the first place, she quickly answered, "I like to drink Coke!"

Success.   Dividends can be important. My mother and my grandmother have made it their strategy to buy stocks that pay good dividends and that have had a history of increasing their dividends to the shareholders. While they realized a large amount of the appreciation will come from the growth of the underlying stock, they do like to have some income stream to carry them through the more volatile periods of the market.

Investment Clubs

While many people can learn a great deal from other people, they can also learn by joining an investment club. Through the years I have been involved with several of these groups, but two investment clubs have been surprising successful.

The first club was started in May 1985 with 15 women in their fifties and sixties. Most of these women knew each other socially, but they thought it would be fun to increase their underlying knowledge of how stocks work. They call themselves the Investment XV Club. They each put in $1,000 and contribute $50 a month. From a beginning balance of $15,000, their account had grown to $469,563 as of June 4, 1999. Even though these women are now near or in their seventies, they still focus on growth stocks. Their current holdings as of June 4, 1999, included the following:

Number of Shares	Company	Cost	Current Market Value
200	SBC Communications	$ 4,049	$10,725
100	America Online	8,408	11,800
200	Estee Lauder	3,732	9,350
50	Amazon.com	7,975	5,418
100	Dillards	1,849	3,625
100	Lucent Technologies	5,995	6,187
50	Yahoo	8,528	7,368
375	Citigroup	12,472	16,359
200	FDX (Fedex)	9,740	10,450
242	Select 10 Strategy	1,000	2,591

146	Global Stock Fund	1,000	2,065
400	Abbott Labs	5,522	18,000
100	Acxiom Corp.	2,438	2,900
400	Baldor Electric	4,699	7,750
100	Boeing Co.	5,345	4,387
100	Chevron	7,821	9,150
300	Cisco Systems	20,533	34,462
200	Coca-Cola	4,214	13,950
200	Cullen Frost	4,759	11,300
100	Walt Disney	2,946	3,062
300	DuPont	14,356	21,075
200	Emerson Electric	5,309	13,425
400	GE	4,597	41,950
200	Harley Davidson	3,796	11,325
600	Intel	13,093	31,875
200	Lilly	14,893	15,050
800	Microsoft	9,058	63,600
400	Procter & Gamble	5,135	38,650
300	Southwest Airlines	3,850	9,750
100	Texaco	2,986	6,425
100	Union Planters	4,468	4,162
400	Wal-Mart	2,381	18,400
	Money market fund	7,255	7,255

The second group is called the Million Dollar Investment Club, and at the rate it is growing will soon reach that goal. This club started in July 1987 (just before the dreaded October crash of '87) with 17 members. Each person contributed an initial $350 (17 people × $350 = $5,950) and added $35 each month. (They have recently increased their monthly contributions to $75 each month.) From a beginning balance of less than $6,000, this club's investment account has grown to $408,391 as of June 4, 1999. My mother is a member, and although the club has many interested members, a woman named Sunny Steed serves as the primary resource for stock recommendations and research. Sunny has picked up investing as a hobby and spends several hours a week at the Pine Bluff, Arkansas, Public Library reading such investment resources as *Money, Forbes, Fortune, The Wall Street Journal, Kiplinger's, Smart Money, Barron's,* various Value Line and Morningstar publications, and many others. She has a wonderful knack for condensing all of the information into a report that keeps club members up-to-date on major events concerning their stock holdings. This club's investment portfolio includes the following:

Number of Shares	Company	Cost	Current Market Value
104	Associates First Cap	$ 3,971	$ 4,316
1	Berkshire Hathaway	1,157	2,337
178	RegionsFinancial Cp	7,242	6,786
100	Tenneco Inc. New	3,808	2,287
160	Staffmark	4,780	1,600
200	Abbot Labs	4,968	9,000
50	Allied Signal	2,861	2,918
100	Alltel	2,621	7,325
1000	Cisco Systems	9,169	114,875
400	Coca-Cola	10,557	27,900
100	DuPont	6,608	7,025
350	Exxon	11,288	28,218
100	Fannie Mae	5,952	6,875
200	Ford Motor Co.	3,625	11,250
200	GTE	4,841	12,675
200	GE	4,960	20,975
400	Intel	6,500	21,250
100	Johnson & Johnson	5,162	9,662
600	McDonald's	6,430	24,600
100	Medtronic	5,070	7,450
600	Merck	12,637	42,375
200	Procter & Gamble	4,984	19,325
300	Simmons First Nat'l	5,411	9,975
200	Southern Co.	2,495	5,650
	Money market fund	1,629	1,629

Both of these clubs are filled with people who want to learn more about investing and are glad to do it by investing $50 to $75 a month. These clubs have given each member a much better understanding of how to invest in the stock market, how to read and understand a research report, and how to build a balanced and diversified stock portfolio. They often buy stocks in these portfolios that they would be less likely to put in their personal accounts because of the risk.

For more information about investment clubs, you can write the National Association of Investment Clubs (NAIC) at:

NAIC
1515 E. 11 Mile Road
P.O. Box 220
Royal Oak, MI 48068
877-275-6242
www.better-investing.org

TRUTH 10: *Money Alone Cannot Make You Happy*

In my job I have the privilege of meeting all kinds of people with various levels of financial resources. Some people are barely getting by while others have far more than they need. But each person's personal level of security or happiness is rarely tied to the amount of money he or she has accumulated. If you are hoping that accumulating a large sum of money will make you happy and you are spending your days doing everything possible to reach some magic number, you are wasting your time.

As my dad is fond of saying, "I have never seen an armored car following a funeral procession!" We can't take it with us. Money is important and is closely tied to our feeling of self-worth and our emotional sense of well-being. And I firmly believe we are all called to be good stewards of the financial resources we have been blessed with. But money will never make you happy. It can make you comfortable, it fills you with adventure and might even give you short-lived security. But money cannot give you the highest and most sought-after treasure of all . . . it will never fill that spot.

This truth is so important that I want to include a personal story that illustrates my point.

As we met for the June 1999 meeting of the Investment XV Club, we gathered around a very solemn table. Just two days before, on June 1, American Airlines Flight 1420 had crashed in their hometown of Little Rock. There were over 130 people aboard and now 11 people had lost their life. One of the surviving passengers, Dr. Tharp Gillespie, is the husband of the presiding secretary of the club, Miriam Gillespie.

As we sat at the table for our regular meeting as we had done since May 1985, we were instantly struck by the amazing gift of life. There was a reverence around that table—an incredible event had taken place. The image broadcast over the news displaying the wreckage of that plane proved to us that miracles do still happen.

The subjects of money and investing did not matter at that moment. Our concern was for Dr. and Mrs. Gillespie and for all of the survivors and the victims of that tragedy.

It shouldn't take a tragedy to put money in perspective, but it often does. Life is the gift. No amount of money can buy you life, or health, or joy, or peace. Enjoy the true treasures that you are given.

These ten truths can add to your personal investment knowledge. Now it is time to understand your investment options.

Your Investment Alternatives

7

" There are times that you can feel uncomfortable about your investments, but eventually, if you distribute your finances between bonds and stocks, you will be OK. "
Gene and Clois Ratliff, 71 and 61
Little Rock, Arkansas

" Although we started like many young people—so obsessed with climbing the ladder of success that we did not take the time to manage our money with enough research to make wise decisions with our financial blessings—we now see the 'errors of our ways.' We now know that making good choices with our money can give us less to worry about and allow us to enjoy our lives more. "
Bryan and Melissa Powell, 29
Jonesboro, Arkansas

A YOUNG WOMAN OR AN OLD HAG?

Turn the page for the **answer!**

THE **ANSWER!**

It is both! There is a beautiful young woman looking back over her shoulder . . . and an old hag looking down with a scarf over her head.

The picture of the young woman and the old hag is a wonderful illustration of how a typical investment portfolio may appear at various points in time. During profitable market conditions, you will feel terrific. Everything is going great and all of your investments bring you pride.

Then a correction or market downturn occurs and you are caught off guard. You become uncertain as to how long the downturn will last and your investment portfolio takes on the appearance of the old hag. Your job will be to remember it is usually a matter of perspective. Sometimes market declines can truly be opportunities to add to your quality holdings while stock prices are low.

“Saving more at an early age would have paid some substantial dividends for the future.**”**

Jon Mark Erstine, 42
Memphis, Tennessee

Investment Alternatives

Checking
Passbook Savings
Money Market Accounts
Certificates of Deposit (CDs)
Savings Bonds
Treasury Bills
Treasury Notes
Treasury Bonds
Corporate Bonds
Municipal Bonds
Preferred Stocks
Common Stocks
Large Capitalization Stocks
Mid-Capitalization Stocks
Small Capitalization Stocks
Micro-Capitalization Stocks
Initial Public Offerings (IPOs)

Mutual Funds
Growth Mutual Funds
Large Capitalization Growth Mutual Funds
Mid-Capitalization Growth Mutual Funds
Small Capitalization Growth Mutual Funds
Growth and Income Mutual Funds
Balanced Mutual Funds
Sector Funds
International Mutual Funds
Insurance as an Investment
Fixed Annuities
Variable Annuities
Life Insurance
Variable Life Insurance
Managed Futures
Precious Metals

Clients walk into my office with a dream and a hope of financial independence, but the sheer number of investment alternatives that are available to help them reach their goals instantly overwhelms them. They know they need to be placing their money into the investments that are best suited to them for reaching their future goals, but they often suffer from a lack of confidence. Some people are even afraid to ask questions, even though they may not understand exactly what a money market is or how it functions. They may not know how to invest in a stock or mutual fund. They often have questions about various fee structures and associated costs. The key is to slow down and relax. This is your money. By taking the time to improve your understanding of some of the basic concepts and then focusing on the historical risk-return numbers in this chapter, you will be more informed and, I hope, more confident about your final decisions.

When I teach an investment workshop, I often begin the session with an illustration like the one on the next page that has a lot of different items.

I allow participants a total of 50 seconds to memorize as many of the items as they can. Then I remove the image and give them one minute to write down as many as they can remember. Some people can remember 10, some can remember 17 or 18, but even the person with the best memory can't come close to remembering and writing down all.

The point is that you don't need to be able to remember all the information in this chapter. But you do need to focus your attention on three of the basic asset classes. Once you have mastered a general understanding of how these three asset classes work and how they are interrelated, you will be that much closer to financial freedom. The three asset classes that I want you to consider are cash, bonds, and stocks.

CASH

Cash is wonderful. You can hold it in your hands. You can deposit it in the local bank and make withdrawals at your convenience. You can use it to buy things or pay off debt, or give it away to help people.

In addition to physical currency, cash is held in electronic forms. We consider checks and debit cards to be cash instruments. In fact, only a very small percentage of the money that actually changes hands is in the form of paper currency.

In 1996 only 17.3 percent of all personal consumption expenditures were handled with cash (paper and coins); 50.6 percent were completed by check; 10.5 percent by Visa; 9.6 percent by other general purpose cards; 7.3

Source: *Puzzlegrams* by Pentagram.

percent by money orders, TCs, food stamps, and preauthorized and remote payments; and 5.4 percent by all other cards, according to Visa.

Cash investments would include:

- Paper currency
- Checking accounts
- Savings and money market accounts
- Some short-term CDs and bonds with maturities of less than one year

All cash investments are considered short-term investments and are geared to meet short-term needs. For example, you usually keep enough paper currency to buy your lunch and fill your car with gas or buy a soft drink at work. You keep enough money in your personal checking accounts, I hope, to pay your fixed bills and to cover your day-to-day living expenses that you don't pay for with paper currency. You should keep enough money in a savings account or a money market account to cover your emergency fund. Most financial planners recommend that you keep three to six months of expenses set aside in your emergency fund. And, depending on your age and your personal risk tolerance level, you should plan to keep enough money in short-term CDs or Treasury bills to give you the security your financial plan deserves.

The key to understanding cash investments is that they carry low risk and low return. They typically have the highest level of safety, but they won't help your money compound at a rapid pace. Inflation is the biggest risk to your cash investments.

These are interest rate yields you might expect from various short-term investments:

Paper Currency	Checking Account	Savings Account	Money Market	Six-Month CD
0%	0–2.5%	2–3.00%	3.00–4.75%	5.00%

These rates of return were as of June 17, 1999, and are subject to change without notice.

Why Do People Keep Cash and Other Short-Term Investments?

1. Many people lived through the Great Depression and either lost money in the stock market or heard their parents talk about losing everything in the market. So they decided that stock market investing was not for them. They feel more comfortable knowing that their investments are FDIC insured up to $100,000, and they are willing to give up the opportunity for higher rates of return.

2. For some people it is a matter of indecision. They receive a bonus or accumulate an extra amount of money in their cash accounts, and because of an inability to make a decision, they leave the money in a low-yielding cash account.

> Your short-term investments should be held to meet your short-term needs.

3. For the last group, it is simply lack of knowledge. They have done an excellent job of accumulating the money, but they have never learned what to do next.

All of us need cash investments. But your cash investments should be used for what they were intended to do. They should be used to provide necessary liquidity for your family. They should be used for your emergency fund. And they should be used by risk averse investors as a percentage of their overall financial plan.

BONDS

The second basic asset class is bonds. Bonds are often considered boring and that is exactly what makes them so attractive. You put $10,000 into a ten-year U.S. government bond and for ten years your semiannual income checks arrive like clockwork, and at the end of the ten years you get your $10,000 back. Not a lot of guesswork, few surprises—you buy your bonds and live on or reinvest the income.

Let's look at how an actual bond investment might work. Assume that XYZ Corporation wants to build a new manufacturing plant. This company has been in business for over 50 years and carries the highest-quality investment ranking. Now it needs to raise $100 million dollars to pay for the new plant and equipment. Where does it find that kind of money?

From investors just like you. Let's say that you have $10,000 to invest and XYZ Corporation is issuing a new $100 million bond to build a new plant. These bonds carry the highest-quality rating and will pay 6 percent interest for ten years. Because corporate bonds don't carry FDIC insurance as a certificate of deposit does and the bond has a ten-year maturity, the 6 percent income yield is appealing. So investors like you invest in this bond issue, thus providing XYZ Corporation the capital it needs to build a new plant.

How Do You Benefit?

Quality bonds are considered less volatile than stocks and are thought to provide a steady income stream.

Bonds give you the opportunity to put a specific amount of money into an investment, receive a specific and usually dependable return, and then get your original investment back on a specific future date.

The XYZ bond might look like this after you make a $10,000 principal investment:

Year	
2001	$600 interest paid as $300 payments semiannually
2002	$600 interest
2003	$600 interest
2004	$600 interest
2005	$600 interest
2006	$600 interest
2007	$600 interest
2008	$600 interest
2009	$600 interest
2010	$600 interest plus your original $10,000 principal to be repaid on the stated maturity date

Bond basics.   Regardless of the type of bond or fixed income instrument you purchase, it will tend to have certain common features:

- Corporate and government bonds trade in $1,000 increments.
- Municipal bonds trade in $5,000 increments.
- Bonds have a "face value" or "par value" or "maturity value," which is what the bonds are expected to be worth when they mature.
- They have a stated maturity date ranging from a few days to 30 to 40 years.
- They have a stated interest rate, which is the percentage they are expected to pay based on the face value of the bond.
- They may be rated by one of the rating services; Standard and Poor's and Moody's are two of the major ones. These services assign a letter rating based on the following scale:

	S&P	Moody's
Highest Quality	AAA	Aaa
	AA	Aa
	A	A
	BBB	Baa
	BB	Ba
Lower Quality	B	B

The ratings continue but AAA through BBB are considered "investment grade bonds" with AAA being the highest quality and moving on to higher-risk and higher-yield bonds.

Most bonds pay semiannual interest with the exception of Treasury bills, which pay interest at maturity, and zero-coupon bonds, which work like savings bonds and are purchased at a discount and grow in value until maturity.

The most difficult concept for investors to grasp is that while bonds are often issued and originally purchased at a round number like $10,000, they quickly begin to trade at different prices in the open market.

Assume you bought the $10,000 XYZ bond described above. XYZ stated it would pay you 6 percent interest for ten years. What happens to the value of that investment if interest rates rise and within two years a similar bond could be purchased with an 8 percent yield?

Who would want to buy your 6 percent bond when they could buy an 8 percent bond? No one would buy it for the full value of $10,000 that you paid, but someone would offer to buy it from you at a discount that would give them a yield equivalent to the 8 percent. So if you needed to sell your 6 percent bond, someone might offer to pay you $8,640.97, which could result in a $1,359.03 principal loss if you needed to sell it. A lot of investors look at the income stream alone and don't realize that bonds actually move up and down in value based on the interest rate movements that are occurring in the economy.

Although you don't need to know all of the ins and outs of how bond prices function, it is helpful to know some of the basics:

- Bond prices move inversely to interest rates.
- As interest rates move higher, bond prices fall.
- As interest rates move lower, bond prices rise.

Bond Strategies

The short-term strategy.   A short-term bond will mature in less than five years.

Short-term bonds will carry the lowest yields and the smallest amount of principal fluctuation.

Risk averse investors often buy high-quality short-term bonds.

The intermediate strategy.   Intermediate bonds offer maturities from five to ten years in length. These bonds should give you a somewhat higher yield than a similar quality short-term bond, but because of their extended maturity dates, they have more volatile price fluctuations. Investors hoping to capture a higher income may buy intermediate bonds. You might also buy intermediate bonds if you thought interest rates were going to remain the same or decline in the future.

The long-term strategy. Long-term bonds vary from 10 to 30 years. They often pay an even higher rate of return than an intermediate bond, but because of their length, they have the most price volatility. You would be interested in long-term bonds if you felt sure that interest rates would be declining or if you simply wanted the higher income.

The laddered bond strategy. This is one of my favorite strategies because I believe it's impossible to predict which way interest rates will move. Notice how volatile interest rates have been over the past 20 years: as low as 5.26 percent in 1998 and as high as 13.91 percent in 1981.

How is an individual investor supposed to know which way interest rates will move? The only assumption I rely on in predicting interest rates is that I will never be able to predict them correctly! As a result, I often use the laddered bond strategy. It's very simple; your only decision is whether you would like to implement a short, intermediate, or long-term laddered strategy. For this illustration I'll use a ten-year intermediate ladder.

Assume you have $100,000 to invest in the bond portion of your asset allocation. Choose the type and quality of bond that you wish to invest in and "ladder" the maturity dates by placing $10,000 into each bond.

Years 2001 through 2005 offer a short-term bond strategy that protects against large swings in principal. Years 2006 through 2010 offer an intermediate bond strategy that will give you slightly higher yields and protect your income stream if interest rates decline.

Historical Chart of the 10-Year U.S. Treasury Bond Yield

1968-1998

Source: *Wiesenberger Investment Performance Digest, 1999 Edition,* Wiesenberger, a Thomson Financial Company, 1455 Research Blvd., Rockville, MD 20850; 800-232-2285.

Maturity Date	Amount Invested	Yield
2001	$10,000	5.00%
2002	10,000	5.25
2003	10,000	5.35
2004	10,000	5.50
2005	10,000	5.60
2006	10,000	5.75
2007	10,000	6.00
2008	10,000	6.10
2009	10,000	6.15
2010	10,000	6.25

To keep this strategy in place, when the 2001 bond matures, you will take that $10,000 and roll it into a new bond in the year 2011. You will continue to do this as the years pass. If interest rates remain the same, your income remains the same. If interest rates rise, your income has the potential to rise as the bonds mature. And even if interest rates drop slightly, you may pick up a little yield by rolling your one year (2001) bond into a new ten-year (2011) bond because a ten-year bond should pay more than a one-year issue.

The beauty of this strategy is its simplicity: You are not forced to make interest rate assumptions, and over time you will earn the average of what bonds are paying.

The zero-coupon bond strategy.   Zero-coupon bonds are bonds that pay no interest. Instead, they are offered to investors at a discount with a specific maturity date when they will grow to their full face value.

For example, a ten-year zero-coupon Treasury note purchased today might have a face value of $10,000. Your purchase cost would be approximately $6,000. At that price this bond would have a yield to maturity of roughly 5.25 percent.

Zero-coupon bonds are often used to prefund specific investment goals such as a child's college education or personal retirement. If you know your child will be attending college in 15 years, a zero-coupon bond can be purchased to assure that you will have a specific amount of money on a specific date. If you want $15,000 available on January 1, 2014, why not consider buying a 15-year zero-coupon bond?

"Zeros," as they are often referred to, can be purchased as Treasury bonds, corporate bonds, or tax-free municipal bonds. They offer a wonderful method of investing money without having to wonder what your rate of return will be. On the other hand, a disadvantage of zeros is that they generate taxable income every year if they are purchased in your personal account. This is income you have not actually received, but you will receive a 1099 unless you purchase these bonds in an IRA where the taxes are deferred or as tax-free municipal zeros. The second disadvantage is that long-term zeros have a higher degree of volatility and their rate of return is low.

The bottom line for bonds and the various bond strategies discussed here is that bonds and other fixed income assets can help you ride through the difficult times in the stock market. When your growth investments are declining or moving sideways, your bond portfolio will always be there to provide the steady rates of return they were created to generate.

STOCKS

Stocks have historically provided the highest rates of investment return of all the major asset classes. For discussion purposes, I define stocks as equity ownership in a publicly traded company. That ownership is typically represented as shares of stock, and these shares can be physically issued in certificate form or they can be held in book entry form at your financial institution.

When you purchase the common stock of a company, you become a partial owner in that company, and as a shareholder you are entitled to several rights. You have the right to receive financial information and the right to vote on various issues affecting your investment. But by far the biggest benefit is that you have the right and opportunity to share in the future growth of some of the largest companies in the United States and the world. This opportunity for growth doesn't come without risk. As a shareholder, you also participate in losses and any difficult periods that may face the company in which you have chosen to invest. Stocks are very different from bonds in that they don't have to pay you anything. Remember that bonds have a written obligation to pay an investor interest. Stocks are under no obligation to pay any dividends or any other form of compensation. While many companies choose to pay their shareholders dividends, those income payments are set once a quarter and may be changed or eliminated at the discretion of the board of directors.

How Is a New Stock Created?

Step 1.   A person develops an idea for a product or service and forms a private corporation.

Step 2.   Revenues grow to a point that the investment banking community begins to take notice, and discussions of future growth and expansion take place.

Step 3.   The company decides to expand the business and needs money to fund the expansion.

Step 4.   The company goes to the investment bankers with a business plan, and the bankers review the company's management team, past track record, and future business plan. If the potential looks attractive, the investment bankers will structure the new stock issue.

Step 5. The issue will be filed with the Securities and Exchange Commission and all of the legal paperwork completed.

Step 6. The new stock issue will be priced and then sold through financial advisers and investment bankers.

Step 7. The public stock will be assigned a ticker symbol and will begin to trade on its assigned exchange.

Why Public Companies Issue Stock and How a Stock Differs from a Bond

If a company's stock is already publicly traded, it may choose to issue a "secondary stock issue." Using our illustration of the XYZ Corporation and the $100 million plant, what if XYZ didn't want to borrow money through the issuance of a debt security—a bond issue? How else could it raise the capital? It could issue additional shares of stock. If the stock was currently trading at $50 a share, the company could issue 2 million shares of stock to raise the $100 million. You might buy this secondary issue in the hope that the new plant would add such a large amount of increased productivity and profitability that it would prove to be a prudent investment.

The benefit to XYZ is that it is not borrowing the money and therefore will not be required to pay any interest on it nor to pay back the principal to shareholders. The disadvantage is that now there are a larger number of shares outstanding in the common stock, which could dilute the capability of the earnings per share. The purchasers or investors in this stock will benefit by becoming equity owners or shareholders of the corporation with the opportunity to benefit from future profits.

If stocks have all these risks, why are they so popular? Over the years hundreds of very smart entrepreneurs have developed products and services and new technologies—these entrepreneurs need capital to move from the drawing board to reality. But once the stock is issued, its price is at the mercy of the buyers and sellers of those shares of stock.

Certain factors that can impact the value of a stock are explained in the following.

EPS—earnings per share. Earnings per share is the net income divided by the number of shares outstanding. If a company earned $1 million and there are 1 million shares of stock outstanding, then this company would report an earnings per share of $1. ($1 million net income divided by 1 million shares outstanding equals $1.)

Determining EPS is the most frequently used method of monitoring whether a company is making money and growing at a reasonable rate. Most long-term investors are looking to buy stock in companies that have had a long history of steady and increasing earnings per share. Investors want to believe that their companies will continue to have similar or better growth potential in the future.

Stable management teams.   Many analysts and investors look for companies that have had the same management teams in place for a long time. Investors like to see that members of senior management personally own a large stake of common stock in the company they are running. Abrupt changes in senior management can cause investors to lose confidence in a company.

Future growth prospects.   Is the company in a growing industry that has a tremendous amount of upside potential or is it in a more mature industry whose growth is slowing but is more assured?

Unforeseen surprises.   The stock market reacts very strongly to unforeseen surprises, both on the upside and the downside. The price of a stock can jump sharply over the news release of a new product or service or a potential merger or acquisition. But prices can drop just as quickly if a company reports any sort of negative news. And stock prices can be impacted by more than a company's business plan and its future. When the overall stock market becomes jittery or overvalued, many stocks may decline in anticipation of a slowing economy or an unexpected rise in short-term interest rates. There are many things that affect stock prices, but the bottom line is this: If people are rushing to buy into the stock of a company—those shares will be rising. And if people are rushing to sell out of the stock of a company—those shares will be falling. It is a matter of supply and demand.

HOW YOU BUY STOCK

Stocks are traded on public exchanges. Some of the larger exchanges include the New York Stock Exchange, the recently merged American Stock Exchange, and the Nasdaq (National Association of Security Dealers Automated Quotes).

First, you need to determine which stock you want to buy. Next, you must look up the ticker symbol, which is usually a three-letter or four-letter symbol used to access the computer information regarding every major publicly traded stock. Just for fun, let's say the name of the company is Allyson.com and the fictitious symbol is ALLY.

Once we know the ticker symbol, we can punch that into the computer (either your financial professional's or through a service you subscribe to like E-trade) and find out the current market value of the stock. There will always be two prices, a bid price and an asked price.

The best way to explain the bid and the asked price is to use the example of selling a car. If you place your 1996 Ford truck on the market, you would likely place an ad in the newspaper listing all its benefits along with your selling price—that is, the price you're asking for the truck. So you decide to publish your sales offer of $12,000. The day the ad runs, your phone rings to announce a buyer interested in seeing your truck. He says, "I like your truck, and I will pay you $11,500 for it. This is called the "buyer's price" or the "bid." There is an obvious distinction between the bid of $11,500 and the asking price of $12,000. The difference between the two prices is called "the spread" and no transaction will occur until the buyer and the seller agree on a single price.

One of four things can happen:

1. The buyer loves the truck and after the seller says "$12,000 is my best offer" for the third time decides to move the bid to $12,000, and the deal is closed.

2. The seller needs to move the truck and is grateful for the bid of $11,500, which he accepts and moves the asking price down to $11,500 so they can make the transaction.

3. Buyer and seller negotiate and meet in the middle at a price of $11,750.

4. Buyer and seller can't agree on a price and both parties walk away; the potential buyer looks for another truck and the seller looks for a more motivated buyer.

The same outcomes can occur with stocks. Assume our fictitious Allyson.com is trading with a bid of $11½ and $12 asked. If you were motivated to buy the stock, you would be required to pay $12 to acquire it. But if you were a seller who was determined to sell, you might only receive $11½ per share. Or you might meet in the middle at $11¾, or possibly no transaction would be done if you couldn't agree on a price. The prices of most stocks are constantly moving during the hours of the open market. The price of each security is determined primarily by supply and demand. When a lot of people want to buy the stock and only a few are willing to sell, the stock price will move up. If a lot of people want to sell their shares of stock and no one is there to buy, the share value will drop.

Now that you understand the bid and the asked, you should also be aware of the two most common type of orders: market orders and limit orders. A market order is by far the most common. It most likely assures you of an execution of your trade. A market order states that you are willing to pay whatever the market requires to fill your order. If you are a buyer, you are willing to take the seller's price; if you are a seller, you are willing to accept the buyer's price.

However, if you are afraid the market could move sharply, you could place a limit order and say, "I want to buy 100 shares of Allyson.com, but only if I can buy it at no more than $11¾. A limit order allows you to specify the target price at which you want to buy or sell your stock. A limit order can help protect you from skyrocketing IPOs (initial public offerings) that you may wish to purchase.

Once you have determined the type of order, you must decide exactly how much money you want to invest. After looking up the exact dollar price of the stock from the newspaper or the Internet, you can determine how many shares you are able to purchase. You often hear financial professionals discuss buying in increments of 100 shares, which are considered "round lots" and are often used as the recommended increments (100 shares, 200 shares, 300 shares, etc.). However, you may purchase stock in any increment, even as few as one share at a time. Most financial professionals wouldn't recommend buying one share at a time because of the higher transaction costs to you and the issuing company. After purchasing your shares, under today's rules, you have three days to pay for your stock. This is called the settlement date, and you are required to pay for our purchase on or before that date. Some investment companies may require you to deposit money before a trade is made, especially if you plan to purchase any of the more volatile technology or Internet companies.

As an owner of shares, you can immediately begin to participate in the movements in the price of the shares; and you begin to receive the company's annual report and its quarterly reports. Whether you are purchasing your first stock or your hundredth, researching the companies, evaluating their potential, and physically placing your investment money on the line and becoming an owner of a corporation is almost always an exciting event. The expectation of profit and the intrigue of being involved in some of the fastest-growing corporations in the world can be a rewarding experience.

How Well Stocks Have Really Performed

The S&P 500 index is often used as a benchmark when discussing the annualized rates of return for common stocks. The past few years have been unbelievable and even the longer term has been outstanding.

For the period ending December 31, 1998:

1-year return	28.58%
3-year return	26.13
5-year return	24.03
10-year return	18.95
20-year return	17.45

Source: © Bloomberg LP. All rights reserved.

Can you imagine having had the foresight to invest in some of the largest companies in the world 20 years ago? If you had somehow been able to mimic the 20-year historical returns of 17.45 percent, your money would have grown exponentially:

1. $1,000 would have grown in 20 years to $24,949

2. $10,000 would have grown in 20 years to $249,494

3. $100,000 would have grown in 20 years to $2,494,941

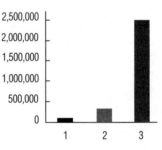

The investment world is filled with "should haves" and "could haves." We all have good 20/20 hindsight. There is no doubt the stock market has been extraordinarily good over the past 20 years. But the fact that it has can't tell you what it will do over the next 5, 10, or 20 years. However, investment research firm Wiesenberger has studied the longer-term relationships between stocks, bonds, and cash from 1960 to 1998. Figure 7.1 illustrates the growth of $10,000 in various categories. It shows how stocks have outperformed U.S. long-term bonds, U.S. housing, three-month Treasury bills, and inflation from 1960 to 1998.

This Wiesenberger chart is one of the finest illustrations of the longer-term returns for various asset classes. Over the long term, stocks have been the clear winner.

FIGURE 7.1   *Equity Investing in the Modern Era, 1960–1998*

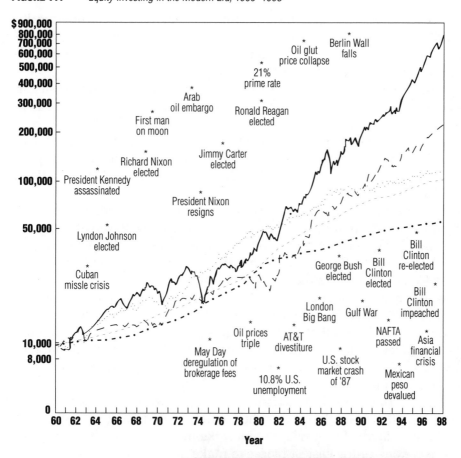

Legend	Ending Value on $10,000 Investment	Annualized Compound Rate of Return
—— S&P 500	$803,609	11.90%
– – · U.S. Long-Term Bonds	211,837	8.14
· · · · U.S. Housing	113,602	6.43
– – – 3-Month Treasury Bills	103,248	6.17
– · · – Inflation	55,780	4.51

Source: Wiesenberger Investment Performance Digest, Wiesenberger, a Thomson Financial Company, 1455 Research Blvd., Rockville, MD 20850; 800-232-2285.

Large Caps, Midcaps, Small Caps

If stocks have been the long-term performance driver in building wealth for ordinary investors, then it's important to discuss the differences between the three major classes of common stock: large capitalization, mid-capitalization, and small capitalization stocks.

These categories are referred to as large cap, midcap, and small cap stocks. But the type of stock that falls into each category and the risk-return ratio of each group varies greatly.

Large cap stocks refer to companies with a market capitalization over $2 billion. These are often well-known names and are usually referred to as blue chip stocks. Some examples include Exxon, IBM, GE, AT&T, DuPont, Merck, McDonald's, and Eastman Kodak.

Midcap stocks refer to companies with a market capitalization from $500 million to $2 billion. These are usually not as well known but may offer a more aggressive growth potential. Examples would include Abercrombie and Fitch, Best Buy, Delta Air Lines, Harley Davidson, Intuit, Lowe's Co., Outback Steakhouse, and Starbucks Corp.

Small cap stocks refer to companies with a market capitalization of less than $500 million. They are less likely to be known by the average investor, but history has shown that they have generated the largest returns since 1926. Examples would include Alaska Air Group Inc., Autobytel.com Inc., Callaway Golf Co., Incyte Pharmaceuticals, Linens 'N Things Inc., and Skytel Communication.

The importance of understanding the capitalization of each stock or mutual fund that you select is that each of these broad categories will come in and out of favor. There will be times like most of 1999 when large cap stocks were one of the easiest places to make money, but there have been many periods when market conditions favored small cap and midcap stocks. How can you choose an appropriate blend to help you meet your future financial goals? Only after a detailed review of your current assets, your stated goals and objectives, and your level of risk tolerance can you or your financial professional structure a portfolio designed to meet your goals.

One final distinction must be made within the types of stocks (or stock mutual funds) you choose to hold.

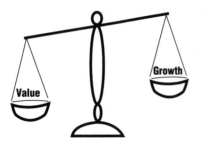

For years students of the markets have attempted to determine who will be the long-term winner between value investors and growth investors. A value stock is typically characterized by being in a sector of the market that is often thought of as boring and dull, such as paper stocks, chemical stocks, and autos. It is often thought that a savvy investor will attempt to buy these companies when they are out of favor and wait patiently for the markets to recognize their true value. Some common large cap value stocks include DuPont, Eastman Kodak, Burlington Northern, Alcoa, and Sears.

The opposite of value investing is growth investing. The years 1998 and early 1999 have proven that when growth stocks are in favor, they can soar. A company may be considered a growth stock if it has a projected earnings per share growth rate of 15 to 50 percent per year. Lately, Internet stocks and most large technology companies fall into this category. Other sectors include drug companies, consumer companies, and some large multinational companies. Well-known large cap growth stock include Merck, Cisco Systems, America Online, Intel, Microsoft, Dell Computers, and Lucent Technologies.

The problem for most investors is that they have very short memories. Although large cap growth stocks have undoubtedly been the best place lately for the person hoping to build wealth, there have been plenty of periods when growth was totally out of favor and value stocks were king. (See Figure 7.2.)

With so many choices and stock strategies available to individual investors, my best advice is to design and implement the strategies that best

FIGURE 7.2   *Large Cap Value versus Large Cap Growth*
Rolling 12-Month Quarterly Excess Returns, January 1, 1975–March 31, 1999

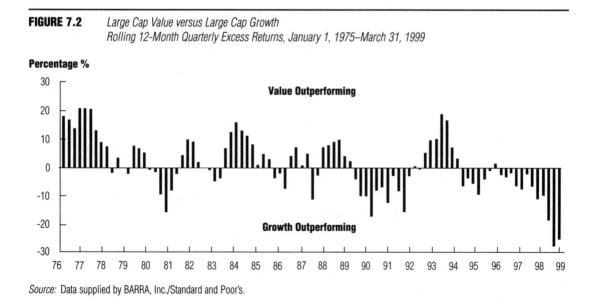

Source: Data supplied by BARRA, Inc./Standard and Poor's.

suit you. Then . . . don't chase every cycle. Let the markets do their job. You should create an asset allocation that you feel comfortable with and then let time and compound interest work their magic.

You may now think you need to own some stocks—with the returns that have been generated over the past 15 years, you may be thinking of putting a large portion of your money into stocks. But there is a catch . . . What is it?

Not all stocks go up in value. There are many companies whose value may rise quickly only to have their product or service become obsolete. Sometimes high-quality stocks can have slow growth periods and the slower than expected earnings growth can affect the stock's price. And sometimes the overall market will decline—even if your stock holdings are continuing to show outstanding earnings growth, the overall tone of the market can force a broad stock decline.

HOW THE THREE LARGEST ASSET CLASSES INTERACT AND WHEN YOU WANT TO HOLD EACH CLASS

Cash and Other Short-Term Investments

- You want short-term investments to meet short-term needs.
- You want to hold cash and cash equivalents for your emergency funds.
- You want to hold short-term investments if you believe interest rates will be moving higher and you don't want to lock your other fixed income investments into longer-term maturities.
- You want to hold cash and short-term investments when you believe the stock market is too high and could fall in the near future.

Bonds and Other Fixed Income Investments

- You want to hold bonds to generate their steady income stream and for their reduced volatility.
- You want to hold shorter-term bonds if you believe interest rates will be moving higher.
- You want to hold longer-term bonds if you believe interest rates will be moving lower.
- You may want to consider a laddered portfolio of bonds if you are uncertain as to which direction interest rates may be moving.

- You may want to use a zero-coupon bond strategy if you don't need the income but still like the idea of receiving a specific amount of money on a specific maturity date.

Stocks and Other Growth Investments

- You want to hold stocks if you believe inflation could be a risk for your future purchasing power.
- You want to hold stocks if you believe that corporations will continue to have an increasing earnings stream.
- You want to hold stocks if you want to profit from the creation and sale of goods and services in the United States and around the world.
- You want to hold stocks to take advantage of the risk-return opportunity in a growing economy.
- You may want to lower your allocation in stocks if you see a slowing economy and/or rising interest rates. Unfortunately, we never know when interest rates will be rising or when the economy will be slowing.

WHAT SHOULD YOU DO?
WORK FROM YOUR PERSONAL WRITTEN FINANCIAL PLAN

This plan will outline exactly where you are today, determine where you need to be in the future, fully explore your personal attitudes toward risk, and outline exactly what rate of return will help you reach your future financial goals. Only with this information can you develop your proper asset allocation.

With your written financial plan, you will be able to determine what amount of your money should be held in cash, what portion should be held in bonds, and what portion should be held in stocks. As you now know, each asset class plays a critical role toward moving you closer to financial independence. Yet if you look back at history, it is very difficult to know which blend of assets will be the best for the future.

You can explore your asset allocation in more detail in the action steps at the end of this chapter, but here are some common asset allocations for various risk tolerance levels that may serve as an example for you.

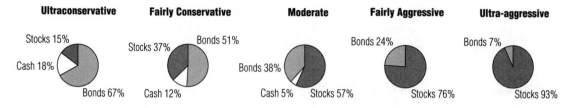

Ultraconservative — Stocks 15%, Cash 18%, Bonds 67%
Fairly Conservative — Stocks 37%, Bonds 51%, Cash 12%
Moderate — Bonds 38%, Cash 5%, Stocks 57%
Fairly Aggressive — Bonds 24%, Stocks 76%
Ultra-aggressive — Bonds 7%, Stocks 93%

These hypothetical illustrations are examples of how various financial portfolios could be allocated among the three basic asset classes. The importance of this information cannot be overemphasized. The single largest factor in the success of your financial plan may be how your personal investments are allocated between cash, bonds, and stocks.

The biggest mistake individual investors make is to put their financial plan into place and then begin to sell assets at the first bond market or stock market downturn. They will often jump out when they should be buying. Structure your investment portfolio so that you are able to sleep at night without being forced to constantly shift assets from one class to another.

ACTION STEP

Risk Tolerance

Defining your personal level of risk tolerance allows you to build a portfolio most suited to helping you reach your future financial goals while allowing you to invest within your comfort zone. This short questionnaire may offer some insight into your personal feelings toward risk. It will also rank some of the common factors that determine your ability to take on risk. These factors include age, income, current savings, and general investment knowledge. Please circle your answer.

1. What is your age?
   1. 65 and over
   3. 36–64
   5. 35 and under

2. What is your time horizon for investing this money?
   1. 1 year
   2. 2–5 years
   3. 5–10 years
   4. 10–20 years
   5. 20 years or longer

3. What is your primary objective for this money?
   1. Safety of principal
   2. Current income
   3. Growth and income
   4. Conservative growth
   5. Aggressive growth

4. Regarding your income, do you expect it to:
   1. Decrease dramatically in the future?
   2. Decrease a slight amount in the future?
   3. Stay about the same?
   4. Increase with the pace of inflation?
   5. Increase dramatically?

5. What amount of money do you have set aside for emergencies?
   1. None
   3. Enough to cover three months of expenses
   5. Enough to cover six or more months of expenses

6.   Which statement best describes your personal investment experience?
   1.   I have never been responsible for investing any money.
   2.   I am a relatively new investor.
   3.   I have invested some of my money through IRAs and through employer-sponsored retirement plans (401(k)s) for quite some time, but now I am ready to develop additional investment strategies.
   4.   I have invested for quite some time and am fairly confident in my ability to make prudent investment decisions.
   5.   I have invested money for years and have a definite knowledge of how the various stock and bond markets work.

7.   Regarding your view of risk, which investment would you be more comfortable making?
   1.   I am comfortable investing in savings accounts and CDs that are FDIC insured.
   2.   I invest in savings accounts and CDs, but I also own various income-producing bonds and/or bond mutual funds.
   3.   I have invested in a broad array of stocks, bonds, and mutual funds, but only those of the highest quality.
   4.   I have invested primarily in growth stocks and growth stock mutual funds.
   5.   I like to pick out new and emerging growth companies and aggressive growth stock mutual funds.

8.   To understand your risk tolerance more clearly, which investment would you be more likely to invest in?
   1.   This investment has a 20-year average annual return of 6 percent. It has achieved those returns with infrequent and very slight downturns. This investment has never experienced a negative return.
   3.   This investment has a 20-year average annual return of 9 percent. It has achieved those returns with a few moderate downturns when the decline lasted less than six months and then began to recover. It has experienced more than one year of negative returns.
   4.   This investment has a 20-year average annual return of 14 percent. It has achieved those returns while cycling through several periods of above-average returns and several periods of substantially negative returns.

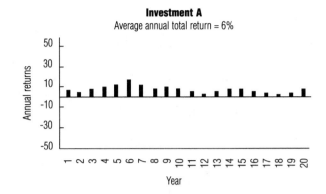

Investment A
Average annual total return = 6%

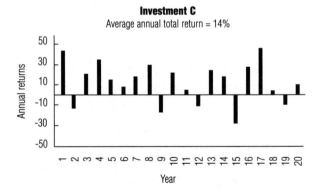

Investment B
Average annual total return = 9%

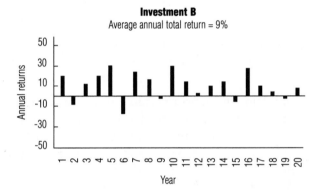

Investment C
Average annual total return = 14%

Given your investment goals, which investment would you choose?

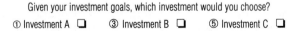

① Investment A ❏   ③ Investment B ❏   ⑤ Investment C ❏

What's Your Score?

To score the risk tolerance test, simply add up the points. You receive one point for each number that you circled. For example, if you circled a 1, you receive 1 point. If you circled a 4, you receive 4 points. The lowest number of points is 8 and the highest number is 40. Please count the number of points you circled and place a star on the risk tolerance scale below.

Ultraconservative		**Moderate**		**Ultra-aggressive**
	Fairly Conservative		**Fairly Aggressive**	

8   10   12   14   16   18   20   22   24   26   28   30   32   34   36   38   40

These questions and this scoring scale are meant to be used only as a guide because your actual investment plan may vary based on additional information that was not asked in the questionnaire. But after you have scored your risk tolerance, the next step is creating a portfolio of investments that matches your tolerance for risk.

Having determined your level of risk tolerance, you can now take one of two steps:

1. You can use your knowledge to begin to build your investment portfolio.
2. You can compare the following asset allocation strategies with your current investment holdings to see if your present strategy matches your objectives and your risk tolerance.

After you have evaluated and scored the questionnaire, you'll find yourself in one of five categories. The asset allocations suggested on the next two pages offer hypothetical examples of the types of allocations available. Your circumstances may change, so your investment allocation should be reviewed periodically and adjusted as needed. The investments you select will determine the overall aggressiveness and volatility of your portfolio. Remember that the value of your portfolio will fluctuate with market conditions.

1. Ultraconservative

As an ultraconservative investor, you prefer income-oriented, guaranteed investments such as CDs and bonds. Your need for income is high and your tolerance for risk is very low. With this in mind, you may wish to consider this sample asset allocation:

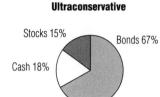

Ultraconservative

Stocks 15%

Bonds 67%

Cash 18%

Cash   18%
Bonds   67%
Stocks   15%

2. Fairly Conservative

As a fairly conservative investor, you are still uncomfortable with the volatility inherent in the stock market. However, you realize that a long-term commitment to quality growth investments should help you reach your financial goals. Therefore, while still primarily interested in fixed income-producing assets, you are willing to increase your allocation to balanced funds and some growth and income funds. If you venture into individual stocks, you are more likely to lean toward large cap, dividend-paying companies. Your basic asset allocation may look like this:

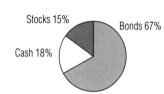

Fairly Conservative

Stocks 37%

Bonds 51%

Cash 12%

Cash   12%
Bonds   51%
Stocks   37%

3. Moderate

Moderate investors see themselves as the tortoise in the "Tortoise and the Hare." You are definitely interested in achieving reasonable returns and you have attempted to measure and quantify the risk. You realize there will be periods of negative returns, yet you are determined to commit to a long-term strategy of investing in a variety of growth investments that include large cap stocks, midcap stocks, and even international stocks. However, to reduce the overall volatility of your portfolio, you'll have a healthy portion held in fixed-income assets. Your basic asset allocation would include:

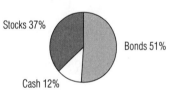

Moderate

Bonds 38%

Stocks 57%

Cash 5%

Cash   5%
Bonds   38%
Stocks   57%

4. Fairly Aggressive

As a fairly aggressive investor (the category I place my family in), you'll be critically aware of the risk-return ratio between your various investment options. You are not at all interested in income, so you spread your money among a variety of more aggressive growth stocks and growth mutual funds. You would be interested in diversifying your money into all the major growth categories (large cap, midcap, small cap, and international). You would want to structure your portfolio to take advantage of growth stock cycles and value stock cycles by owning both types. And because of the higher level of volatility, you'd want to be sure you set a consistent schedule to monitor your progress. Your basic asset allocation might include:

Fairly Aggressive

Cash 3%

Bonds 21%

Equity 76%

Cash   3%
Bonds   21%
Equity   76%

5. Ultra-aggressive

As an ultra-aggressive investor, you're interested in high return. You are aware of the risks, but you believe in making the most of every dollar. You are interested in investing in growth sectors such as technology and health care. You look to new industries like the Internet and biotechnology for your excitement. However, you are not carried away. You place a considerable portion of your portfolio into large cap and midcap growth stocks. You realize the importance of diversification and know there will be wild swings in the month-to-month value of your accounts. Your basic asset allocation might be:

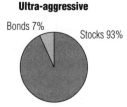

Ultra-aggressive

Bonds 7%

Stocks 93%

Cash   0%
Bonds   7%
Stocks   93%

Determine Your Current Asset Allocation

The following table will allow you to determine your current asset allocation. Remember that asset allocation is the predominant factor that controls risk and the potential for return. Once you have completed this table, go back to page 155 and compare your current asset allocation to the suggested allocations for each type of investor.

To complete this table, list the name and current dollar value of each investment you hold in the appropriate column. Next, calculate the subtotals for each category and then add all three subtotals to find the total dollar value of your portfolio. Finally, divide the subtotal of each category into the total value of your portfolio to discover your current asset allocation.

Cash		Bonds		Stocks	
Name	**Dollar Value**	**Name**	**Dollar Value**	**Name**	**Dollar Value**

Totals and
Percentages   _____   _____   _____

Your current asset allocation is:

Cash: _____%

Bonds: _____%

Stocks: _____%

Will Your Current Asset Allocation Help You Reach Your Financial Goals?

Rewrite your current asset allocation. Does your allocation match your risk tolerance? Will your current allocation have the potential to help you reach your financial goals?

Cash %   Bonds %   Stocks %

_____   _____   _____

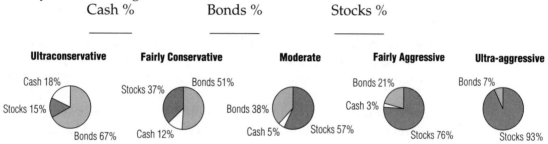

| Ultraconservative | Fairly Conservative | Moderate | Fairly Aggressive | Ultra-aggressive |

Each asset allocation model offers the potential for various risk-reward scenarios. I can never overemphasize that past performance can never predict or guarantee future results, but history can be a helpful guide.

For historical information, I relied on Investment View Hypothetical Software distributed by Chase Global Data and Research of Concord, Maine.

For the cash portion of the illustration I chose to use the three-month CD index. For the bond portion I used the Lehman Long-Term Treasury Bond Index, and for the stock portion I chose the S&P 500 Composite Index with the dividends reinvested. I used the longest time horizon available beginning December 31, 1979, and ending December 31, 1998. This gives a 19-year history and includes a few difficult periods for stocks, including 1987 and 1990.

The following data are examples of the blended rate of return for each risk tolerance and an example of how a single $10,000 investment would have grown, assuming all dividends and interest were reinvested and no taxes were paid. This information is provided to illustrate how these strategies would have worked over the past 19 years.

	19 YEARS	
Risk tolerance	**Return from January 31, 1979 through January 31, 1998**	**What $10,000 would have grown to:**
Ultraconservative	12.63%	$ 95,829
Fairly Conservative	14.63	127,999
Moderate	15.63	157,910
Fairly Aggressive	16.58	184,321
Ultra-aggressive	17.33	208,474

Over the past 19 years the risk-return theory played out exactly as it's supposed to. Investors who were willing to invest a larger percentage of their asset allocation into stocks enjoyed a considerably higher rate of return.

Armed with this information, you should be better able to determine if your current asset allocation will help you reach your stated future financial goals. If not, you will need to create an asset allocation that will both match your risk tolerance and offer the potential for the necessary rates of returns.

As a contingency plan, I recommend you or your financial adviser run numbers that are 3 to 6 percent lower than those that we have experienced in recent history. For example:

Risk tolerance	**This lower return**	**What $10,000 would have grown to in 19 years:**
Ultraconservative	8.0%	$43,157
Fairly Conservative	9.0	51,416
Moderate	10.0	61,159
Fairly Aggressive	10.7	68,992
Ultra-aggressive	11.2	75,160

These numbers may be more in line with the long-term benchmarks. The truth is that no one knows what the future holds. But good planning still increases your opportunity for success.

The Five Laws of
Successful Investing

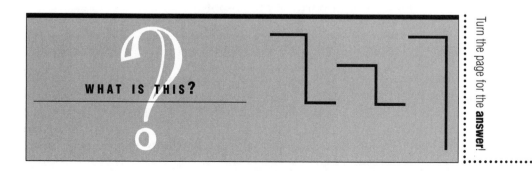

WHAT IS THIS?

Turn the page for the **answer!**

THE ANSWER!

It is an "E"! Just turn the page a quarter turn and you will clearly see the outline of an "E." Yet, many of you may have seen "Zs." As with the other visual illusions in this book, it's time to change your perspective. Let's turn to the five laws of successful investing.

The five laws of successful investing are intended to answer some of your questions or concerns. This chapter will help you understand some of the most important aspects of investing.

> **"**Although I was widowed at 45 and had never made an investment or a bank deposit, I was forced to learn fast. I was a depression kid and knew the value of a dollar. My dad had taught me that if you take care of the nickels, the dollars will take care of themselves.**"**
> **Bequita Gray,** 74
> *Little Rock, Arkansas*

SUCCESSFUL INVESTING: *Five Laws*

The five laws of successful investing are like the laws of nature: gravity, for example, proves that if you drop an apple, it will fall to the ground. This is a fact; it is part of life that we must accept and work within. By understanding the law of gravity, we can make our daily lives safer by working within certain parameters. For example, we don't let small children play on tall ladders because they could fall and hurt themselves. We don't throw things over a friend's head because we know that gravity could pull the object down and injure that friend.

Just as certain things occur naturally in nature, there are a few certainties for you to consider when it comes to investing. I call these the five laws of successful investing, and if you choose to work within this framework, you will increase your opportunity for profit.

LAW 1: *Risk Exists*

This makes sense academically, but in the real world of investing many high-risk investments turn out to be exactly what you would expect, and those excessive risks can quickly turn into losses.

Over the past few years I have turned to Modern Portfolio Theory to help me understand this concept. Modern Portfolio Theory is a broad strategy that tries to help investors match their risk tolerance to the type of investments they choose to help them reach their target rates of return.

There are four basic premises to Modern Portfolio Theory:

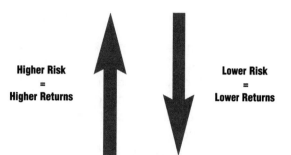

Higher Risk
=
Higher Returns

Lower Risk
=
Lower Returns

1. Investors Are Risk Averse

As we stated in Chapter 1, people hate to lose money. If, as a financial adviser, I am able to make nine fabulously profitable recommendations for a client and one losing recommendation, it will be the losing transaction that we discuss during our regular reviews. I am not blaming them. I hate to lose money too. The act of realizing a capital loss by selling a stock below its original purchase price is emotionally difficult.

The bottom line for risk is that you can usually assume the average investor will be more concerned with the prospect of losing money than with the returns. If you find this hard to believe, just wait until you suffer your first significant loss.

Modern Portfolio Theory attempts to identify and quantify risk. By quantifying the risk of various investments, you are able to make a more informed decision as to which investments more closely match your attitudes toward risk. If you can understand the risk involved, you will more likely withstand the volatility.

2. Markets Are Basically Efficient

Saying markets are efficient is a fancy way of saying that there is so much information available through research reports and TV and the Internet that it is virtually impossible to receive any significant information before the rest of the world receives it too.

Some of my customers think their financial adviser should somehow be able to beat the market, assuming that this could be done by strategically timing buys and sells or by using some other form of sophisticated system of stock screening and analysis.

But reality proves this to be false. Above-average returns are difficult if not impossible to achieve over the long term. (As we discussed in Myth # 8, the hot investment of one year rarely repeats its performance for the long term.)

3. Investors Should Utilize Asset Allocation Strategies

If timing the market is not the proper strategy and if markets are so efficient that you will rarely be able to profit by choosing the top one of two stocks, how are you supposed to invest your money?

Asset allocation should be your ever present mantra. Asset allocation is exactly what it says: you look at the current investable assets you are holding and determine how they are allocated or distributed. For example, the three primary asset allocation categories, as noted earlier, are cash, bonds, and stocks.

These asset classes respond differently to different economic conditions and serve a different function in the structuring of your portfolio. It is usually the weighting within these asset classes that determines your longer-term success as an investor.

"A rising tide raises all ships," according to Warren Buffett. If stocks are moving up and you have a diversified portfolio of stocks, you should profit—not so much on the basis of the individual securities you own as on the basis of security. In bad stock market declines, you can reduce your risk by having a smaller allocation in stocks and a higher allocation in cash and bonds. Conversely, in good times you'll want to increase your allocation in growth investments.

The difficulty is finding an overall asset allocation strategy that matches your risk tolerance. Risk is easily the most challenging part of investing. You already know the typical explanation that more risk can mean a higher rate of return. And, conversely, a lower risk factor should offer lower anticipated returns.

4. Investors Need to Implement the Idea of Optimality

According to optimality, "for any level of risk that one is willing to accept, there is a rate of return that should be achieved" (Philip Wilson, Wilson Associates International).

This is one of the most exciting premises. If I know a stock is an aggressive investment with a fabulous performance history but also a lot of volatility; I still might purchase the stock if I am willing to stomach the wild swings in return for the higher profit potential.

Internet stocks are excellent examples of how you might incorporate the theory of optimality into your financial plan. The growth performance of this sector has been fabulous; you can clearly see the concept of asset class in place here. It didn't really matter which Internet company you owned. If you owned a basket of them, you most likely made money. But if you bought any of these companies, you did so with the full knowledge that they could have dropped in value just as quickly. Optimality says some investments are risky, so buy the ones that could prove to be worth the risk.

Before we can continue with our discussion on risk, I must introduce you to the concept of the standard deviation—a mathematical term that can send cold chills up a college freshman's spine and even make highly educated business professionals a bit uncomfortable. But I believe understanding this concept could be a turning point in your comfort level and confidence level when it comes to investing in the volatile world of stocks.

The standard deviation is a measure of the volatility of any given investment. A statistician reviews each price swing that a specific stock has had over a specific period of time and plots the average rate of return. Then the statistician monitors the price swing (deviation) in relationship to the average price; the stocks that have smaller price swings (deviation) have less risk. The stocks with greater price swings (deviation) away from the average price tend to have more risk.

Even if you can't follow this definition, you only need to remember this: The lower the standard deviation . . . the lower the risk. The higher the standard deviation . . . the higher the risk.

The standard deviation is nothing more than measuring the volatility of price swings and assigning them a mathematical value so we investors can compare the inherent risk associated with our various investments.

If I'm thinking about investing in a volatile stock, I can check to see how high the standard deviation has been and then I'm able to make a more informed decision. If the standard deviation is quite high, I will ask the optimality question, Do I believe the potential return is worth taking the risk? The other thing the standard deviation allows me to do is build a broader portfolio of lower-risk investments and add a few higher standard deviation stocks without compromising my overall risk tolerance (assuming the stocks with higher risk offer a commensurately higher rate of return).

The beauty of today's technology is that the standard deviation can be measured and plotted on a chart without having to do the calculations yourself. For illustration, let's review the top ten holdings of the S&P 500 Index and compare their actual rates of return and volatility over the stated time horizon.

Because one of these companies was not publicly traded in December 1998, we must use a slightly different time horizon of January 1989 through December 1998. Over that time frame the ten largest holdings of the S&P 500 Index had the following standard deviations and returns:

Rates of Return	Standard Deviation	Average One-Year Rolling Rates*	Min. Return	Max. Return
Microsoft	26.65%	56.57%	16.00%	97.14%
General Electric	14.84	22.85	−1.56	47.26
Merck	26.26	20.66	−22.38	63.69
Exxon	11.72	13.26	−6.02	32.54
Intel	28.68	41.25	−5.82	88.52
Coca-Cola	15.74	28.16	2.27	54.06
Wal-Mart	25.43	21.87	−19.85	63.80
IBM	33.35	9.50	−45.35	64.35
Pfizer	26.65	33.03	−10.79	76.86
Philip Morris	24.62	15.64	−24.86	56.15

*The average rolling one-year returns are calculated by taking the actual return for each available one-year time frame. In this example, you take the return from January 1989 through January 1990, then from February 1989 through February 1990, then March 1989 through March 1990, for each 12-month period through December 1998. Then take an average of all of those one-year returns, which gives you the average one-year rolling returns.

Source: Wilson Associates International.

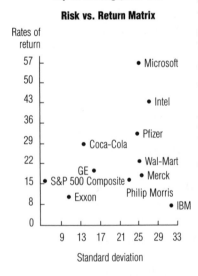

Top 10 Holdings, S&P 500

Risk vs. Return Matrix

Source: Wilson Associates International.

Compare the minimum and maximum rates of return for each stock in the chart above. Notice which stocks had the lowest minimum one-year rates of return and which stocks had the highest maximum one-year rates of return. Does it surprise you to find IBM at the bottom of the list on the low side of performance and Microsoft and Intel on the top of the list on the high side for performance?

The most interesting thing is that one of the finest companies in America (IBM) had the highest standard deviation of these ten stocks over this specific time horizon.

Obviously, these are all very well-known companies, but how can we look at these companies to gain a greater knowledge of their past risk/return potential?

What does this chart mean? *The higher the dot, the higher the rate of return.* The further the dot is to the right, the more the stock has deviated from it's average rate of return and therefore the higher the risk.

Over the last ten years, IBM has had a lower-than-average rate of return at 7.45 percent with a much higher-than-average deviation of 33.10 percent. With an average rolling one-year rate of return of 7.45%, this plots the return considerably lower than the nine other stocks, and over that time IBM's stock had some dramatic price swings. These price swings increased the standard deviation of the stock, therefore increasing the risk. That plotted the standard deviation sharply to the right side of the risk scale, which is the exact opposite of optimality. What you want to see are dots that carry above-average returns with below-average risks. In other words, most investors want to move up the chart and to the left.

You might find it helpful to know what a common index average rate of return over this time was and its corresponding standard deviation. Let's look at the S&P 500 Index over the same time horizon and use that as a benchmark for comparison.

S&P 500 Index	Average Rolling One-Year Return
Rate of return	17.44%
Standard deviation	10.29%
Minimum return	0.52%
Maximum return	34.36%

Source: Wilson Associates International.

This benchmark information can be very helpful when building a portfolio of common stock investments. I see many people now jumping into very high standard deviation stocks like technology and Internet issues. They have read how much money has been made in these stocks. It all seems so simple; buy them and they are bound to go up.

What these investors may or may not realize is that these stocks are exactly the ones that have the highest deviation. If the stock market begins to lose any momentum or the companies have even one lackluster earnings report, the value of these stocks can plummet.

Does that mean you should not own them? Absolutely not. If you look one last time at the Risk versus Return Matrix, you'll see a square dot marked with a "Top 10 Holdings for the S&P." This is the overall risk-return rating for the entire hypothetical portfolio of the top ten holdings in the S&P 500 Index. Notice that by blending in higher risk-higher return investments like Microsoft and Intel with some of the older names like Coca-Cola, Exxon, and GE, the risk has been pushed toward the left and the rate of return has remained more than acceptable.

Top 10 Holdings of the S&P 500 Index	
Average rate of return	26.10%
Standard deviation	15.16%
Minimum return	1.17%
Maximum return	51.04%

Source: Wilson Associates International.

The point: You want to understand and quantify the amount of risk you are exposing yourself to in order to achieve the rates of return necessary to meet your stated goals.

If you would like further data on where to find the average standard deviation, you may look in the following: Wilson Associates International, CDA Technologies, Morningstar, and Value Line.

LAW 2: *The Importance of Diversification*

Some people believe there are at least two major sources of risk in investing: market risk and business risk.

Market Risk

Market risk involves a decline in the overall market in which you are investing. For example, if you have money in the stock market and the stock market begins to decline, you will most likely lose money. You can attempt to protect yourself from market risk in two ways.

1. Diversify the actual markets in which you are investing your money. This is called asset allocation. Determine what percentage of your assets you want in cash, in bonds, and in stocks. You can also add more asset classes like real estate and precious metals; and the most sophisticated investors may look at other commodities and financial futures contracts (often called managed futures). You can thus reduce market risk by diversifying the asset classes in which you invest your money.

2. You may be able to reduce some market risk through sector rotation. Though markets often fall in unison, there are usually one or two sectors of the market that do well when other sectors are performing poorly. The stock market is often dividend into the following sectors:

   - Basic materials
   - Energy
   - Technology
   - Health care
   - Consumer cyclicals (Durable)
   - Consumer cyclicals (Nondurable)
   - Consumer noncyclicals
   - Utilities
   - Financials
   - Transportation
   - Telecommunications

You might see a steep decline in basic materials or energy while such sectors as heath care or technology are rebounding. An Action Step at the end of this chapter will help you categorize your current stocks into their appropriate sector and then map out the percentages of each sector you currently hold to determine your sector weightings.

Business Risk

The second major form of risk is business risk, which occurs when you invest in a business and that business goes out of business!

Companies come and go. If you invest in a new or even an old, well-known company whose product or service is no longer needed, you could lose all of your money. You can reduce or almost eliminate business risk by diversifying your money among several businesses in several different industry sectors of the market and the economy. Buying a mutual fund is a wonderful example of diversification. A mutual fund might purchase 75 to 100 stocks. If one company gets into trouble and goes down in value because of a business risk problem, you have the remaining holdings to rely on for performance.

LAW 3: *Begin with Quality*

Some of my favorite words in a research report are "the world's largest."

- The world's largest retailer is Wal-Mart.
- The world's largest maker of hamburgers is McDonald's.
- The world's largest software manufacturer is Microsoft.
- The world's largest soft drink company is Coca-Cola.
- The world's largest electrical manufacturer is General Electric.
- The world's largest computer chip maker is Intel.
- The world's largest pharmaceutical company is Merck.
- The world's largest bank is Citigroup.
- The world's largest energy company is Exxon.

While these stocks come in and out of favor with various analysts, I am constantly looking for companies that my customers can hold for a lifetime. These are called *core holdings*. They tend to be large, well-known companies whose future is expected to continue and whose profits are expected to increase over time.

These quality holdings may not give you the overnight returns that so many investors are hoping to find. But they may protect your portfolio against inflation, and they should provide returns that will match the overall returns of the large stocks in general. Investors who begin with quality can begin to move up the risk-return scale.

I see far too many people who make their first venture into the stock market by buying a "hot tip" they have overheard from a coworker or neighbor. They have no idea what the company does nor have they looked at any research. They simply buy the stock and hope for the best.

Obviously, this is not the best strategy. I recommend you begin with quality. Buy the stocks of companies whose products and services you use every day. These should be the companies you will be proud to tell your families and friends you own. Then you can increase your risk and venture into smaller, more speculative stocks after doing your homework.

LAW 4: *Compound Interest—Time Is on Your Side*

The easiest way I can explain compound interest is to illustrate it by using three different rates of return. Assume you have $1,000 to invest and plan to invest an additional $1,000 every year for a total of 30 years.

Year	3.75% Return	5.25% Return	11.00% Return	Year	3.75% Return	5.25% Return	11.00% Return
1	$1,000.00	$1,000.00	$1,000.00	16	$21,392.74	$24,143.49	$39,189.95
2	2,037.50	2,052.50	2,110.00	17	23,194.97	26,411.02	44,500.84
3	3,113.91	3,160.26	3,342.10	18	25,064.78	28,797.60	50,395.94
4	4,230.68	4,326.17	4,709.73	19	27,004.71	31,309.48	56,939.49
5	5,389.33	5,553.29	6,227.80	20	29,017.39	33,953.23	64,202.83
6	6,591.43	6,844.84	7,912.86	21	31,105.54	36,735.77	72,265.14
7	7,838.61	8,204.20	9,783.27	22	33,272.00	39,664.4	81,214.31
8	9,132.55	9,634.92	11,859.43	23	35,519.70	42,746.78	91,147.88
9	10,475.03	11,140.75	14,163.97	24	37,851.68	45,990.98	102,174.15
10	11,867.84	12,725.64	16,722.01	25	40,271.12	49,405.51	114,413.31
11	13,312.88	14,393.73	19,561.43	26	42,781.29	52,999.30	127,998.77
12	14,812.12	16,149.41	22,713.19	27	45,385.59	56,781.76	143,078.64
13	16,367.57	17,997.25	26,211.64	28	48,087.55	60,762.81	159,817.29
14	17,981.35	19,942.10	30,094.92	29	50,890.83	64,952.85	178,397.19
15	19,655.65	21,989.07	34,405.36	30	53,799.24	69,362.88	199,020.88

This illustration demonstrates the power of compound interest. If you add interest to a single amount and then allow the new total to earn the same rate of return, the overall effect can be incredible.

I chose the numbers above to show how various types of investments might behave. Cash investments have averaged around 3.5 percent over the past 30 years. Bonds have averaged around 4.5 percent and stocks have averaged around 11.0 percent over the past 70 years. I'm not suggesting that these will be the rates of return you should expect to make on any specific asset class. But you can certainly see the impact of compound interest depending on the rate of return you actually achieve.

The second illustration can be found in almost every investment strategy book I have ever read, but its impact is so powerful that I am including it here as well. It's from *Financial Peace* by Dave Ramsay, "Who is the Smarter—Ben or Arthur?" Bernard Zick, who has a master's degree in business administration (MBA) and is an expert on the time value of money, gave this consumer quiz in his monthly newsletter.

Ben, 22, will invest $1,000 per year compounded annually at 10 percent for eight years until he is 30. For the next 35 years, until he is 65, Ben will invest not one penny more.

Arthur, 30, will invest $1,000 per year for 35 years until he is 65. His investment also earns 10 percent compounded interest each year.

At 65, will Arthur or Ben have the most money? The answer shown in Figure 8.1 is yet another example of the power of compound interest and the importance of getting started now.

The third illustration of the power of compound interest is the "Rule of 72." If you'd like to know how quickly your investment portfolio will double, you can take your anticipated rate of return and divide it into 72.

72 divided by 6%—your money doubles in   12 years
72 divided by 7%—your money doubles in   10.2 years
72 divided by 8%—your money doubles in   9 years
72 divided by 9%—your money doubles in   8 years
72 divided by 10%—your money doubles in 7.2 years
72 divided by 11%—your money doubles in 6.5 years
72 divided by 12%—your money doubles in 6 years

The Rule of 72 shows the true power of compound interest. The higher your average annual rate of return, the faster your investment money will grow. This concept is even more impressive when you use real money.

FIGURE 8.1   *Example of Compound Interest*

Age	Ben Invests	Year-End Value	Arthur Invests	Year-End Value
22	$1,000	$ 1,100	0	0
23	1,000	2,310	0	0
24	1,000	3,641	0	0
25	1,000	5,105	0	0
26	1,000	6,716	0	0
27	1,000	8,487	0	0
28	1,000	10,436	0	0
29	1,000	12,579	0	0
30	0	13,837	$1,000	$ 1,100
31	0	15,221	1,000	2,310
32	0	16,743	1,000	3,641
33	0	18,418	1,000	5,105
34	0	20,259	1,000	6,716
35	0	22,285	1,000	8,487
36	0	24,514	1,000	10,436
37	0	26,965	1,000	12,579
38	0	29,662	1,000	14,937
39	0	32,628	1,000	17,531
40	0	35,891	1,000	20,384
41	0	39,480	1,000	23,523
42	0	43,428	1,000	26,975
43	0	47,771	1,000	30,772
44	0	52,548	1,000	34,950
45	0	57,802	1,000	39,545
46	0	63,583	1,000	44,599
47	0	69,941	1,000	50,159
48	0	76,935	1,000	56,275
49	0	84,628	1,000	63,002
50	0	93,091	1,000	70,403
51	0	102,400	1,000	78,543
52	0	112,640	1,000	87,497
53	0	123,904	1,000	97,347
54	0	136,295	1,000	108,182
55	0	149,924	1,000	120,100
56	0	164,917	1,000	133,210
57	0	181,409	1,000	147,631
58	0	199,549	1,000	163,494
59	0	219,504	1,000	180,943
60	0	241,455	1,000	200,138
61	0	265,600	1,000	221,252
62	0	292,160	1,000	244,477
63	0	321,376	1,000	270,024
64	0	353,514	1,000	298,127
65	0	388,865	1,000	329,039

. . . and he never caught up!!!!

If you started your portfolio at age 30 with $25,000 and were able to earn a 10 percent average annual rate of return and assuming no additions are made, your portfolio would double every 7.2 years.

30.0 years old	$ 25,000
37.2 years old	$ 50,000
43.4 years old	$100,000
50.6 years old	$200,000
57.8 years old	$400,000
64.1 years old	$800,000 WOW!

LAW 5: *The Final Responsibility Is Yours*

You are the steward of the resources you have been given. Therefore, the final responsibility is yours. As a financial adviser, I work very closely with my customers to help them structure detailed financial plans that will allow them to have a written road map for attempting to accomplish their future financial goals.

But all I can provide is a blueprint. They have to earn the income to fund the plan. They have to take the time to educate themselves so they'll understand their investments. They must take the time to know how to read their statements. Does that mean you must become an expert? No.

However, no one will ever care more about your money than you. Yours is the most important role of all.

12 Review Your Stock Sector Analysis

This action step will allow you to identify those areas of the stock market that you have chosen to overweight and areas to underweight in your investment dollars.

To complete this action step you need a complete list of all your current individual stock holdings. First, you want to break them down into separate categories. To help with this task I have listed each category with some examples of the various types of stocks that will fall into each sector.

Capital Goods Sector

Aerospace/Defense
Conglomerates
Electrical Equipment
Electronics—Defense
Engineering and Construction
Heavy Duty Trucks
Machine Tools
Machinery—Diversified
Manufacturing—Diversified Industrials
Office Equipment and Supplies
Pollution Control

Technology

Communication Equipment Manufacturers
Computer Systems
Computer Software and Services
Electronics—Instruments
Electronics—Semiconductors

Transportation Sector

Airlines
Railroads
Truckers
Transport Misc.

Basic Materials Sector

Aluminum
Building Materials
Chemicals
Containers
Gold Mining
Metals
Paper and Forest Products
Steel

Energy Sector

Oil and Gas Drilling
Oil—Domestic Integrated
Oil—International Integrated
Oil Well Equipment and Services
Oil Exploration and Production

Financial Sector

Banks—Money Center
Banks—Major Regional
Insurance Brokers
Insurance—Life
Insurance—Multiline
Insurance Property and Casualty
Investment Banking/Brokerage
Personal Loans
Savings and Loans
Financial—Misc.

Utilities

Electric Companies
Natural Gas Dist.

Consumer Cyclicals/Durables Sector

Automobiles
Auto Parts—After Market

Hardware and Tools
Homebuilding
Household Furnishings and Appliances
Manufactured Housing

Consumer Cyclicals/Nondurable Sector

Broadcast Media
Commercial Services
Distributors—Commercial Products
Entertainment
Hotel/Motels
Leisure Time
Publishing
Restaurants
Retail
Specialty Printing
Toys

Health Care Sector

Health Care Diversified
Health Care Drugs
Health Care Misc.
Health Care HMOs
Hospital Management
Medical Products and Supplies

Telecom Sector

Telecommunications
Telephone

Then, list the name and current dollar value of each stock you hold in the appropriate column. Next, calculate the subtotals for each stock sector and add the subtotals to find out the total dollar value of your stock portfolio. Finally, divide the subtotal of each category into the total value of your stock portfolio to discover your current stock sector allocation.

Capital Goods	Technology	Transportation	Basic Materials	Energy	Financial

Utilities	Con. Cyc. Durables	Con. Cyc. Nondurables	Con. Noncyclical	Health Care	Telecomm.

The point of this review is to make sure your stock holdings are broadly diversified among several industries. Different sectors of the stock market provide higher returns at various points in a market cycle. If you can properly diversify your stock holdings, you should be better positioned to capture those returns and to defend against any unexpected downturns in any one sector.

Analyzing Your Investment Choices

> **"**A little learning is a dangerous thing. I grew up in the days when men handled all the finances and women knew little about them. Those days are gone forever! I began to learn when I had to, when my widowed mother turned her finances over to me (and I still don't know nearly enough.) Learn, study, read a lot, join an investment club (the best learning tool). Actually, handling your own money can turn you into a quick study.**"**
> **Mrs. Donald Nilles,** 70ish
> *Little Rock, Arkansas*

> [What was the best investment you ever made?] **"**Our college education. It improved our self-esteem, our ability to earn a better income, and allowed us to invest in the stock market and other securities for our future.**"**
> **Larry and Ann Dodgen,** 64 and 62
> *Paragould, Arkansas*

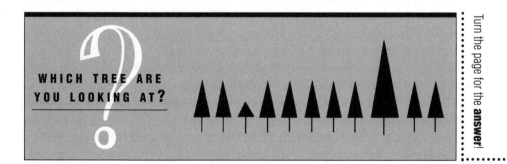

WHICH TREE ARE YOU LOOKING AT?

Turn the page for the **answer!**

THE ANSWER!

This picture is less of a gimmick and more of an illustration of what the human eye is drawn to. Most of you will look at the small tree or the large tree. The human brain is drawn to those things that stand out or are considered to be different.

Now that you've read about the three major asset classes—cash, bonds, and stocks—it's time to learn more about each class and the inherent risk-reward relationship of each investment alternative.

It's time for you to be different from the average investor. If you take the time to review the following pages, you'll undoubtedly advance your financial knowledge.

> **"**The best financial advice I ever received came from my dad. He said. 'Waste not, want not.' And investing in Xerox stock put our children through college.**"**
> **Anonymous,** 73
> *Little Rock, Arkansas*

THE HISTORICAL PERFORMANCE OF VARIOUS INVESTMENTS

Now that you understand more of how the three basic asset classes work, you can begin to structure your investment portfolio. Your portfolio is made up of specific investments. Each type of investment carries its own set of risks and benefits. You measure the risks with the standard deviation and you measure the benefits with past performance.

It's necessary to make informed decisions. *Knowledge instills confidence.* If you understand how each type of investment works, how much volatility each has produced, and what rate of return each has generated, you'll be better equipped than most investors to not be swayed by the difficult periods.

Don't be intimidated by the information here. When some of you look at the charts, the bar graphs, and the numbers, your eyes may roll back into your head. Don't lose hope! If you take the time to review the explanations in each section and then walk through the worksheets at the back of this chapter, you will have learned how to judge many of the important factors in choosing investments that match your tolerance of risk and your performance expectations.

The information here is a reference tool. By comparing and contrasting the risks and the benefits of your various options, you'll be able to implement your plan and fund specific investments that will help you reach your future financial goals.

This chapter offers technical skills for reviewing various investment options so you can make more informed decisions. Whether you are using a financial professional or investing on your own, these pages illustrate the advantages and disadvantages of each alternative as well as demonstrate rates of return and varying degrees of risk.

Many sources of historical investment data are available at your public library or through the Internet. Some of these are published by Ibbotson, Wiesenberger, Morningstar, and Lipper. The information here was compiled by using data available from Wilson Associates International, which has specialized in creating software for the investor who is interested in maximizing returns while attempting to minimize risk. The software Wilson provides to any subscriber for a fee has provided me with considerable information. It is with thanks to the company that I present the following research.

How to Read the Research

It may be helpful to compare two very different investment alternatives. For this exercise I compare the Generic Money Market Index to Standard and Poor's 500-Stock Index.

Page 185 illustrates the Generic Money Market Index. Just under the title is the date. The *date* is very important because you want to know if the investment has had a track record long enough to give you valid information. The time horizon for the Generic Money Market Index is ten years, December 1988 through December 1998.

Next is the *Definition*. The definition should help explain what the investment is and what its primary function will be in your investment portfolio and overall asset allocation.

Then you will see the *Index*. The Index provides the benchmark from which you can evaluate the performance of your specific investment. For example, if you were investing in a money market fund, you would compare your money market fund's performance to other money market funds with the same objective.

Category is the basic asset category into which each specific investment alternative falls.

In *Performance* you will find four separate listings:

- Year-to-date—In this case it represents the 1998 total return.
- Last 12 months
- Last three years—Represents the trailing three-year total return.
- Last five years—Represents the trailing five-year total return.

The performance data allow you to compare various investment alternatives on a one-year, three-year, and five-year basis and look at the actual returns they have generated since 1995. You can evaluate each alternative's short-term performance—was the performance fairly consistent or did the return vary greatly from year to year?

You will then see *Rate of Return (1 Year)*. This figure looks back over the trailing ten-year time horizon and at every one-year "rolling" holding period and then takes an average of that return. From these data the Generic Money Market has generated an average one-year rolling return of 5.11 percent and the S&P 500 has generated an average one-year rolling return of 17.56 percent.

Next is the *Standard Deviation*. As you remember from Chapter 8, the standard deviation is a mathematical measurement of risk. The lower the standard deviation, the lower the volatility or risk. The higher the standard deviation, the higher the volatility or risk. As you would expect, the Generic Money Market Index has a very low standard deviation of 1.6 percent. Compare that with the S&P 500, which has a standard deviation of 10.30 percent.

The next section illustrates how a $1,000 increment would have theoretically grown over the stated ten-year period.

Below is a comparison of the Generic Money Market Index to the S&P 500 Index:

	Generic Money Market	**S&P 500 Index**
Original Investment	$1,000	$ 1,000
5 years	1,283	2,246
10 years	1,645	5,044
15 years	2,111	11,328

Remember that these theoretical growth rates are using the compounded average annual rolling rate of return for the trailing ten-year time period. These numbers are meant to be averages and are only used for illustration. Your actual rates of return will vary greatly depending on the actual future returns of the specific asset categories that you choose.

The *Monthly Rates* are interesting because they show the actual rates of return that each investment alternative produced on a month-by-month basis. The Generic Money Market generated very consistent positive monthly rates of return, while the S&P 500 posted 36 negative monthly returns out of 120 monthly periods. This table clearly illustrates the varying degrees of volatility that two different choices offer.

The *Annual Rate of Return* information is listed for 1989 to 1998. These tables can help you compare the volatility on an annual basis by counting how many negative periods were generated versus positive periods. For example, the Generic Money Market Index posted zero negative annual returns (page 185), while the S&P 500 posted one negative annual return in 1990 and one flat return in 1994 (page 192).

The point of this research is to allow you to better understand your investments and the recommendations of your personal financial adviser (if you use one).

At a glance you can compare two of the basic factors of risk and return for the Generic Money Market and the S&P 500:

	Generic Money Market Index	S&P 500 Index
Standard deviation	1.6%	10.30%
Return	5.11%	17.56%

So the choice becomes how you best structure your investments so they give you the highest rate of return with the lowest possible risk. In the investment community we call that *optimizing* your portfolio. Optimization is a mathematical method of creating the optimal or ideal blend of investments that will generate the highest possible rate of return for your specific level of risk tolerance.

FIGURE 9.1   *Building Blocks for a Diversified Investment Portfolio*

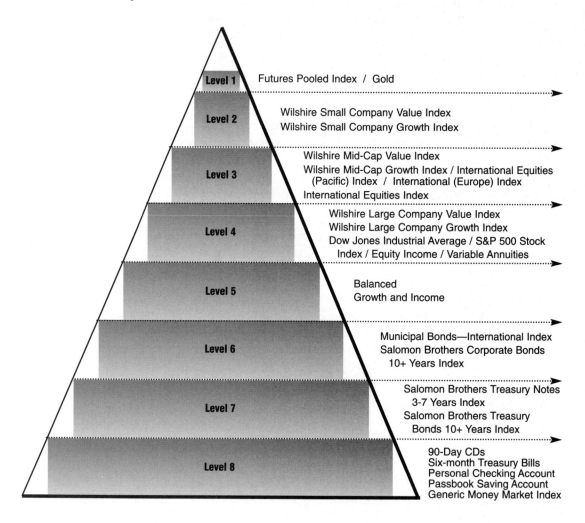

Generic Money Market Index

Horizon: December 1988–December 1998

Definition: This money may be held in a bank or other financial institution such as a brokerage account. These accounts may or may not be FDIC insured. They invest in short-term instruments with maturities of less than one year. Their primary function is to provide the investor with a higher rate of return than a passbook savings account while delivering high liquidity.

Who uses money markets? Money markets are used for emergency funds. If you are saving for a short-term need, you'll want to save in a short-term vehicle, and a money market is a great place to save for your next vacation or a new piece of furniture. But the primary use of a money market is to let you earn a reasonable rate of interest on your secure money.

Index: Money Market Average

Category: Cash Equivalents

Performance:

Year-to-Date	5%	Last 3 Years	16%
Last 12 Months	5%	Last 5 Years	27%

Rate of Return (1 Year)	5.11%
Standard Deviation	1.60%
Original Portfolio Amount	$1,000
Portfolio Value in 5 Years	$1,283
Portfolio Value in 10 Years	$1,645
Portfolio Value in 15 Years	$2,310

Standard Deviation

1.60%

		Monthly Returns										Annual Return
	Jan.	**Feb.**	**Mar.**	**Apr.**	**May**	**Jun.**	**Jul.**	**Aug.**	**Sep.**	**Oct.**	**Nov.**	**Dec.**	
1989	0.71	0.70	0.73	0.76	0.79	0.79	0.71	0.74	0.67	0.70	0.66	0.65	8.97
1990	0.62	0.65	0.64	0.64	0.67	0.66	0.66	0.62	0.62	0.61	0.61	0.61	7.87
1991	0.60	0.54	0.51	0.47	0.47	0.44	0.47	0.44	0.43	0.40	0.40	0.37	5.70
1992	0.34	0.31	0.31	0.31	0.28	0.28	0.28	0.25	0.25	0.22	0.22	0.25	3.37
1993	0.25	0.25	0.22	0.22	0.22	0.22	0.22	0.22	0.22	0.22	0.22	0.22	2.70
1994	0.21	0.24	0.24	0.24	0.27	0.29	0.32	0.32	0.34	0.37	0.39	0.42	3.71
1995	0.44	0.44	0.46	0.46	0.46	0.46	0.45	0.45	0.45	0.45	0.45	0.44	5.54
1996	0.42	0.42	0.39	0.39	0.39	0.41	0.41	0.41	0.40	0.40	0.40	0.42	4.96
1997	0.40	0.40	0.39	0.42	0.41	0.41	0.43	0.43	0.43	0.43	0.43	0.42	5.12
1998	0.42	0.42	0.42	0.42	0.42	0.41	0.41	0.41	0.41	0.41	0.38	0.38	5.03

90-Day CDs

Horizon: December 1988–December 1998

Definition: This money is usually held at a bank. Ninety-day CDs allow investors to try to guarantee their principal through FDIC insurance, and they typically carry maturity schedules from 30 days to 10 years. An interest penalty may apply if the money is withdrawn before the scheduled maturity date.

Who uses 90-day CDs? These short-term certificates of deposit are often used by investors who want absolute safety of their principal. They buy these short-term investments to provide a certain level of income while ensuring that their money will soon be maturing and available for other opportunities. Many people buy these CDs when saving for an event that is less than five years away, such as the purchase of a new car or a down payment on a new home.

Index: Certificates of Deposit

Category: Cash Equivalents

Performance:

Year-to-Date	6%	Last 3 Years (HPR*)	18%
Last 12 Months	6%	Last 5 Years (HPR)	31%

Rate of Return (1 Year)	5.74%
Standard Deviation	1.58%
Original Portfolio Amount	$1,000
Portfolio Value in 5 Years	$1,322
Portfolio Value in 10 Years	$1,747
Portfolio Value in 15 Years	$2,310

$1,322 $1,747 $2,310

5 yrs.   10 yrs.   15 yrs.

Standard Deviation

1.58%

*HPR = Holiday period return.

	Jan.	Feb.	Mar.	Apr.	May	Jun.	Jul.	Aug.	Sep.	Oct.	Nov.	Dec.	Annual Return
Monthly Returns													
1989	0.73	0.76	0.82	0.85	0.84	0.77	0.76	0.72	0.72	0.74	0.71	0.70	9.48
1990	0.70	0.63	0.72	0.68	0.71	0.70	0.70	0.69	0.66	0.68	0.68	0.67	8.54
1991	0.64	0.55	0.55	0.52	0.51	0.48	0.51	0.51	0.47	0.47	0.44	0.41	6.23
1992	0.36	0.33	0.35	0.35	0.35	0.32	0.32	0.29	0.27	0.29	0.29	0.29	3.89
1993	0.29	0.26	0.26	0.26	0.26	0.26	0.26	0.26	0.26	0.28	0.28	0.28	3.27
1994	0.28	0.25	0.31	0.33	0.35	0.38	0.40	0.40	0.40	0.45	0.47	0.52	4.63
1995	0.51	0.49	0.53	0.51	0.53	0.50	0.52	0.49	0.47	0.49	0.49	0.49	6.18
1996	0.48	0.43	0.46	0.43	0.45	0.45	0.47	0.47	0.44	0.46	0.44	0.46	5.59
1997	0.46	0.41	0.45	0.45	0.47	0.47	0.49	0.49	0.46	0.48	0.48	0.50	5.75
1998	0.49	0.43	0.49	0.47	0.49	0.46	0.48	0.48	0.46	0.45	0.43	0.45	5.73

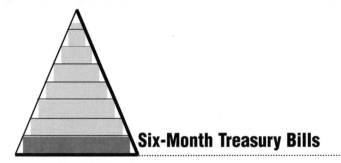

Six-Month Treasury Bills

Horizon: December 1988-December 1998

Definition: These are debt instruments of the U.S. government. They are thought to carry the highest quality rating of the full faith and credit of the U.S. government. Treasury bills have varying maturity schedules from 30 days to 1 year. These debt instruments are used as a short-term investment for many investors' asset allocation models. Treasury bills pay interest at maturity and are sold at a discount.

 Who buys six-month Treasury bills? Short-term Treasury bills are used by people who want to invest in the highest-quality bonds that will give them a reasonable rate of interest. You would buy six-month Treasury bills if you knew you were buying a specific item within the next year and you wanted keep your money liquid. These bonds may be sold prior to maturity at the current market price without an interest penalty. Also, the interest is exempt from state income tax.

Index: U.S. Government Treasury Bills

Category: Cash Equivalent

Performance:

Year-to-Date	5%	Last 3 Years (HPR)	17%
Last 12 Months	5%	Last 5 Years (HPR)	29%

Rate of Return (1 Year)	5.50%
Standard Deviation	1.45%
Original Portfolio Amount	$1,000
Portfolio Value in 5 Years	$1,307
Portfolio Value in 10 Years	$1,709
Portfolio Value in 15 Years	$2,233

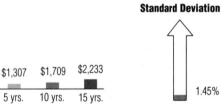

$1,307 $1,709 $2,233

5 yrs.   10 yrs.   15 yrs.

Standard Deviation

1.45%

	Jan.	Feb.	Mar.	Apr.	May	Jun.	Jul.	Aug.	Sep.	Oct.	Nov.	Dec.	Annual Return
1989	0.69	0.69	0.72	0.75	0.74	0.74	0.73	0.69	0.69	0.68	0.68	0.64	8.78
1990	0.67	0.63	0.66	0.69	0.68	0.65	0.68	0.67	0.63	0.66	0.63	0.62	8.17
1991	0.59	0.52	0.58	0.52	0.51	0.48	0.51	0.48	0.47	0.47	0.44	0.44	6.19
1992	0.41	0.35	0.38	0.35	0.34	0.34	0.34	0.31	0.28	0.28	0.28	0.28	4.02
1993	0.28	0.25	0.28	0.25	0.28	0.25	0.28	0.28	0.25	0.27	0.27	0.27	3.25
1994	0.27	0.24	0.30	0.30	0.32	0.35	0.37	0.40	0.40	0.42	0.42	0.47	4.34
1995	0.47	0.44	0.52	0.51	0.51	0.48	0.43	0.43	0.40	0.47	0.45	0.47	5.72
1996	0.47	0.42	0.44	0.41	0.44	0.41	0.43	0.43	0.45	0.45	0.45	0.45	5.36
1997	0.47	0.40	0.44	0.44	0.46	0.43	0.45	0.45	0.45	0.45	0.42	0.44	5.44
1998	0.44	0.42	0.44	0.44	0.46	0.43	0.43	0.43	0.43	0.43	0.40	0.40	5.27

Table header: Monthly Returns

Salomon Brothers Treasury Notes 3–7 Years Index

Horizon: December 1988–December 1998

Definition: Same quality as Treasury bills but have varying maturity schedules from three to seven years. Investors use these notes to fulfill the allocation need for high-quality intermediate-term bonds. Due to the longer maturity date, Treasury notes tend to have a somewhat higher return than Treasury bills. Treasury notes pay interest semiannually.

Who buys three–seven-year Treasury notes? Any investor who wants to position a portion of her asset allocation in the intermediate fixed-income sector will be drawn toward this investment. People in retirement who are looking for the highest quality income-producing assets will buy intermediate Treasury bonds. The income is exempt from state income taxes.

Index: Domestic Debt Index

Category: Domestic Bonds

Performance:

Year-to-Date	9%	Last 3 Years (HPR)	23%
Last 12 Months	9%	Last 5 Years (HPR)	39%

Rate of Return (1 Year)	8.67%
Standard Deviation	4.37%
Original Portfolio Amount	$1,000
Portfolio Value in 5 Years	$1,515
Portfolio Value in 10 Years	$2,296
Portfolio Value in 15 Years	$3,480

$1,515 — 5 yrs. $2,296 — 10 yrs. $3,480 — 15 yrs.

Standard Deviation 4.37%

	Monthly Returns												Annual Return
	Jan.	**Feb.**	**Mar.**	**Apr.**	**May**	**Jun.**	**Jul.**	**Aug.**	**Sep.**	**Oct.**	**Nov.**	**Dec.**	
1989	1.11	−0.66	0.48	2.02	2.37	3.06	2.49	−2.00	0.44	2.40	1.06	0.16	13.59
1990	−0.98	0.16	0.03	−0.53	2.38	1.48	1.69	−0.78	1.07	1.59	1.69	1.57	9.72
1991	1.07	0.35	0.50	1.22	0.52	−0.06	1.35	2.12	2.13	1.22	1.42	2.85	15.69
1992	−1.36	0.26	−0.70	1.10	1.76	1.78	2.25	1.37	1.69	−1.66	−0.67	1.43	7.37
1993	2.49	1.75	0.37	1.03	−0.41	1.75	0.13	1.87	0.42	0.13	−0.67	0.44	9.64
1994	1.20	−1.70	−1.95	−0.85	0.11	−0.07	1.42	0.27	−1.13	−0.09	−0.70	0.41	−3.10
1995	1.91	2.25	0.54	1.29	3.50	0.70	−0.12	0.88	0.69	1.28	1.51	1.07	16.60
1996	0.98	−1.28	−0.87	−0.61	−0.18	1.16	0.23	0.00	1.52	2.01	1.39	−0.85	3.50
1997	0.39	−0.02	−0.78	1.26	0.80	0.97	2.35	−0.68	1.29	1.38	0.16	0.96	8.32
1998	1.65	−0.32	0.27	0.47	0.74	0.74	0.35	2.37	2.93	0.17	−0.55	0.33	9.49

Salomon Brothers Treasury Bonds 10+ Years Index

Horizon: December 1988–December 1998

Definition: Same quality as Treasury notes but with varying maturities from 10 to 30 years. Investors use these instruments to fulfill their allocation need for high quality longer-term income-producing assets. Treasury bonds pay interest semiannually.

Who buys ten-year Treasury bonds? This investment is chosen by individuals who want to increase their current income by investing in longer-term bonds. The income is exempt from state taxes. Many investors buy these bonds for their IRA accounts, thus deferring all income taxes.

Index: Domestic Debt Index

Category: Domestic Bonds

Performance:

Year-to-Date	14%	Last 3 Years (HPR)	30%
Last 12 Months	14%	Last 5 Years (HPR)	57%

Rate of Return (1 Year)	11.03%
Standard Deviation	8.14%
Original Portfolio Amount	$1,000
Portfolio Value in 5 Years	$1,668
Portfolio Value in 10 Years	$2,848
Portfolio Value in 15 Years	$4,806

					Monthly Returns								**Annual Return**
	Jan.	**Feb.**	**Mar.**	**Apr.**	**May**	**Jun.**	**Jul.**	**Aug.**	**Sep.**	**Oct.**	**Nov.**	**Dec.**	
1989	2.26	−2.01	0.98	2.22	3.93	5.80	2.29	−2.63	0.31	4.10	0.83	−0.19	19.04
1990	−3.51	−0.51	−0.16	−2.36	4.42	2.31	1.02	−4.24	1.27	2.36	4.01	2.03	6.39
1991	1.17	0.32	0.40	1.45	−0.13	−0.06	1.53	3.28	3.25	0.08	0.62	5.97	19.21
1992	−3.10	0.58	−1.12	0.07	2.58	1.49	4.06	0.81	1.48	−2.07	0.39	2.68	7.89
1993	3.07	3.33	0.05	0.94	0.25	4.24	1.59	3.98	0.48	0.50	−2.60	0.46	17.31
1994	2.37	−3.98	−4.48	−1.15	−0.60	−0.88	3.15	−0.70	−3.08	−0.46	0.55	1.66	−7.63
1995	2.77	2.78	0.73	1.74	7.87	1.10	−1.54	2.12	1.72	2.84	2.11	2.57	30.05
1996	0.04	−4.75	−2.01	−2.02	−0.18	2.05	−0.01	−1.23	2.80	4.06	3.19	−2.43	−0.87
1997	−0.60	−0.11	−2.44	2.31	1.18	1.90	5.88	−2.82	2.79	3.39	1.31	1.69	15.11
1998	2.02	−0.74	0.24	0.36	1.89	2.35	0.23	4.48	3.73	−1.60	0.87	−0.25	14.25

Municipal Bonds—National Index

Horizon: December 1988–December 1998

Definition: These are debt instruments of state, county, and local governments. They vary widely in quality and the ratings from S&P and Moody's should be reviewed. Most municipal bond buyers are interested in the tax-free income that is generated from municipal bonds. The maturity dates vary from a few months to 30 years or more. Most municipal bonds pay interest on a semiannual basis.

Who buys municipal bonds? People who are interested in tax-free income.

Index: Municipal Bonds—National

Category: Domestic Bonds

Performance:

Year-to-Date	5%	Last 3 Years (HPR)	18%
Last 12 Months	5%	Last 5 Years (HPR)	28%

Rate of Return (1 Year)	6.91%
Standard Deviation	3.93%
Original Portfolio Amount	$1,000
Portfolio Value in 5 Years	$1,397
Portfolio Value in 10 Years	$1,950
Portfolio Value in 15 Years	$2,724

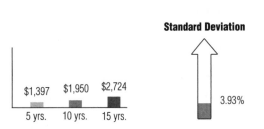

	Monthly Returns												Annual Return
	Jan.	Feb.	Mar.	Apr.	May	Jun.	Jul.	Aug.	Sep.	Oct.	Nov.	Dec.	
1989	1.38	−0.68	−0.05	2.10	1.74	1.23	1.04	−0.86	−0.17	1.04	1.46	0.68	9.22
1990	−0.80	0.93	0.04	−1.01	2.24	0.87	1.44	−1.66	0.21	1.31	2.03	0.44	6.13
1991	1.19	0.59	0.19	1.32	0.84	−0.19	1.22	1.20	1.19	0.81	0.15	2.11	11.12
1992	0.04	0.14	0.00	0.85	1.23	1.60	3.08	−1.50	0.30	−1.48	2.12	1.00	7.55
1993	0.99	3.38	−1.05	0.93	0.44	1.55	−0.06	1.99	1.10	0.18	−1.03	1.49	10.29
1994	0.99	−2.38	−3.93	0.32	0.79	−0.53	1.54	0.25	−1.42	−1.63	−1.82	1.95	−5.88
1995	2.52	2.64	0.91	0.06	2.79	−0.85	0.71	0.99	0.55	1.30	1.62	1.01	15.15
1996	0.55	−0.58	−1.36	−0.37	0.08	0.82	0.87	0.00	1.22	1.04	1.60	−0.32	3.57
1997	0.05	0.80	−1.14	0.70	1.30	1.03	2.65	−0.99	1.13	0.58	0.50	1.48	8.34
1998	0.89	0.02	0.05	−0.54	1.47	0.36	0.17	1.45	1.09	−0.23	0.24	0.21	5.28

Salomon Brothers Corporate Bonds 10+Years Index

Horizon: December 1988–December 1998

Definition: These are debt instruments of various corporations whose quality vary greatly. Corporate bonds usually carry a rating from S&P or Moody's from AAA to C. Investors buy corporate bonds to increase their potential for a higher level of income. Corporate bonds pay interest semiannually.

Who buys ten-plus-year corporate bonds? These bonds are often purchased by investors who desire a higher level of income than is currently being paid by Treasury bonds of the same length. The income from corporate bonds is fully taxable by states and the federal government.

Index: Domestic Debt Index

Category: Domestic Bonds

Performance:

Year-to-Date	9%	Last 3 Years (HPR)	25%
Last 12 Months	9%	Last 5 Years (HPR)	51%

Rate of Return (1 Year):	10.74%
Standard Deviation:	6.72%
Original Portfolio Amount	$1,000
Portfolio Value in 5 Years	$1,665
Portfolio Value in 10 Years	$2,774
Portfolio Value in 15 Years	$4,619

$1,665 $2,774 $4,619

5 yrs. 10 yrs. 15 yrs.

Standard Deviation

6.72%

	Jan.	Feb.	Mar.	Apr.	May	Jun.	Jul.	Aug.	Sep.	Oct.	Nov.	Dec.	Annual Return
1989	1.93	−1.07	0.70	1.94	3.65	3.61	1.83	−1.45	0.44	2.76	0.93	0.18	16.43
1990	−1.70	0.02	0.07	−1.64	3.77	2.09	1.06	−2.78	0.62	0.77	2.54	1.75	6.56
1991	1.65	1.60	1.44	1.48	0.60	−0.07	1.54	2.62	2.50	0.62	0.99	4.02	20.65
1992	−1.33	1.17	−0.57	0.24	2.51	1.58	2.96	0.85	0.96	−1.74	0.88	2.18	10.00
1993	2.51	2.72	0.32	0.57	0.33	3.04	1.18	3.15	0.25	0.61	−1.78	0.60	14.23
1994	2.33	−2.93	−3.95	−1.09	−0.98	−0.59	3.16	−0.16	−2.71	−0.38	0.21	1.52	−5.67
1995	2.52	3.20	1.02	1.85	6.46	0.91	−0.96	2.16	1.62	1.61	2.50	2.22	28.01
1996	0.14	−3.58	−1.19	−1.67	0.03	1.74	0.11	−0.63	2.68	3.61	2.79	−1.80	1.99
1997	−0.17	0.39	−2.16	1.69	1.42	1.98	5.36	−2.47	2.36	0.91	1.10	1.58	12.41
1998	1.00	−0.01	0.57	0.73	1.66	0.95	−0.64	−0.55	3.84	−2.21	3.61	−0.04	9.11

Table title: **Monthly Returns**

S&P 500 Stock Index

Horizon: December 1988–December 1998

Definition: The Standard and Poor's 500 Stock Index is one of the most widely followed stock benchmarks. This index dates back to 1923 and currently includes 500 stocks from 83 industries. The top ten holdings of this index at the end of 1998 were Microsoft, General Electric, Merck, Exxon, Intel, Coca-Cola, Wal-Mart, IBM, Pfizer, and Phillip Morris.

Who buys the S&P 500? Those who are often referred to as the "if you can't beat 'em, join 'em" investors. The S&P 500 has had a marvelous long-term track record; it allows you to become instantly diversified in 500 of the country's publicly traded companies. You might invest in the S&P 500 if you simply want to match the returns of this index.

Index: Index of 500 Large and Medium Capitalized Companies

Category: Domestic Equities

Performance:

Year-to-Date	29%	Last 3 Years (HPR)	111%
Last 12 Months	29%	Last 5 Years (HPR)	193%

Rate of Return (1 Year)	17.56%
Standard Deviation	10.30%
Original Portfolio Amount	$1,000
Portfolio Value in 5 Years	$2,246
Portfolio Value in 10 Years	$5,044
Portfolio Value in 15 Years	$11,328

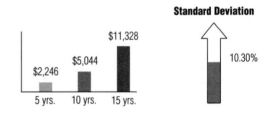

	Monthly Returns												**Annual Return**
	Jan.	**Feb.**	**Mar.**	**Apr.**	**May**	**Jun.**	**Jul.**	**Aug.**	**Sep.**	**Oct.**	**Nov.**	**Dec.**	
1989	7.32	−2.49	2.33	5.19	4.05	−0.57	9.03	1.95	−0.41	−2.32	2.04	2.40	31.69
1990	−6.71	1.29	2.65	−2.49	9.75	−0.67	−0.32	−9.04	−4.87	−0.43	6.46	2.79	−3.11
1991	4.35	7.15	2.42	0.24	4.31	−4.58	4.66	2.37	−1.67	1.34	−4.03	11.44	30.47
1992	−1.86	1.29	−1.94	2.94	0.49	−1.49	4.09	−2.05	1.18	0.35	3.40	1.23	7.62
1993	0.84	1.36	2.11	−2.42	2.68	0.29	−0.40	3.79	−0.77	2.07	−0.95	1.21	10.08
1994	3.40	−2.71	−4.36	1.28	1.64	−2.45	3.28	4.10	−2.44	2.25	−3.64	1.48	1.32
1995	2.59	3.90	2.95	2.95	4.00	2.32	3.32	0.25	4.22	−0.36	4.39	1.93	37.58
1996	3.40	0.93	0.96	1.47	2.58	0.38	−4.42	2.11	5.63	2.76	7.56	−1.98	22.96
1997	6.25	0.78	−4.11	5.97	6.09	4.48	7.96	−5.60	5.48	−3.34	4.46	1.72	33.15
1998	1.11	7.21	5.12	1.01	−1.72	4.06	−1.06	−14.46	6.41	8.13	6.06	5.76	28.58

Dow Jones Industrial Average

Horizon: December 1988–December 1998

Definition: The Dow Jones Industrial Average follows the 30 stocks that make up this index. These stocks represent some of the largest and best-known companies in the United States. Examples include Eastman Kodak, Exxon, Coca-Cola, IBM, General Electric, and General Motors. The index had its origin in 1896 and is one of the most followed and quoted stock indexes.

Who buys the stocks in the Dow Jones? Those who adhere to the "buy what you know and use" strategy. Many investors feel comfortable knowing they are owners of such high-quality companies. You would buy these stocks to participate in the large cap portion of your asset allocation.

Index: Dow Jones Industrial Average

Category: Domestic Equities

Performance:

Year-to-Date	18%	Last 3 Years (HPR)	90%
Last 12 Months	18%	Last 5 Years (HPR)	173%

Rate of Return (1 Year)	17.83%
Standard Deviation	9.53%
Original Portfolio Amount	$1,000
Portfolio Value in 5 Years	$2,271
Portfolio Value in 10 Years	$5,159
Portfolio Value in 15 Years	$11,719

Standard Deviation

9.53%

$11,719 · $5,159 · $2,271

5 yrs. 10 yrs. 15 yrs.

	Jan.	Feb.	Mar.	Apr.	May	Jun.	Jul.	Aug.	Sep.	Oct.	Nov.	Dec.	Annual Return
1989	8.36	−3.25	1.88	5.87	2.93	−1.24	9.44	3.23	−1.28	−1.47	2.61	2.03	32.24
1990	−5.62	1.72	3.38	−1.54	8.61	0.44	1.16	−9.72	−5.87	−0.07	5.15	3.22	−0.61
1991	4.23	5.64	1.39	−0.61	5.12	−3.73	4.33	0.88	−0.62	1.99	−5.43	9.74	24.32
1992	1.96	1.62	−0.75	4.06	1.35	−2.05	2.26	−4.02	1.12	−1.39	2.44	0.66	7.21
1993	0.27	1.84	2.63	−0.22	2.91	0.36	0.66	3.15	−1.97	3.53	0.09	2.59	16.89
1994	5.98	−3.68	−4.44	1.25	2.08	−2.88	3.85	3.96	−1.12	1.69	−4.32	3.27	5.05
1995	0.25	4.35	4.32	3.94	3.33	2.63	3.34	−2.08	4.50	−0.70	6.71	1.42	36.67
1996	5.44	1.67	2.40	−0.32	1.33	0.75	−2.22	1.58	5.28	2.50	8.17	−0.64	28.67
1997	5.66	0.95	−3.79	6.46	4.59	5.13	7.17	−7.30	4.69	−6.33	5.12	1.53	24.90
1998	−0.02	8.08	3.40	3.00	−1.80	1.01	−0.77	−15.13	4.54	9.56	6.10	1.16	18.17

Table title: **Monthly Returns**

Wilshire Large Company Growth Index

Horizon: December 1988–December 1998

Definition: Also known as large caps. You're able to calculate a company's capitalization by multiplying the current stock price by the number of shares outstanding. Some investment analysts consider a company with a market capitalization of over $2 billion to be a large cap stock. These companies are often well known and their stocks are usually referred to as blue chip stocks. These stocks are growth oriented and are often in the fastest-growing industries. Example of growth industries are technology, consumer cyclical nondurables, health care, telecommunications, and some financials.

Who buys large company growth stocks? Almost all investors who are seeking a growth-oriented investment option will look favorably on the large company growth sector, hoping to focus on companies with rapid and consistent earnings growth.

Index: Domestic Equity Index of Large Cap Growth Companies

Category: Domestic Equities

Performance:

Year-to-Date	42%	Last 3 Years (HPR)	141%
Last 12 Months	42%	Last 5 Years (HPR)	243%

Rate of Return (1 Year)	19.43%
Standard Deviation	12.41%
Original Portfolio Amount	$1,000
Portfolio Value in 5 Years	$2,430
Portfolio Value in 10 Years	$5,906
Portfolio Value in 15 Years	$14,354

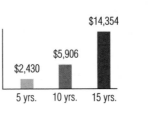

Standard Deviation 12.41%

	Monthly Returns												Annual Return
	Jan.	**Feb.**	**Mar.**	**Apr.**	**May**	**Jun.**	**Jul.**	**Aug.**	**Sep.**	**Oct.**	**Nov.**	**Dec.**	
1989	6.60	−2.39	3.30	5.72	5.55	−0.90	11.11	−0.97	−0.21	−1.56	2.15	1.05	35.21
1990	−7.41	0.22	4.06	−1.36	10.99	1.04	−1.17	−9.71	−6.67	−0.60	8.34	4.74	0.34
1991	6.80	8.42	4.42	−0.22	4.93	−4.79	5.16	3.73	−2.37	1.07	−1.73	15.01	46.63
1992	−1.65	0.93	−2.65	0.24	0.59	−2.84	4.05	−1.30	1.69	2.00	4.42	0.60	5.93
1993	−1.06	−1.49	1.28	−5.59	3.66	−1.29	−2.74	3.64	−0.65	2.75	0.33	1.03	−0.54
1994	2.00	−1.04	−4.72	0.77	1.27	−3.22	2.89	5.59	−1.79	2.82	−2.46	1.31	2.97
1995	2.84	3.63	2.92	2.25	3.87	3.93	3.07	0.24	5.54	0.65	3.86	−0.09	37.88
1996	3.83	1.65	0.33	2.38	4.46	0.56	−5.05	2.98	7.12	0.89	8.17	−2.48	26.95
1997	7.95	−0.36	−4.63	8.18	6.30	4.27	8.79	−6.39	5.09	−4.63	5.74	0.71	33.69
1998	3.17	8.64	3.83	0.69	−2.38	7.28	−0.61	−13.54	7.25	8.15	7.38	8.27	42.21

Wilshire Large Company Value Index

Horizon: December 1988–December 1998

Definition: Also known as large caps. The companies in this index are similar to those in the Wilshire Large Company Growth Index. They typically have a market cap over $2 billion and may also be referred to as blue chip stocks. Examples of value companies are those in capital goods, transportation, energy, utilities, consumer cyclical durables, and some financials.

Who buys large company value stocks? People who believe that some large company cyclical companies have fallen in price to a level that is attractive to investors.

Index: Domestic Equity Index of Large Cap Value Companies

Category: Domestic Equities

Performance:

Year-to-Date	11%	Last 3 Years (HPR)	74%
Last 12 Months	11%	Last 5 Years (HPR)	139%

Rate of Return (1 Year)	15.55%
Standard Deviation	11.47%
Original Portfolio Amount	$1,000
Portfolio Value in 5 Years	$2,060
Portfolio Value in 10 Years	$4,245
Portfolio Value in 15 Years	$8,745

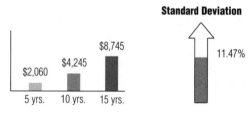

Standard Deviation

11.47%

	Monthly Returns												Annual Return
	Jan.	Feb.	Mar.	Apr.	May	Jun.	Jul.	Aug.	Sep.	Oct.	Nov.	Dec.	
1989	6.60	-2.39	3.30	5.72	5.55	-0.90	11.11	-0.97	-0.21	-1.56	2.15	1.05	35.21
1990	-7.41	0.22	4.06	-1.36	10.99	1.04	-1.17	-9.71	-6.67	-0.60	8.34	4.74	0.34
1991	6.80	8.42	4.42	-0.22	4.93	-4.79	5.16	3.73	-2.37	1.07	-1.73	15.01	46.63
1992	-1.65	0.93	-2.65	0.24	0.59	-2.84	4.05	-1.30	1.69	2.00	4.42	0.60	5.93
1993	-1.06	-1.49	1.28	-5.59	3.66	-1.29	-2.74	3.64	-0.65	2.75	0.33	1.03	-0.54
1994	2.00	-1.04	-4.72	0.77	1.27	-3.22	2.89	5.59	-1.79	2.82	-2.46	1.31	2.97
1995	2.84	3.63	2.92	2.25	3.87	3.93	3.07	0.24	5.54	0.65	3.86	-0.09	37.88
1996	3.83	1.65	0.33	2.38	4.46	0.56	-5.05	2.98	7.12	0.89	8.17	-2.48	26.95
1997	7.95	-0.36	-4.63	8.18	6.30	4.27	8.79	-6.39	5.09	-4.63	5.74	0.71	33.69
1998	3.17	8.64	3.83	0.69	-2.38	7.28	-0.61	-13.54	7.25	8.15	7.38	8.27	42.21

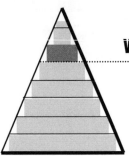

Wilshire Mid-Cap Growth Index

Horizon: December 1988–December 1998

Definition: A type of index that allows investors to buy common stocks of medium-sized companies that the money manager considers to have the potential for above-average growth. These companies usually don't pay dividends. This type of investment would be used to fill the allocation for midcap growth companies.

Who buys midcap growth companies? You may be interested in midcap companies if you have already filled your large cap growth asset allocation and are willing to increase your risk in an attempt to increase your potential for higher returns.

Index: Domestic Equity Index of Midcap Growth Companies

Category: Domestic Equities

Performance:

Year-to-Date	−1%
Last 12 Months	−1%

Last 3 Years (HPR)	36%
Last 5 Years (HPR)	91%

Rate of Return (1 Year)	14.75%
Standard Deviation	15.03%
Original Portfolio Amount	$1,000
Portfolio Value in 5 Years	$1,990
Portfolio Value in 10 Years	$3,958
Portfolio Value in 15 Years	$7,876

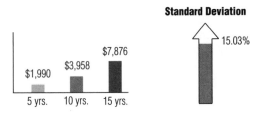

Standard Deviation 15.03%

	Monthly Returns												**Annual Return**
	Jan.	**Feb.**	**Mar.**	**Apr.**	**May**	**Jun.**	**Jul.**	**Aug.**	**Sep.**	**Oct.**	**Nov.**	**Dec.**	
1989	4.98	0.31	1.93	5.61	4.36	−3.35	7.36	3.26	0.10	−4.08	−0.36	0.59	21.98
1990	−9.20	2.64	4.59	−4.85	10.68	0.02	−3.89	−13.79	−8.64	−4.89	11.19	5.96	−12.91
1991	9.44	9.29	6.35	−0.77	5.55	−4.47	5.43	3.81	0.11	2.62	−4.18	13.34	55.41
1992	2.99	1.69	−3.99	−2.38	−1.25	−4.54	5.48	−2.09	1.75	4.08	7.66	3.06	12.29
1993	2.26	−3.37	3.07	−4.18	5.70	0.66	−0.89	5.07	2.51	0.53	−1.56	5.53	15.76
1994	3.53	0.53	−5.95	0.40	−1.53	−5.04	2.44	8.56	−0.79	2.44	−4.43	1.66	0.91
1995	0.02	6.00	3.69	1.49	1.64	6.29	8.40	1.53	2.79	−3.52	5.25	0.36	38.96
1996	1.73	3.74	1.21	5.93	2.99	−5.45	−8.56	7.29	4.73	−2.83	5.63	−1.32	14.66
1997	2.90	−1.89	−6.11	3.42	8.27	3.47	7.07	−0.77	6.58	−4.77	0.59	0.85	20.13
1998	−0.70	8.24	1.60	0.70	−5.62	−0.60	−5.94	−20.29	4.95	7.91	5.78	6.76	−1.08

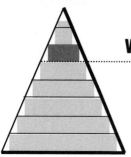

Wilshire Mid-Cap Value Index

Horizon: December 1988–December 1998

Definition: This type of index seeks undervalued companies or medium-sized companies that may have recently been out of favor.

Who buys midcap value stocks? People who believe that some of the medium-sized cyclical companies have fallen in price to a level that has become attractive to investors.

Index: Domestic Equity Index of Value Midcap Companies

Category: Domestic Equities

Performance:

Year-to-Date	–3%	Last 3 Years (HPR)	50%
Last 12 Months	–3%	Last 5 Years (HPR)	101%

Rate of Return (1 Year)	15.26%
Standard Deviation	14.78%
Original Portfolio Amount	$1,000
Portfolio Value in 5 Years	$2,034
Portfolio Value in 10 Years	$4,137
Portfolio Value in 15 Years	$8,414

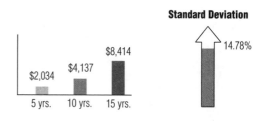

	Monthly Returns												Annual Return
	Jan.	**Feb.**	**Mar.**	**Apr.**	**May**	**Jun.**	**Jul.**	**Aug.**	**Sep.**	**Oct.**	**Nov.**	**Dec.**	
1989	3.85	0.77	1.61	5.29	3.43	1.45	4.22	4.22	–1.17	–3.53	–0.03	–0.09	21.51
1990	–6.98	1.06	0.20	–6.08	5.49	–1.06	–3.29	–8.37	–5.58	–3.35	7.92	3.79	–16.36
1991	6.36	9.12	3.00	2.21	4.89	–1.20	4.63	3.52	0.12	2.08	–2.36	8.53	48.53
1992	1.63	1.53	–0.16	2.79	1.49	–0.40	4.05	–1.30	0.80	1.07	4.16	5.12	22.63
1993	3.11	2.56	4.51	–2.59	0.45	2.29	1.44	2.18	0.92	–1.02	–3.87	2.49	12.84
1994	1.67	–2.47	–1.68	1.72	–1.08	–0.92	3.59	2.37	–2.81	–0.86	–3.36	1.34	–2.74
1995	3.71	4.17	–0.10	2.56	3.79	2.67	4.13	2.96	2.86	–0.08	4.57	0.89	37.12
1996	1.01	1.19	1.31	–1.71	1.31	0.62	–4.59	3.43	2.72	2.47	5.63	0.12	13.97
1997	2.29	2.14	–3.23	2.97	6.21	3.88	5.82	–1.15	4.94	–2.57	4.76	5.55	35.83
1998	–3.36	6.11	4.50	–1.05	–2.85	–1.96	–5.36	–13.91	4.52	5.33	3.41	3.69	–2.87

Wilshire Small Company Growth Index

Horizon: December 1988–December 1998

Definition: This type of investment allows the investor to buy a set of smaller common stocks that the money manager considers to have the potential for above-average growth. These companies usually don't pay dividends. This type of investment would be used to fill the allocation for small cap growth.

Who buys small company growth stocks? You'd be interested in this sector of the market after you've filled the large cap and midcap portions of your asset allocation. Small cap growth stocks have had some of the most dramatic returns, but they are not for the faint of heart. In a down market, small size and illiquidity can cause fast and sharp declines in small cap stocks.

Index: Domestic Equity Index of Small Cap Growth Companies

Category: Domestic Equities

Performance:

Year-to-Date	−2%	Last 3 Years HPR)	29%
Last 12 Months	−2%	Last 5 Years (HPR)	75%

Rate of Return (1 Year)	13.09%
Standard Deviation	17.40%
Original Portfolio Amount	$1,000
Portfolio Value in 5 Years	$1,849
Portfolio Value in 10 Years	$3,420
Portfolio Value in 15 Years	$6,326

Standard Deviation 17.40%

$1,849 $3,420 $6,326
5 yrs. 10 yrs. 15 yrs.

			Monthly Returns										**Annual**
	Jan.	Feb.	Mar.	Apr.	May	Jun.	Jul.	Aug.	Sep.	Oct.	Nov.	Dec.	Return
1989	4.79	0.49	2.58	5.46	4.89	−3.40	5.12	2.81	1.31	−6.25	−0.27	0.63	18.91
1990	−9.94	4.22	5.72	−4.56	10.03	−0.67	−5.46	−16.25	−12.07	−5.88	11.59	7.00	−19.02
1991	10.92	10.26	7.51	−0.98	5.00	−5.77	5.64	4.70	0.25	2.68	−5.02	12.56	56.80
1992	5.69	2.40	−5.50	−5.08	−1.65	−5.17	4.92	−2.18	2.77	4.89	8.85	3.82	13.20
1993	2.40	−4.82	3.51	−3.27	5.92	1.12	0.21	5.13	4.22	0.32	−2.32	4.91	17.98
1994	2.84	1.18	−7.00	0.50	−2.78	−5.83	3.16	8.62	−0.05	2.63	−4.74	3.13	0.54
1995	−1.84	6.00	3.95	1.50	2.42	7.06	8.56	0.53	2.46	−5.31	4.76	1.25	35.19
1996	−1.65	5.03	2.47	7.53	4.42	−5.98	−10.50	7.89	3.41	−3.53	5.73	0.21	14.05
1997	2.10	−5.91	−5.80	2.27	13.72	4.72	6.62	1.92	6.22	−6.12	−2.30	−0.71	15.86
1998	−0.14	9.61	3.12	−1.46	−6.24	−0.30	−8.04	−20.48	6.11	4.58	7.87	7.17	−2.46

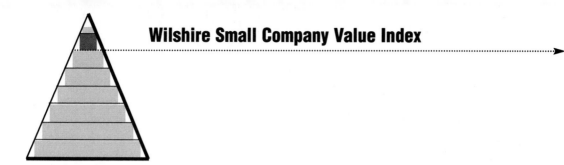

Wilshire Small Company Value Index

Horizon: December 1988–December 1998

Definition: This type of investment seeks undervalued companies or smaller companies that may recently have been out of favor.

Who invests in small company value stocks? Investors are often looking for situations where a lot of bad news about a small publicly traded company has emerged. In such a case, investors hope the market was overreacting to a short-term problem and that by investing in such a company, they will be rewarded when the market recognizes the future potential of the company.

Index: Domestic Equity Index of Small Cap Value Companies

Category: Domestic Equities

Performance:

Year-to-Date	−5%	Last 3 Years (HPR)	45%
Last 12 Months	−5%	Last 5 Years (HPR	85%

Rate of Return (1 Year)	14.77%
Standard Deviation	15.65%
Original Portfolio Amount	$1,000
Portfolio Value in 5 Years	$1,991
Portfolio Value in 10 Years	$3,965
Portfolio Value in 15 Years	$7,896

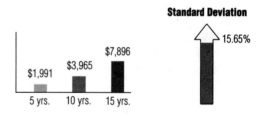

Standard Deviation 15.65%

	Monthly Returns												Annual Return
	Jan.	**Feb.**	**Mar.**	**Apr.**	**May**	**Jun.**	**Jul.**	**Aug.**	**Sep.**	**Oct.**	**Nov.**	**Dec.**	
1989	2.98	0.88	1.45	3.75	3.54	1.17	3.77	4.37	5.10	−9.27	−0.01	−0.14	18.12
1990	−7.01	2.00	0.54	−4.75	3.50	−1.68	−4.98	−6.99	−6.87	−3.44	5.96	3.56	−19.39
1991	4.76	8.74	3.27	3.41	3.89	−0.62	4.99	3.92	0.66	1.99	−2.02	8.09	49.00
1992	3.47	2.41	1.24	2.70	1.85	0.04	3.82	−0.59	0.76	0.88	4.63	4.88	29.23
1993	3.37	2.28	3.41	−2.70	0.70	1.30	2.02	2.56	2.14	−0.23	−3.42	2.12	14.12
1994	0.90	−1.66	−3.17	1.30	−0.59	0.03	2.87	2.37	−2.00	−1.67	−2.69	2.58	−1.96
1995	2.05	3.50	−0.53	2.70	2.29	2.68	3.43	2.40	3.16	−0.57	3.66	1.57	29.62
1996	0.79	0.82	1.57	−0.31	1.46	0.27	−4.63	3.77	2.90	1.24	6.26	0.66	15.43
1997	1.48	2.30	−2.69	1.83	7.00	3.65	5.40	1.11	5.51	−2.74	2.03	4.04	32.44
1998	−2.85	7.07	4.09	−0.45	−2.70	−1.71	−7.28	−11.93	2.97	3.63	2.87	2.95	−4.87

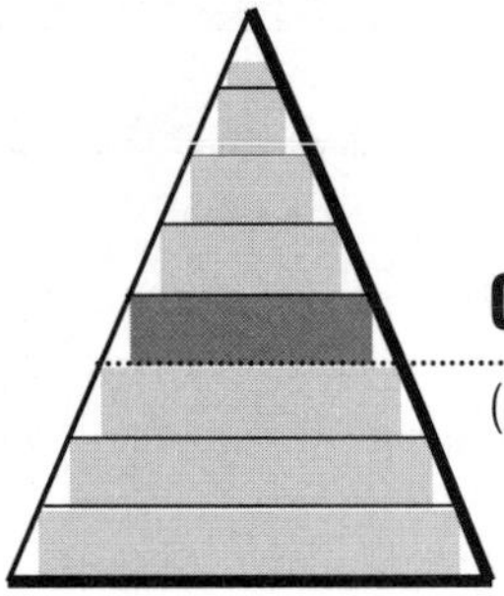

Growth and Income

(Equity Index with an objective of growth and income)

Horizon: December 1988–December 1998

Definition: These funds seek companies that are paying steady and/or increasing dividends and also growing their revenues and earnings at a pace that will offer the potential for above-average returns.

Who buys growth and income investments? Almost all investors can use some investments in this category. Even conservative investors can venture into this sector as a hedge against inflation.

Index: Open-End Fund Equity Index with an Objective of Growth and Income

Category: Domestic Equities

Performance:

Year-to-Date	17%	Last 3 Years (HPR)	76%
Last 12 Months	17%	Last 5 Years (HPR)	128%

Rate of Return (1 Year)	14.15%
Standard Deviation	9.32%
Original Portfolio Amount	$1,000
Portfolio Value in 5 Years	$1,938
Portfolio Value in 10 Years	$3,757
Portfolio Value in 15 Years	$7,282

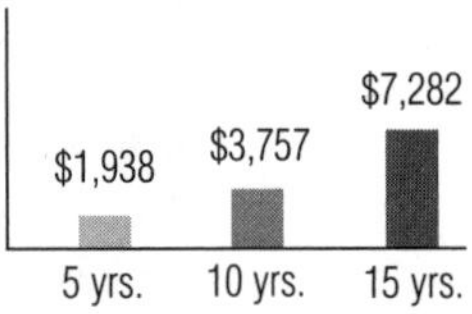
$1,938
$3,757
$7,282
5 yrs.
10 yrs.
15 yrs.

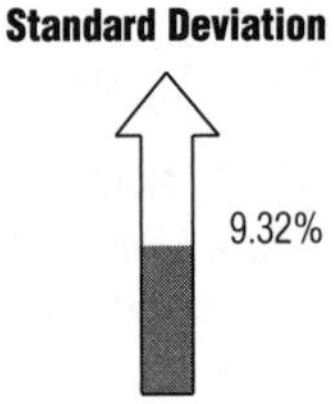
Standard Deviation
9.32%

	Monthly Returns												
	Jan.	**Feb.**	**Mar.**	**Apr.**	**May**	**Jun.**	**Jul.**	**Aug.**	**Sep.**	**Oct.**	**Nov.**	**Dec.**	**Annual Return**
1989	5.84	–1.43	1.99	4.17	3.31	–0.47	6.92	1.98	–0.41	–2.72	1.40	1.34	23.70
1990	–5.81	1.22	1.99	–2.49	7.62	–0.20	–0.58	–7.96	–4.79	–1.27	5.71	2.76	–4.85
1991	4.52	6.28	2.01	0.32	3.99	–4.30	4.18	2.41	–0.81	1.62	–3.93	9.43	27.91
1992	–0.30	1.65	–1.73	1.88	0.75	–1.82	3.13	–1.83	1.07	0.13	3.41	1.17	7.57
1993	1.27	1.13	2.66	–1.67	2.17	0.55	0.29	3.67	–0.06	1.46	–1.55	0.93	11.26
1994	2.91	–2.03	–4.10	1.05	0.99	–2.24	2.70	3.76	–2.07	1.20	–3.43	0.50	–1.14
1995	1.55	3.69	2.41	2.54	3.34	2.10	3.42	0.57	3.26	–1.16	4.12	1.53	30.91
1996	2.91	1.34	1.15	1.54	1.99	–0.27	–4.09	2.70	4.70	2.05	6.61	–1.26	20.71
1997	2.69	0.47	–3.52	4.07	5.93	3.98	7.32	–3.91	5.13	–3.41	2.80	1.83	25.10
1998	0.27	6.66	4.46	0.73	–1.90	1.92	–2.34	–14.21	5.11	7.06	5.15	4.51	16.58

Balanced

(Index with an objective of equity and debt instruments)

Horizon: December 1988–December 1998

Definition: A balanced investment seeks to invest in all three major asset categories—cash, bonds, and stocks. Different managers use different strategies for achieving more than adequate returns while reducing risk by having some exposure to less risky assets like cash and bonds.

Who buys balanced investments? These could be considered for those who'd like to make more than they can in a guaranteed investment like a CD or a Treasury bond. They know they're assuming more risk, but are quantifying that risk and using it to try to increase their potential for higher returns. This strategy can also be implemented by those who don't want to worry about their asset allocations but would rather let the money manager make those decisions.

Index: Open-End Fund Equity Index with an Objective of Equity and Debt Instruments

Category: Domestic Equities

Performance:

Year-to-Date	13%	Last 3 Years (HPR)	53%
Last 12 Months	13%	Last 5 Years (HPR)	86%

Rate of Return (1 Year)	12.02%
Standard Deviation	7.04%
Original Portfolio Amount	$1,000
Portfolio Value in 5 Years	$1,764
Portfolio Value in 10 Years	$3,111
Portfolio Value in 15 Years	$5,486

Standard Deviation

7.04%

$1,764 $3,111 $5,486

5 yrs. 10 yrs. 15 yrs.

	Monthly Returns												**Annual Return**
	Jan.	**Feb.**	**Mar.**	**Apr.**	**May**	**Jun.**	**Jul.**	**Aug.**	**Sep.**	**Oct.**	**Nov.**	**Dec.**	
1989	4.50	−1.36	1.55	3.49	3.25	0.38	5.61	0.96	−0.22	−1.72	1.30	1.09	20.21
1990	−4.59	0.75	1.38	−1.97	6.31	0.32	−0.11	−6.01	−3.13	−0.32	4.81	2.48	−0.79
1991	3.76	4.94	1.87	0.48	3.32	−3.38	3.48	2.46	0.00	1.54	−2.45	7.92	26.10
1992	−0.85	1.34	−1.42	1.42	1.16	−0.79	3.00	−1.08	1.04	−0.15	2.26	1.36	7.41
1993	1.31	1.10	1.97	−0.66	1.41	1.02	0.40	3.02	0.17	1.03	−1.51	1.34	11.03
1994	2.76	−2.01	−3.66	0.29	0.63	−1.69	2.30	2.55	−1.91	0.37	−2.44	0.89	−2.16
1995	1.10	2.99	1.71	1.91	3.31	1.70	1.99	0.86	2.28	−0.60	3.13	1.42	24.03
1996	1.74	0.30	0.43	0.98	1.23	0.09	−2.70	1.85	3.72	1.84	4.61	−1.10	13.53
1997	2.87	0.13	−2.80	2.80	4.32	2.79	5.74	−2.72	3.94	−1.74	1.53	1.36	19.32
1998	0.57	4.05	2.81	0.62	−1.10	1.43	−1.58	−8.73	4.12	4.06	3.67	3.39	13.28

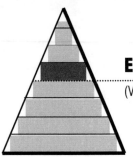

Equity Income/Variable Annuities

(Variable annuity equity index of higher-yielding domestic companies)

Horizon: December 1988–December 1998

Definition: Variable annuities became available in the 1950s. They have become popular retirement planning invest-ments because of their tax-deferred contracts. These investments are offered through life insurance companies and they also carry a broad variety of estate benefits. The investment subaccounts within these variable annuity contracts often function much like mutual funds. The subaccount listed here is one that considers growth and income important.

Who buys variable annuities using an equity type of subaccount? If you are seeking to maximize the amount of money you can save on a tax-deferred basis, variable annuities should interest you. Plus, the added mortality benefits are a ter-rific way to protect your estate.

Index: Variable Annuity Equity Index of Higher-Yielding Domestic Equities

Category: Domestic Equities

Performance:

Year-to-Date	11%	Last 3 Years (HPR)	61%
Last 12 Months	11%	Last 5 Years (HPR)	115%

Rate of Return (1 Year)	12.93%
Standard Deviation	11.06%
Original Portfolio Amount	$1,000
Portfolio Value in 5 Years	$1,837
Portfolio Value in 10 Years	$3,373
Portfolio Value in 15 Years	$6,194

$1,837 — 5 yrs. $3,373 — 10 yrs. $6,194 — 15 yrs.

Standard Deviation

11.06%

	Monthly Returns												Annual Return
	Jan.	Feb.	Mar.	Apr.	May	Jun.	Jul.	Aug.	Sep.	Oct.	Nov.	Dec.	
1989	5.43	−3.89	5.81	8.55	−0.80	−0.27	5.82	1.63	−1.31	−5.37	0.78	1.15	17.90
1990	−6.74	0.91	0.39	−3.56	6.57	−1.16	−2.11	−8.10	−7.08	−2.54	7.03	2.33	−14.36
1991	5.10	6.47	2.66	0.26	4.36	−4.27	4.93	1.95	−0.85	1.63	−4.06	7.64	28.09
1992	0.64	2.64	−1.34	2.86	0.47	−1.00	3.01	−0.64	−0.17	0.53	3.36	2.07	12.99
1993	2.02	2.08	2.97	−0.70	1.59	0.87	0.94	3.50	−0.37	0.74	−1.90	1.99	14.47
1994	3.34	−2.38	−4.05	2.15	0.72	−1.29	3.11	3.61	−1.79	1.26	−3.25	0.71	1.78
1995	1.74	3.57	2.69	2.55	3.07	1.09	3.07	0.96	3.04	−0.93	4.18	2.66	31.37
1996	2.53	0.37	1.08	0.93	1.11	−0.37	−4.21	2.00	3.86	1.89	5.97	−1.32	14.36
1997	3.70	1.04	−3.41	3.33	5.59	4.15	6.79	−3.70	5.03	−3.31	3.20	2.16	26.63
1998	−0.12	5.70	4.79	0.03	−1.81	0.91	−2.63	−13.01	5.23	6.79	4.17	2.37	11.29

International Equities Index

Horizon: December 1988–December 1998

Definition: According to the 1999 edition of the *Investment Performance Digest* by Wiesenberger, the first stock exchange is thought to have begun in France in 1138—the Paris Exchange. International stock markets have changed dramatically since then, evolving into an estimated $17 trillion of market capitalization worldwide.

Who buys international equities? The world is a very large place with investment opportunities lurking at every corner of the planet. If you limit yourself to stocks in the United States only, you are missing out on over 50 percent of investment opportunities. You should invest in international stocks to hedge against difficult periods in our national economy. While often viewed as incredibly risky, the standard deviation of international stocks (10.14 percent) has been slightly lower than the standard deviation of the S&P 500 (10.30 percent).

Index: Open-Ended Funds International Equities Index

Category: International Equities

Performance:

Year-to-Date	5%	Last 3 Years (HPR)	23%
Last 12 Months	5%	Last 5 Years (HPR)	29%

Rate of Return (1 Year)	8.77%
Standard Deviation	10.14%
Original Portfolio Amount	$1,000
Portfolio Value in 5 Years	$1,522
Portfolio Value in 10 Years	$2,318
Portfolio Value in 15 Years	$3,529

Standard Deviation

10.14%

	Monthly Returns												**Annual Return**
	Jan.	**Feb.**	**Mar.**	**Apr.**	**May**	**Jun.**	**Jul.**	**Aug.**	**Sep.**	**Oct.**	**Nov.**	**Dec.**	
1989	3.49	−0.11	0.10	2.77	−1.85	−0.57	9.22	−0.29	3.57	−4.10	3.58	4.74	21.79
1990	−1.86	−2.16	0.09	−2.05	7.84	2.04	3.81	−10.43	−10.36	6.23	−1.84	0.28	−9.71
1991	2.38	7.62	−1.56	0.97	1.38	−4.58	4.00	−0.50	2.50	0.62	−3.25	4.84	14.68
1992	1.36	0.95	−3.08	2.20	4.53	−2.41	−2.70	0.30	−2.13	−2.15	0.29	1.22	−1.90
1993	−0.10	2.34	5.40	4.03	2.00	−1.33	3.04	7.58	0.57	5.61	−2.37	11.45	44.55
1994	2.72	−2.50	−4.75	0.61	0.24	−0.99	2.67	4.16	−0.97	1.57	−4.33	−2.85	−4.79
1995	−4.23	0.88	3.41	3.40	1.54	−0.07	4.21	−1.71	1.29	−2.23	0.61	2.89	10.07
1996	3.41	0.19	1.66	3.54	0.09	0.64	−4.06	1.50	1.70	−0.88	3.71	0.64	12.27
1997	0.96	1.93	−0.42	0.40	5.54	4.92	2.98	−7.87	6.22	−9.22	−1.02	1.13	4.34
1998	0.30	6.94	4.97	4.97	−3.15	−2.92	1.93	−18.09	−1.86	7.52	5.01	1.91	4.78

International Equities (Europe) Index

Horizon: December 1988–December 1998

Definition: European markets are made up of 15 primary countries: Austria, Belgium, Denmark, Finland, France, Ireland, Italy, Netherlands, Norway, Portugal, Spain, Sweden, Switzerland, and the United Kingdom.
 Who buys European stocks? Investors interested in focusing on the growing economy of Europe with an interest in a well-balanced asset allocation in a large portfolio.

Index: Open-Ended International Equities (Europe) Index

Category: International Equities

Performance:

Year-to-Date	20%	Last 3 Years (HPR)	74%
Last 12 Months	20%	Last 5 Years (HPR)	106%

Rate of Return (1 Year)	11.29%
Standard Deviation	11.36%
Original Portfolio Amount	$1,000
Portfolio Value in 5 Years	$1,707
Portfolio Value in 10 Years	$2,915
Portfolio Value in 15 Years	$4,978

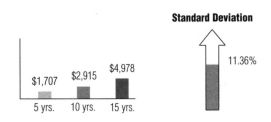

	Monthly Returns											Annual Return
	Jan.	Feb.	Mar.	Apr.	May	Jun.	Jul.	Aug.	Sep.	Oct.	Nov.	Dec.	
1989	4.21	−0.07	0.62	3.54	−3.36	2.93	8.21	−0.80	3.58	−7.50	4.31	7.03	23.93
1990	0.12	−1.73	2.64	−1.48	5.45	3.57	4.08	−11.06	−11.23	5.94	−0.67	−1.10	−7.09
1991	0.99	7.06	−4.82	−0.24	0.97	−6.46	4.67	1.28	2.72	−1.88	−2.75	5.54	6.33
1992	0.76	1.04	−3.04	4.73	4.23	−2.65	−4.67	−1.58	−2.67	−6.70	0.33	2.80	−7.82
1993	0.82	0.94	4.54	2.68	1.45	−1.14	2.02	7.64	−1.16	3.99	−2.81	6.85	28.42
1994	7.20	−2.90	−2.18	3.68	−3.69	−1.89	4.84	2.21	−3.23	3.43	−4.05	−0.72	1.92
1995	−1.21	1.62	1.78	4.40	2.67	1.32	5.10	−2.53	2.47	−1.08	−1.05	2.08	16.39
1996	1.12	3.08	2.27	1.71	2.45	0.75	−2.52	3.08	1.33	1.86	4.29	2.13	23.64
1997	0.47	1.30	2.28	−1.58	4.03	4.32	2.45	−4.37	8.54	−3.75	0.80	1.76	16.73
1998	3.31	7.97	7.64	2.61	2.97	−0.50	1.32	−13.77	−5.43	6.43	4.46	3.75	20.29

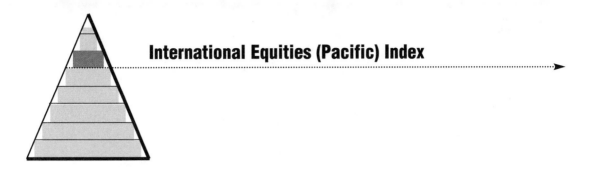

International Equities (Pacific) Index

Horizon: December 1988–December 1998

Definition: The Pacific markets are made up of five areas: Australia, Hong Kong, Japan, New Zealand, and Singapore.
Who buys stocks from the Pacific region? These areas of the world are often viewed as some of the most volatile (notice the 20.87 percent standard deviation, double the S&P 500), yet many investors believe some of the best technology products and other quality products are being produced by companies trading on these markets. Therefore, if you are an aggressive investor seeking to take advantage of opportunities in the Pacific region, you may want to weigh the risks.

Index: Open-Ended Funds International Equities (Pacific) Index

Category: International Equities

Performance:

Year-to-Date	−5%	Last 3 Years (HPR)	−30%
Last 12 Months	−5%	Last 5 Years (HPR)	−29%

Rate of Return (1 Year)	−0.75%
Standard Deviation	20.87%
Original Portfolio Amount	$1,000
Portfolio Value in 5 Years	$963
Portfolio Value in 10 Years	$928
Portfolio Value in 15 Years	$894

Standard Deviation
20.87%

$963 $928 $894
5 yrs. 10 yrs. 15 yrs.

			Monthly Returns									Annual
	Jan.	**Feb.**	**Mar.**	**Apr.**	**May**	**Jun.**	**Jul.**	**Aug.**	**Sep.**	**Oct.**	**Nov.**	**Dec.**	**Return**
1989	0.26	1.68	−1.61	0.58	−2.74	−2.11	9.97	−0.66	9.18	−2.85	2.72	4.24	19.17
1990	−2.34	−5.48	−8.16	−1.13	10.98	3.67	4.45	−10.08	−14.88	20.39	−8.29	−1.75	−16.35
1991	2.41	9.22	−2.22	4.35	−0.97	−2.08	1.07	−6.15	6.58	0.65	−6.27	2.28	7.94
1992	−1.34	−3.75	−7.98	−1.32	6.76	−3.38	−5.90	8.41	−3.13	−1.19	0.37	−0.31	−13.11
1993	−1.08	3.63	10.17	11.63	3.75	−3.14	5.41	4.26	0.00	4.20	−6.85	12.79	52.43
1994	3.11	−0.32	−6.32	4.62	2.78	0.21	1.16	3.91	−2.72	1.15	−6.73	0.05	0.14
1995	−9.44	−0.20	3.22	2.33	1.86	−0.97	5.75	−1.66	0.54	−2.04	−0.14	3.95	2.38
1996	5.80	−1.21	0.60	3.44	−1.34	−0.90	−5.58	0.95	2.46	−2.46	4.32	−1.28	4.32
1997	−1.46	1.12	−4.39	−0.02	8.47	3.29	1.33	−12.84	−0.54	−18.80	−4.86	−3.45	−30.08
1998	−2.86	10.99	−2.61	−4.69	−9.47	−6.52	−1.72	−11.64	5.92	14.58	6.01	0.81	−4.60

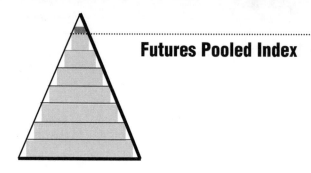

Futures Pooled Index

Horizon: December 1988–December 1998

Definition: Managed futures are often used to hedge your investment portfolio against violent swings in the more traditional investment markets of stocks and bonds. These pools invest in a broad variety of commodities ranging from lumber and pork bellies to stock market futures contracts and Treasury bond futures contracts. Although they are viewed as a volatile investment option, managed futures can actually reduce the overall volatility of a portfolio.

    Who buys managed futures? While usually associated with very large pension plans and foundations with assets over $1 million, lately individual investors have begun to see the value of investments with the potential for growth that are not tied directly to the performance of the stock and bond markets. Because a managed future fund can invest in many markets—such as those trading in lumber, heating oil, or even orange juice contracts—you have the potential to make money regardless of the stock market's direction.

Index: Futures Managers Index of Pooled Accounts

Category: Commodities

Performance:

Year-to-Date	6%	Last 3 Years (HPR)	36%
Last 12 Months	6%	Last 5 Years (HPR)	44%

Rate of Return (1 Year)   8.94%
Standard Deviation   6.39%
Original Portfolio Amount $1,000
Portfolio Value in 5 Years $1,535
Portfolio Value in 10 Years $2,355
Portfolio Value in 15 Years $3,613

Standard Deviation

$1,535 $2,355 $3,613   6.39%

5 yrs.   10 yrs.   15 yrs.

	Monthly Returns												Annual Return
	Jan.	**Feb.**	**Mar.**	**Apr.**	**May**	**Jun.**	**Jul.**	**Aug.**	**Sep.**	**Oct.**	**Nov.**	**Dec.**	
1989	4.64	−4.53	2.70	−1.35	10.20	0.16	4.45	−4.46	−2.27	−3.96	1.84	3.32	10.10
1990	1.86	1.86	1.52	3.73	−4.67	1.18	4.19	5.00	1.77	2.46	0.52	−1.12	19.51
1991	−3.55	−0.65	4.64	−0.20	−1.09	0.77	−3.42	−3.11	4.59	−1.50	0.42	14.66	10.72
1992	−6.43	−3.53	−0.56	−1.71	−0.07	5.14	6.36	3.55	−0.76	−0.31	0.60	−0.57	1.03
1993	−0.78	54.20	−0.53	2.96	0.65	1.33	3.89	−0.27	−0.77	−0.41	0.06	3.09	15.15
1994	−2.14	−2.62	1.66	−1.39	1.66	3.32	−1.69	−1.62	1.26	−0.16	0.89	−1.18	−2.18
1995	−1.72	2.05	6.35	1.40	1.23	1.65	−1.31	0.72	−1.76	−0.44	1.13	3.58	9.00
1996	1.98	−4.08	0.66	3.84	−1.77	−0.08	−0.46	0.28	2.92	5.44	4.28	−1.30	11.89
1997	3.39	1.99	−0.41	−1.40	−0.41	0.80	5.08	−2.95	1.13	−0.09	0.86	1.41	9.49
1998	1.21	0.02	1.06	−2.47	2.21	0.68	−0.58	4.91	2.02	−2.87			

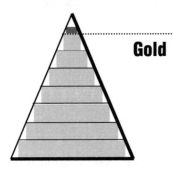

Gold

Horizon: December 1988–December 1998

Definition: Gold as a commodity has been thought of as money for thousands of years. Gold should be purchased mainly when you believe it will appreciate in value. It pays no dividends. The numbers shown below reflect the unmanaged index of monthly gold prices.

Who buys gold? Most investors who buy gold accumulate it as an inflation hedge on the assumption that gold can protect them during uncertain economic periods. If you believed a steep decline for all financial assets was about to occur, you might allocate a portion of your assets to gold.

Index: Gold

Category: Commodities

Performance:

Year-to-Date	0%	Last 3 Years (HPR)	26%
Last 12 Months	0%	Last 5 Years (HPR)	26%

Rate of Return (1 Year)	−2.79%
Standard Deviation	8.42%
Original Portfolio Amount	$1,000
Portfolio Value in 5 Years	$868
Portfolio Value in 10 Years	$753
Portfolio Value in 15 Years	$654

$868 $753 $654

5 yrs. 10 yrs. 15 yrs.

Standard Deviation

8.42%

	Monthly Returns												Annual Return
	Jan.	Feb.	Mar.	Apr.	May	Jun.	Jul.	Aug.	Sep.	Oct.	Nov.	Dec.	
1989	−2.56	−3.33	−0.83	−1.46	−4.16	6.01	−3.99	−2.36	1.87	2.41	8.75	−3.23	−3.76
1990	4.87	−2.78	−9.30	1.73	−3.02	−3.12	5.71	4.14	5.33	−7.73	1.99	0.44	−3.13
1991	−5.24	−0.15	−1.94	0.51	1.81	1.47	−2.93	−2.86	2.14	0.71	2.47	−4.21	−8.29
1992	0.92	−1.19	−2.33	−1.56	0.33	1.75	4.25	−4.74	2.34	−2.73	−1.57	−0.38	−5.12
1993	−0.72	−0.85	3.13	4.90	6.53	0.26	6.15	−7.50	−4.30	3.98	0.34	5.25	17.36
1994	−3.23	0.96	2.02	−3.28	2.98	0.18	−1.08	0.44	2.36	−2.77	−0.18	−0.15	−1.97
1995	−1.98	0.41	4.13	−0.57	−1.40	0.73	−0.94	−0.26	0.44	−0.36	1.35	−0.29	1.14
1996	4.89	−1.21	−1.08	−1.27	−0.18	−2.19	0.88	0.29	−1.92	0.15	−2.18	−0.45	−4.38
1997	−6.52	3.81	−2.46	−2.76	1.60	−3.20	−2.47	−0.30	2.07	−6.24	−4.68	−2.97	−22.08
1998	5.83	−2.43	1.22	3.21	−5.50	0.91	−2.50	−5.33	7.48	−0.52	0.81	−2.47	−0.19

13 Reviewing a Recommendation

When you are attempting to review a new investment recommendation, you may want to use this short worksheet to review the investment's performance, its risk, how it will fit into your current asset allocation, and its cost.

Name of the asset: _____

Performance:

Year-to-date: _____

Last 12 months: _____

Last 3 years: _____

Last 5 years: _____

Standard deviation: _____

How will this asset fit into your current asset allocation?

Would it qualify as:

Cash _____

A bond _____

A stock _____

What is the initial cost of purchasing this investment? _____

What is the ongoing cost of holding this investment? _____

What Type of Investment Makes Sense?

> **"**Don't let your emotions get in the way of your decisions to buy or sell stocks; this is one of the cardinal rules of investing.**"**
>
> **Mel Kemp,** 70ish
> *Little Rock, Arkansas*

> **"**A few years ago I invested $500,000 in five different mutual funds. Today, three and one-half years later, the total value of these investments has reached $952,293.59—almost double my original cost. This far exceeds my wildest dreams. The best advice I have received is to invest for the long term and don't worry about the day-to-day fluctuations of the market. I hope I'm not too old at 83 to be able to absorb new ideas and ways of making decisions in the world of finance.**"**
>
> **Anonymous,** 83

VISUAL VIBRATIONS?

Turn the page for the **answer!**

> **"**Beginning at age 35, I started investing only $50 a month in a deferred annuity, which today—I'm now 64—is worth $85,000. I would encourage anyone in business for themselves to set aside a percentage in a tax-deferred retirement account. The time to start investing is when you're young—you will never miss the money, but you will have a great retirement income and security for the future.**"**
> **M.A.S.,** *64*

Once you choose the basic asset allocations for investing in the various asset classes, you still have an additional investment decision to make: the form in which you'll hold the investments.

There are five basic structures that you may purchase:

1. Individual securities
2. Mutual funds
3. Individual professional money managers
4. Unit trusts
5. Annuities

INDIVIDUAL SECURITIES

As an investor, you are able to pick and choose from the thousands of individual stocks and bonds that have been issued by all of the publicly traded companies. These securities are usually traded on the major exchanges, such as the New York Stock Exchange (NYSE), the American Stock Exchange (AMEX), or the Nasdaq, and these securities are purchased as shares of stock. You may purchase as few as one share at a time.

The advantage of buying individual securities is that, by researching these companies with your financial adviser, you are able to narrow your focus to the stocks that you believe have the potential to be the most profitable. There are some tax advantages as well. If you buy shares of a publicly traded company, you may choose to hold them for years and years. For example, if you purchased shares of stock in XYZ Corporation for a total of $1,000 and ten years later the stock had grown to $25,000, you would be required to pay taxes only on the dividends you received; you would not be required to pay capital gains taxes until you sold the stock.

While the primary advantage of buying individual securities is the potential for growth, the primary disadvantage is the risk of losing your original money. If a company goes out of business, you risk losing all of your money. Other disadvantages include the difficulty in selecting the proper balance of individual companies and the proper balance within industry sectors.

MUTUAL FUNDS

A mutual fund allows ordinary investors to buy a group of stocks or bonds that have been pooled into a single investment with a common investment objective. Some of the most commonly stated investment objectives include:

- Aggressive growth
- Growth
- Growth and income
- Index
- Global
- International growth
- Sector

The stated objectives are printed in the prospectus of the mutual fund, and those objectives should help you choose the mutual funds that could help you reach your future financial goals.

Just like individual securities, mutual funds are traded in shares. Each share is made up of a fractional ownership of each individual company. As an example, if you were to buy a mutual fund that mimicked the S&P 500 Index, you would be buying a fund that had taken a group of investors' money and pooled it together with the common purpose of owning all 500 stocks in the Standard & Poor's Index. It would obviously be difficult to

A Look at Stock Funds

Type of Stock Fund	Capital Gains Potential	Income Potential	Total Potential	Risk Level
Aggressive Growth	Very High	Low	Very High	Very High
Growth	High	Low	High	High
Growth & Income	Moderate	Moderate	Moderate	Moderate
Index	Varies	Varies	Varies	Varies
Global	High	Moderate	High	High
International	Very High	Low	Very High	Very High
Sector	Varies	Varies	Varies	Varies

Source: Reprinted by permission of Standard & Poor's, a division of the McGraw-Hill Companies.

venture out on your own and attempt to purchase all 500 stocks. It would be expensive to buy and hard to monitor. But you could easily buy into an S&P 500 Index fund so that the mutual fund manager does all of the buying, and the fund reports its performance and keeps track of all tax and dividend records.

There are many advantages to owning mutual funds. The most obvious include instant diversification, because most mutual funds own a broad array of stocks and/or bonds, and professional money management, because you are able to hire some of the most skilled portfolio managers in the country. You can find mutual funds with excellent long-term track records and, of course, you can choose the mutual funds whose objectives are most closely aligned with your risk tolerance and stated investment objectives.

Disadvantages may include the ongoing costs of management and administrative fees, tax bills for capital gains that you didn't actually earn,

Type of Fund	Number of Funds Available
Sector	634
Mixed equity	970
World equity	1,697
Money market	974
Tax-free fixed income	2,401
Taxable fixed income	2,343
General equity	4,099

Source: Data supplied by Lipper, Inc., Denver, CO.

and the difficulty in selecting among the more than 13,000 mutual funds and hundreds of mutual fund companies.

In fact, the difficulty in selecting the mutual funds that may be best suited to your stated investment goals may prove to be one of the most difficult decisions. With so many mutual funds and classes of shares to choose from, how can you ever choose the correct one? It is important to remember that you will never be able to always be in the number one mutual fund, and I definitely don't recommend that you jump from fund to fund in search of large profits. Just because a fund manager has had a terrific 12-month run doesn't mean you should switch all of your money to his fund. Instead, buy quality funds with excellent long-term track records and begin to add to those on a regular basis.

INDIVIDUAL PROFESSIONAL MONEY MANAGERS

Individual professional money managers differ from mutual funds in that you hire them to personally manage your money. With a mutual fund investment you pool your money with thousands of other investors who share a similar investment objective. A professional money manager segregates your money into an account that will be invested to meet your personal investment goals—a highly personalized service.

Those with at least $100,000 in investable assets may choose to hire a professional money manager. These money managers are the same types of companies that invest pension money for major corporations or endowment money for major foundations. By hiring one of these professional money managers, you are gaining access to some of the finest investment strategies in the country.

In an effort to hire the proper manager or group of managers, your financial adviser will subject you to a detailed questionnaire that explores your risk tolerance and your investment objectives. The adviser will review your time horizon for money and your tax situation.

The advantages of purchasing your investments through a professional money manager are similar to those of mutual funds: instant diversification because most professionally managed accounts will own a broad array of stocks and/or bonds, access to some of the most skilled portfolio managers in the country, excellent long-term track records, and, of course, your choice of the money managers whose objectives are most closely aligned with your risk tolerance and your stated investment objectives.

In addition to these advantages, a professional money manager can be more flexible in the timing of the buys and sells that affect your annual tax bill. You can request a money manager to take any gains or losses that would be beneficial to you in any specific tax year.

The disadvantages include the ongoing costs for this specialized service and the difficulty in selecting the money manager that most closely aligns itself with your goals.

UNIT TRUSTS

A unit trust is similar to the structure of a mutual fund in that it will purchase a pool of stocks or bonds with a common investment objective such as growth or income. However, a unit trust differs from a mutual fund in that once the investment is placed into the trust, none of the holdings will be sold until the termination of the entire unit trust.

A unit trust will hold a specific number of individual stocks or bonds for a specific and stated amount of time. Most stock unit trusts will have a holding period that may vary from 1 year to 18 months to 2 years, although some bond or fixed-income unit trusts may be structured with a 5-year to a 30-year termination date.

Unit trusts have become an increasingly popular investment over the last five to ten years. They have been a successful structure for some of the most popular investment strategies. You may have heard of the "Dogs of the Dow," a strategy whereby an investor chooses to invest in the 10 stocks from the 30 stocks in the Dow Jones with the highest dividend yields. They hold those stocks for one year and then reallocate their money to the new list of the 10 highest-yielding stocks in the Dow Jones at that time.

This is considered a conservative, contrarian strategy because you are choosing to buy stocks that are currently out of favor. And the long-term performance numbers have been shown to be competitive. According to *U.S. News & World Report* (July 8, 1996), this strategy would have provided a 17.7 percent average annual return since 1973 versus the Dow Jones Industrial Average performance of 11.9 percent over the same time horizon.

Other unit trusts may be designed to allow individual investors to buy a group of stocks in a specific industry, such as a financial stock unit trust, an Internet unit trust, or a technology unit trust.

The advantages of a unit trust include instant diversification, the ability of a skilled money management team to build the portfolio, and you can buy a unit trust with a specific investment objective that fits into your overall portfolio.

One additional advantage is that with some unit trusts, a tax-deferred rollover feature is available for investors who choose to continue with a unit trust strategy by rolling over into a new portfolio on termination of their original unit trust.

The tax-deferred rollover may be available when duplicated stocks are exchanged from one unit trust to the next; only the gain on those stocks sold from the terminating trust will be taxable. The cost basis (original purchase price) of those stocks that remain the same will be carried over until either they are sold from the portfolio or the investor decides to sell the investment.

The disadvantages include the cost of ownership and the specific termination date, which can incur a capital gains liability.

ANNUITIES

There are three main types of annuities: fixed, variable, and immediate.

A *fixed annuity* is a long-term investment vehicle intended to provide a guaranteed return of principal and modest long-term growth. It is generally appropriate for conservative investors who need to grow their assets to provide for future income in retirement. A fixed annuity works very much like a CD or a bond. However, in this case you invest your money with an insurance company, which in turn agrees to pay you a fixed rate of interest on that money for a specified period of time. The major difference between a fixed annuity and a CD or bond is that the annuity grows on a tax-deferred basis. You are not taxed on the income generated by the fixed annuity until you choose to either liquidate the annuity or withdraw money from it. (This tax treatment is similar to that you are accustomed to receiving on your IRA, 401(k), or 403(b).)

The advantage of tax deferral is that your money compounds faster because you are earning interest on your principal, interest on your interest, and interest on the money you would have otherwise had to pay in taxes. The disadvantage of tax deferral is that withdrawn earnings are taxed at ordinary income tax rates and, if withdrawn before age 59½, may be subject to a 10 percent tax penalty. Generally, if you are investing for the long term, the advantage of faster compounding outweighs the disadvantage.

A *variable annuity* is another long-term investment vehicle issued by insurance companies. Moderate and aggressive investors wishing to create future retirement income may be interested in variable annuities. In many ways, a variable annuity works like a family of mutual funds. You choose to invest your variable annuity monies into one or more of the available variable annuity investment portfolios. Each of these portfolios is in turn invested by professional money managers in a diversified array of stocks and/or bonds according to their stated portfolio investment objectives and guidelines. With your investment adviser, you should determine the most appropriate allocation of your funds among the investment options based on your tolerance for risk and your stated investment objectives.

Similar to the difference between a CD and a fixed annuity discussed above, one major difference between a mutual fund and a variable annuity is tax deferral. You aren't taxed on the income, dividends, or capital gains generated within the variable annuity portfolios until you choose to either liquidate the annuity or withdraw money from it. In addition to the tax-deferral advantage provided in a fixed annuity, variable annuities offer an additional tax-deferral advantage. Within a variable annuity, you can also move money between various investment portfolios without triggering tax on the earnings!

In addition to tax deferral, variable annuities offer guaranteed death benefits. In the event of your death, your heirs are protected from the effects of a market downturn. For example, let's assume you buy a $10,000 variable annuity and invest that money into a few growth portfolios. Two months after your purchase, an unexpected economic event occurs and the stock market drops substantially. The variable annuity portfolios, being invested in growth stocks, reflect this market drop and the value of your variable annuity drops to $9,000. If you were to sell your annuity at this point, you would receive the $9,000 minus any investment charges and surrender charges. However, if you were unlucky enough to die at this time, your beneficiaries would be paid no less than the original investment of $10,000. (Some variable annuity contracts provide even more sophisticated death benefit guarantees that allow you to guarantee specific minimum rates of return or to lock in high market performance as a death benefit to your heir.)

Both fixed and variable annuities offer one additional benefit that is unique in the investment arena—the option of creating an income steam that you can't outlive. At that point in the future when you want to generate regular income for retirement, you may ask the insurance company responsible for your annuity to "annuitize" your contract. The insurance company will then take the current value of your contract and use it to provide you with regular income payments. You can arrange for these payments to be monthly, quarterly, or annual. You can choose to have these payments locked in at a constant guaranteed amount, or you can choose to have them fluctuate with the value of selected investment portfolios. Most important, you can choose to have this income stream guaranteed for a specific period of time (say, 20 years), your lifetime (or the lifetime of both yourself and your spouse), or a lifetime with a minimum specified period of time (for example, your lifetime but not less than 20 years). If you select a lifetime guarantee, you have created regular income that you can't outlive.

The payments that you receive from your annuitized fixed or variable annuity are made on a very tax-advantaged basis. A portion of each payment that you receive is treated as return of principal and is not subject to income tax.

The last type of annuity is an *immediate annuity*. An immediate annuity is the same thing as an annuitized fixed or variable annuity except that the insurance company will start payments right away instead of allowing the money to accumulate for years and allowing you to choose when (or if) to trigger the regular income payments.

As a review, within an annuity

- your money grows tax deferred;
- you can attempt to protect your estate from a market decline;
- you can name your beneficiary(ies) and avoid probate; and
- you may choose to annuitize (take a lifetime income benefit) assuring that no matter how long you live, you will always have a steady income on which you can rely.

But . . . there are no perfect investments or investment structures. Disadvantages of the immediate annuity include the increased cost of managing your money because of the cost of insurance and the smaller size of the subaccounts. This structure does tie up your money until you are 59½. And, finally, you are counting on the financial stability of the underlying insurance company.

Let's review the five basic structures:

1. Individual securities
2. Mutual funds
3. Individual professional money managers
4. Unit trusts
5. Annuities

With so many advantages and disadvantages, the sheer number of choices can be overwhelming. Think back to the picture of all the images on page 132. You don't have to remember all of the details. The key is to choose the investment alternatives that will best allow you to reach your future financial objectives while working within your stated tolerance for risk. Finally finding the correct blend is a wonderful achievement and a grand step toward your plan's success.

PART THREE

Putting Your Plan
Into Action

Choosing Your
Financial Adviser

> **"**Don't try and do it alone. Find someone you can feel comfortable about discussing your life with. Money is personal and you shouldn't ever feel intimidated when dealing with a professional.**"**
> **Anonymous**

> **"**I was very fortunate to have a grandmother who was very involved in the stock market. Her advice was to buy quality stocks and forget about them. One such example of this strategy would be the Royal Dutch Petroleum stock that she transferred to me 50 years ago and I still own.**"**
> **Anonymous,** 64
> *Little Rock, Arkansas*

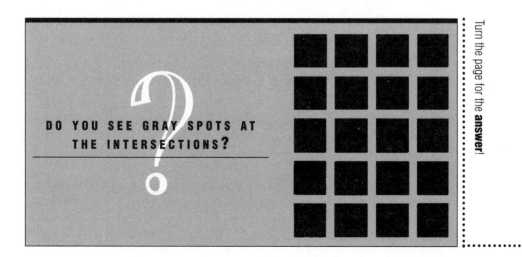

DO YOU SEE GRAY SPOTS AT THE INTERSECTIONS?

Turn the page for the **answer!**

Your brain tells you there are no spots, but your eyes support the illusion, and you are forced to admit that you see the imaginary gray spots.

The same is true when you consider using a financial adviser. An adviser may be seen as an unnecessary expense or as an invaluable tool for your financial success.

Some investors view the Internet as making unnecessary the need for a qualified financial adviser. In fact, the sheer volume of material available on the Internet punctuates the need for advice. The Internet is available 24 hours a day to provide information, but it cannot provide experience.

As your net worth grows, the intangible benefits of hiring a financial adviser may begin to outweigh the costs. As always, it is a matter of perspective. What do you see?

> **"**Pay yourself first and leave it alone. Feel secure about your financial adviser.**"**
> **Charles and Emma Randle,** 71 and 67
> *Jonesboro, Arkansas*

HOW TO CHOOSE A FINANCIAL ADVISER

I hope by now you understand the premise of this book.

- Part 1: You must have a written financial plan.

- Part 2: I've dispelled some investment myths and reinforced some investment truths that could help you increase your knowledge and therefore increase your confidence in dealing with your money. Be sure you understand the five laws of successful investing.

- Part 3: I've outlined the specific roles that each of the three basic asset classes of cash, bonds, and stocks play in your portfolio. You should understand the risk-return levels of several different investment alternatives.

By now, some of you may be thinking, "I've read the first three parts of this book, and once I complete the action steps, I'll have the necessary components to create my own written financial plan. I think I'll try to do this by myself."

I would like to counter the theory of doing it on your own with two motivational stories.

A group of pioneers were gambling on whose horse had more strength. The contest involved harnessing horses and seeing how many pounds of lumber each horse could pull over a certain distance. One horse was able to pull 7,000 pounds, another was able to pull 8,000 pounds, but the winner took a total of 9,000 pounds and pulled it to the finish line.

Being gamblers, the men wondered just how much dead weight the two top horses could pull together. They decided that if one horse could pull 9,000 pounds, then two horses could surely pull 18,000 pounds. And the bidding began. Some said 17,000 pounds and some said 19,000 and one brave soul even ventured as high as 20,000 pounds. But when the day was over, those two horses were able to pull a whopping 30,000 pounds of timber from one point to the next point. *30,000 pounds.* The men were stunned! No one even came close to estimating the power of this team. That is how I feel about the power of a quality financial adviser as part of your investment strategy.

So what was the magic equation that gave this team of animals such strength? Was it their being harnessed together, pulling stride for stride, toward a common goal? Was it the ability of one horse to continue to pull when the other needed to regain a foothold? Was it the comaraderie? Or was it simply teamwork?

Regardless of the reason, the outcome was obvious. The two horses were able to accomplish significantly more together than they ever could have accomplished while they worked alone.

This is how I view your relationship with your personal financial adviser. Your written financial plan serves as the harness and the bridle. The plan document is your guide. Your risk tolerance sets the pace, and the economy and interest rates determine how hard you have to work together to achieve your financial goals. Regardless of external circumstances, I have no doubt that you will be able to accomplish more working as a team than you would be able to accomplish alone.

I love the "horse story." I believe it is true, and I am convinced that quality advice will bring value to your long-term investment strategy.

The second story that I would share with those of you who are still thinking of trying to reach your financial goals on your own is a recent personal experience.

I was in the hospital on October 1, 1997, for a scheduled C-section. I was nervous and somewhat anxious when the instructor asked me if the student nurse could start the IV, saying, "This is her first one. Would you mind if she gives it a try?" As my heart beat a little faster, I facetiously said, "I would be honored." The student nurse was in a panic, and her fear clearly showed in her face. Even though she did her best, in the end it was the instructor who successfully started my IV.

This recent event still evokes a painful twinge. Starting and implementing your financial plan is a lot like the scenario I just described. The student nurse knew all of the terminology and even knew how to use the appropriate tools. But she lacked one key ingredient: experience. I didn't relish the thought of being someone's guinea pig. And the same would be true if you made the fateful decision to go it alone.

If you do it on your own, you probably will be creating your very first financial plan. Do you really want to be your own test case?

Why not find someone who has the tools and the team and the credentials and the *experience* to help you design and implement a professionally created written financial plan?

WHAT IS A FINANCIAL ADVISER?

Your financial adviser is exactly that—a person who has gone through a training program to help people achieve their financial goals.

Your financial adviser should be able to walk you through the seven-step process of creating your financial plan, as outlined in Chapters 1 through 4. As you go through this process with your financial adviser, you should begin to recognize the value of the advice and the experience the adviser brings to your investment strategy.

Every investment company and every financial adviser brings their own skills, talents, products, and services to the table. You'll want to know what services you can expect.

Seven-Step Process for Successful Financial Management

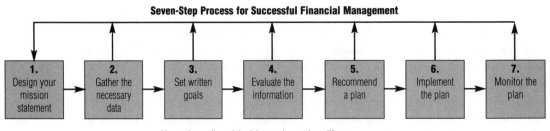

You and your financial adviser review and modify as necessary.

WHAT SERVICES CAN YOU EXPECT?

You can expect to receive advice and any needed implementation in the following areas:

Retirement planning	Laddered maturity programs
Estate planning	Fixed/Variable annuities
Trusts	Insurance
Professional money management	Unit investment trusts
Tax-free investing	Money market funds
Equity research	Mutual funds
Over-the-counter securities	Futures
Initial public offerings	Managed futures
Global equities	Precious metals
Options	Active assets accounts
Fixed-income securities	Margin accounts
Municipal bonds	Individual retirement accounts (IRAs)
U.S. government and agency bonds	Rollover IRAs
Zero-coupon bonds	Roth IRAs
Certificates of deposit (CDs)	Education IRAs
Corporate bonds	SEP-IRAs
Convertible securities	401(k) plans
Home equity line of credit	

We like to call advisers who offer the above services full service advisers. If clients need something done that moves them closer to achieving their financial goals, then full service advisers want to offer that product or service.

If you want to invest but are uncertain which vehicle would be most appropriate, your financial adviser will be glad to make recommendations.

If you are wondering if mutual funds would be a good choice, you can sit down with your financial adviser and discuss the pros and cons.

If you have not yet started creating a comprehensive financial strategy, your financial adviser should be able to guide you through the process.

And the wonderful thing is that you get to choose your financial adviser.

INTERVIEWING PROSPECTIVE ADVISERS

Over the last 17 years, I have worked with and met hundreds of financial advisers, and I can attest to their differences. Each financial adviser has his or her own personality and his or her own set of values on which recommendations are based.

Your job, when interviewing a prospective adviser, is to ask certain important questions. Here are a few examples:

- May I see a copy of your vocational mission statement?
- What type of services and products do you specialize in?
- Do you hold any special investment planning credentials?
- Are you capable of helping me create a written financial plan?
- How will you correspond with me? Telephone? Mail? Annual or semiannual meetings?
- What are the costs?
- How do you get paid?
- Do you like working with investors like me?
- Would you be willing to create a written proposal for my review without any obligation?

If this conversation were occurring in my office, I might ask you the following questions:

- What does your money mean to you?
- What are you planning for?
- What are your expectations for your money?
- What would your expectations of me include?

Then we would move into the seven-step process for creating a written proposal discussed in Chapters 1 to 4. At the next meeting you might review the written proposal and determine if my recommendations match your expectations.

MATCHING YOUR FINANCIAL ADVISER TO YOUR NEEDS

Creating and implementing a financial plan is a lifelong process, so you want to find someone that you will enjoy working with over a long period of time. You may hit it off from the moment you meet, or it may take some time to develop a sense of confidence. But in my office *the client comes first.* It is my goal to find out your goals and try to help you achieve them.

If I were selecting a financial adviser, I'd want one who was trustworthy; a person of integrity; helpful; courteous; responsive; caring; intelligent; proactive . . . and more.

The money is yours and you can choose with whom to place your confidence and your money. Therefore, your financial adviser will do everything possible to create a comfortable environment to meet your needs.

What Will It Cost?

Most full-service financial advisers are paid by a combination of commissions and fees. How you will be charged should be thoroughly discussed and is a welcome question.

I am never afraid to discuss costs with my clients. I can't compete with the discount brokers or the Internet providers on a cost basis, so I must compete on a value-added basis.

After surgery on my knee as the result of a skiing accident, I never asked the surgeon the cost of the surgery. I wanted the best surgeon. Cost was not an issue; outcome was.

The same should be true in dealing with your financial adviser. You'll want to talk about outcome, which planners call *net total return.*

THE INITIAL MEETING

The first meeting with your financial adviser will possibly be the most telling one of all. New clients typically decide whether they will do business with a specific financial adviser within the first few seconds of their meeting. First impressions do make a difference, and I believe it is of the utmost importance that you feel at ease with your adviser from the very start.

Some of my clients may have felt uneasy before our first meeting, and I understand their concern. Money is a very personal and private matter. Right or wrong, it contributes to our feeling of self-esteem. Money does indeed carry very powerful emotions.

Some people walk in afraid that I will shake my head in dismay at the poor job they have done of managing their money. Others walk in knowing they have done a superb job of accumulating a large amount of money and are afraid I will try to change everything they have done. Neither of these apprehensions is true.

Initial meetings are a lot like going to a doctor for the first time. You know you need a physical but you aren't thrilled at the thought of having to "strip." Doctors are aware of your discomfort, so they take certain steps to put you at ease:

- They have an attractive work environment.
- They have appropriately trained and friendly staff.
- They are especially well educated and display their diplomas conspicuously.
- The nurses and doctors are dressed appropriately; a doctor's lab coat establishes confidence.
- They have all the necessary tools and equipment to take care of you.
- They treat you with respect and dignity.

The same steps should be taken by your financial adviser. He or she is there to basically give you a financial "physical." We are aware that this can be a new experience so we will do our best to

- have an attractive work environment;
- have appropriately trained and friendly staff;
- have a level of education and other certifications and qualifications to put you at ease;
- be dressed appropriately;
- have all the necessary computer tools and expertise; and
- treat you with respect and dignity.

This initial meeting is one of the favorite parts of my work. When a prospective client walks into my office with a purse or briefcase full of financial documents and a long list of questions and concerns, I find it an incredible pleasure to begin to work through the seven steps to create this person's financial plan.

I or a member of my team begins by asking, "What does your money mean to you?" and "What are your expectations for this money?" Then I begin to work on creating the client's money mission statement. I take out the detailed financial questionnaire and step-by-step uncover the necessary financial information.

Then I work to establish two types of written goals and objectives. First, I qualify your goals ("I want to plan for my retirement." Or "I want to put my children through college.") Then I quantify your goals. ("I will need to accumulate $750,000 to meet my retirement goal." Or "I will need $100,000 in 15 years to fully fund my child's college tuition and other expenses.")

Your financial adviser then evaluates the information and recommends a specific plan of action. You decide whether to implement the plan and can set up a schedule to monitor the plan.

Opening your account or accounts with your financial adviser. Once you have met with your adviser and have agreed to follow the outlined financial strategy, you open your new account and begin to fund it with your assets. You may write a check or you may transfer various assets into your new account. You may currently be holding the physical certificates of various investments in your lockbox, or you may be holding assets in one or more brokerage accounts that you want to consolidate. Whatever the case, you must determine the *type* of account that best suits your needs.

An asset management account. Almost all major investment firms offer some sort of asset management account that they recommend for accounts with assets over $5,000. These accounts offer some added "bells and whistles" that are ideal for people attempting to simplify their money management. These accounts hold a broad variety of investment alternatives such as stocks, bonds, mutual funds, annuities, and unit trusts. And they usually have some sort of interest-bearing checking or money market account associated with them. This feature allows fast access to your investment money should you need it while allowing your emergency money to draw a competitive rate of return.

Other services that may be included:

- A debit card
- Unlimited check-writing privileges
- Borrowing on margin*
- Internet services*
- Electronic bill payment services*
- Summary statements of capital gains and loss*

Most full-service firms charge an annual fee for an asset management account. You will want to check with your financial adviser to find out the costs.

---

*May sometimes carry additional charges.

At most full-service firms you are still able to hold assets in a standard personal account. This type of account is different from the premier account that I just described in that it is designed with little or no frills. This type of account is used by the newer investor who doesn't yet have the assets to qualify for the premier account or doesn't anticipate needing any additional services.

IRAs.   Under the tax law changes of 1997, there are now three primary types of individual retirement accounts (IRAs): the Traditional IRA, the Roth IRA, and the Education IRA.

The *Traditional IRA* is the standard retirement account that you are probably familiar with. If you choose to fund money into this type of account, you may deposit up to $2,000 for yourself (if you have had earned income of at least $2,000), and you may also invest $2,000 for your spouse. With the Traditional IRA you are allowed to deduct these contributions from your adjusted gross income in the year in which you make the deposit. Unfortunately, when you begin to withdraw this money, you will be taxed at your ordinary tax bracket at that time.

The *Roth IRA* was created under the Taxpayer Relief Act of 1997. It allows you to invest up to the same $2,000 but with no tax deduction. With the Roth IRA, the benefit comes when you begin to withdraw the money to fund your retirement years. The income you withdraw from your Roth IRA is totally tax exempt!

Both Traditional and Roth IRAs carry the potential for penalties of 10 percent for any premature withdrawals made before age 59½. There are some exceptions to this rule, so please consult a qualified tax consultant for more information.

The *Education IRA* also has income limits, but it provides a wonderful way to accumulate a portion of the future savings that you may need to pay for higher education. The Education IRA allows you to deposit $500 per child into an IRA, and this money will grow on a tax-deferred basis. If it is used to fund your child's education, the future value can be withdrawn tax free.

Be aware that the level of your current income affects whether you can participate in or benefit from any of these IRAs.

One last note regarding IRAs: As the popularity of 401(k) plans has grown, people are retiring with enormous balances in their company-sponsored retirement plans. Most people have been placing a portion of their income into these plans for years and, with the recent rise in the stock market, the value of these accounts has become very significant. When you retire, you will often be faced with some important decisions regarding what you should do with your 401(k) rollover. Many investors are rolling these accounts into a Traditional IRA so they can increase the number of their investment options and can exercise more control over their investment management.

If you choose to roll your 401(k) plan to an investment company, by all means feel free to ask it for a sample 401(k) rollover proposal and look at the recommendations. Make sure that how the company wants to invest your money suits you.

CONCLUSION

I conclude with an example of a couple who have worked with their financial adviser to achieve their financial goals. In October 1993 I was given the chance to create a financial plan for them as new customers. Each partner had a very successful career and both had been disciplined about saving and investing for their future, but they had never had anyone offer to do a complete financial review. They had 15 years to wait before retirement and were committed to achieving their goal of financial independence by age 65.

We gathered all the data; we determined what it would take to make them feel financially independent at retirement; we established their level of risk tolerance; and we created an appropriate asset allocation for them. Finally, we reviewed their budget and detailed a systematic investment plan for the exact amount of money that would be necessary to give them the opportunity to reach their financial goals.

Their plan was specific. The written plan stated an anticipated rate of return. It outlined the exact dollar amount they needed to save on a monthly basis, and it listed the couple's financial goals in specific future dollar amounts.

Five and one-half years later, this couple had far exceeded their goal for saving. They are still several years away from retirement, and the future looks very bright.

What did they do right? They made wise choices. They made the effort to find a financial adviser they felt could help them achieve their future goals. Then they stuck to the plan. They didn't jump from one investment strategy to the next. They held for the long term. They held up their end of the bargain and were diligent in having money drafted from their check-

The wheelbarrow was invented in the 1200s and cut the amount of labor in half. Your financial adviser is like a wheelbarrow.

ing account on a regular basis. And they monitored the plan on a regular basis. They knew what they were doing. The details to their success are outlined in Case Study 4 on page 252.

It is no accident that this couple is well on their way to reaching their financial goals.

Let's Get Real: Case Studies

> "As a 30-year-old single female, making a financial budget and plan was the best decision I could have made. It was a positive step toward retirement. It teaches me self-discipline, to save every month, and to watch how my money is spent and saved."
>
> **Jill Lewis,** 36
> *Kennett, Missouri*

> "The best advice we ever received was to institute a systematic savings and investment program. After designing the concept, we put it in written form. Then we matched our investment purchases with our level of comfort pertaining to risk. We wish that we had gotten this organized and systematic a few years earlier. Just as one cannot build a house without a blueprint, you cannot build a secure financial future without a written plan. Set your goal. Write your plan on paper, then work from your paper. This is the advice I would give anyone building for retirement."
>
> **Don and Karen Hudson,** 58 and 48
> *Jonesboro, Arkansas*

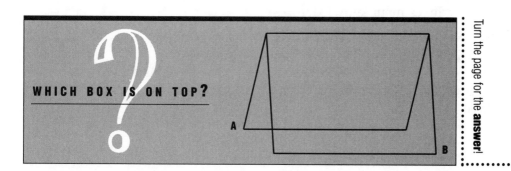

WHICH BOX IS ON TOP?

A

B

Turn the page for the **answer!**

If you stare at this figure long enough, you'll see the images swap places. At first it may appear that A is on top, but then B jumps out at you.

The case studies in this chapter work in much the same way. By giving you the opportunity to explore exactly how other people have chosen to map out their financial plan, you will have a better idea of how to manage your own money.

The beauty of the process is that the more you learn, the more you will be in control.

> **"**We didn't start our saving program soon enough. It can be said that it is all relative, because there wasn't much to start with. Nevertheless, the sooner people start, the better their financial status is at retirement.**"**
> **M.S.F.,** 55
> *Dallas, Texas*

Let's look at some sample financial plans. Although they are provided for illustrative purposes only, you should find them useful whether you're preparing your own plan and/or working with an adviser.

When you begin to create your personal financial plan, it's important to outline the necessary assumptions and policy statements. This section of your plan will restate the following facts about you:

- Age
- Employment
- Current income
- Level of risk tolerance and investment style
- Anticipated returns and contingency returns
- Current savings
- Investment knowledge

Next, follow these seven steps:

Step 1: Prepare your money mission statement.

Step 2: Gather your data, a recap of all your debts and assets. In this section, highlight your current asset allocation and your current budget (see Chapter 2).

Step 3: Establish and write your quantified goals (see Chapter 3).

Step 4: Evaluate the information (see Chapter 4).

Step 5: Develop a plan (see Chapter 4).

Step 6: Implement your plan. This is often the most difficult step because it involves taking action, and that can be uncomfortable.

Step 7: Monitor and update your plan. This is the most overlooked aspect of planning. Markets move and the economy changes, but you could easily get left behind if you don't monitor your progress.

The six mathematical steps for developing your plan are these:

1. After you have determined your current income need, you must be able to estimate how much future income you may need during the first year of retirement. To do this, choose an inflation rate (I use 3 percent) and then inflate your current income for the number of years until you plan to retire to get an estimated future income need.

2. Once you know your estimated future income need, then subtract any future income that you expect to receive during your retirement years. Future income might include pension income, Social Security income, and income from rental properties, royalties, part-time jobs, or any other source of earned income. However, this section **does not** include any investment income because you are attempting to determine exactly how much additional investment income you will need to supplement your pension and Social Security.

3. Now that you have determined the supplemental income you'll need, you must determine exactly how much money you'll need to accumulate to provide you with this supplemental income. As discussed from the beginning of this book, this is the calculation that will answer the question: "Where do I need to be?" Once you figure out this number, you'll know exactly how much money you'll need. What a great day!

This calculation is accomplished by dividing the expected supplemental income need by a "systematic withdrawal rate"—an important factor in establishing how much money you need to accumulate.

To help you determine your systematic withdrawal rate, let's look at it in a little more detail. To make it simpler, assume a client only needs $6,000 of additional supplemental income:

$6,000 Supplemental income needed
÷ 6% Systematic withdrawal rate
= $100,000 Future principal needed

In other words, if this person could accumulate a nest egg of $100,000 and earn 6 percent on that nest egg, that person should have the necessary $6,000 of supplemental income he or she needs.

Even if you don't totally understand the mathematics, you can usually understand the reverse of the math.

A $100,000 investment
Earning 6% interest
Generates $6,000 in income per year

This theory assumes you don't want to touch any principal during your lifetime. The 6 percent systematic withdrawal rate that is shown is the default rate that I use. The higher the systematic withdrawal rate, the lower the amount a client will need to accumulate. Conversely, the lower the systematic withdrawal rate, the less risk the client has for not achieving the necessary rate of return.

For example, if a client needs $10,000 in additional income:

Income needed	$ 10,000	$ 10,000	$ 10,000
Systematic withdrawal rate	4%	6%	8%
Quantitative need	$250,000	$166,666	$125,000

As you can see, the 4 percent systematic withdrawal rate requires a larger nest egg than the 8 percent systematic withdrawal rate.

You'll want to set your systematic withdrawal rate based on a percentage of something lower than your anticipated rate of return. If you plan to keep all of your money in savings accounts and CDs that are anticipated to earn 5.5 percent, you may want to use a 3 percent systematic withdrawal rate.

If you are a moderate investor and plan to use a blend of stocks and bonds with an 8 percent anticipated return, you may want to set a 5 percent systematic withdrawal rate.

If you are a fairly aggressive investor who plans to continue to hold a large portion of your asset allocation in stocks and you anticipate a 10 to 12 percent return, then you may use a 7 to 8 percent systematic withdrawal rate.

The systematic withdrawal rate is one of the keys to determining your future needs. You should be confident that you will be able to earn at least as much as you are taking out, and I encourage you to attempt to earn more than you expect to withdraw so that your income can actually grow to help you keep up with inflation.

4. Once you know how much money you need to accumulate, you need to calculate how you will get there. Step 4 calculates how much your current assets will be worth in the future. This is a simple future value calculation: you take the value of your current assets and inflate them based

on your anticipated rate of return (4%, 6%, 8%, 10%, 12%, etc.) for the appropriate number of years. To calculate this number you can use a financial calculator or you may turn to Appendix A and use the Inflation and Future Value Calculator. As an example of using the calculator, if you have current assets of $25,000 today and you are planning to retire in 40 years:

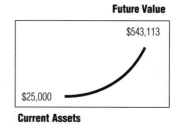

Future Value

$543,113

$25,000

Current Assets

Current assets	$25,000
Anticipated rate of return	8%
40-year factor per $1,000	$21,724.52
Times 25 (because you have $25,000 today) = $543,113	

5. If your current assets won't grow to a balance that will help you meet your supplemental income needs, then you have a shortfall. The amount of your shortfall is calculated by writing down your future accumulation need and subtracting the estimated future value of your current assets.

For example: If you know you need to accumulate a total nest egg of $2,500,000 over the next 40 years and we know you have an estimated future value of $543,113, then:

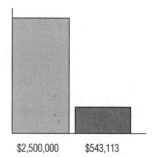

$2,500,000 $543,113

Estimated future need:	$2,500,000
Minus the estimated future value:	$543,113
Leaves a shortfall of:	$1,956,887

6. The final step allows you to calculate how much money you will need to save on an annual or monthly basis to fill in the gap between what you expect to have and what you expect to need. For example, if we know you have a shortfall of $1,956,887 and still have 40 years to fill in that gap, then you can turn to Appendix B to determine approximately what you should be saving and investing every month. In this case, assuming a 10 percent annual return over 40 years, you would need to save and invest $307.09 per month to fund your retirement goal.

Anticipated return	10%
For 40 years you would need to save	$0.157 per month for every $1,000 needed
Multiply $0.157 by 1,956 =	$307.09 per month

CASE STUDY 1 *Lauren Skyler*

Assumptions and policy statement for Lauren Skyler

- 36 years old—single
- Counselor/Social worker
- Current income $30,000 per year
- Plans to retire at age 65
- Considers herself a moderate investor
- Would like to anticipate an average total return of 10 percent, but will run a contingency plan at 8 percent
- Is currently saving $100 per month from current income
- Is very good with numbers but is a relatively new investor

Step 1: Money Mission Statement

"I am committed to creating a written financial plan that will allow me to reach my future financial goals."

Step 2: Gather Data

Total debts	Home: $5,000 left; car $5,000 left
Total cash	$1,200
Total CDs	$0
Total stocks	$18,836
Total	$20,036

Current Asset Allocation

Cash $1,200

Stocks $18,836

Lauren Skyler has an annual income of $30,000 per year or $2,500 per month.

She works within a fairly set budget (shown in Figure 12.1) and hopes that her income will increase over time as she adds more people to her current counseling schedule.

FIGURE 12.1   *Lauren Skyler's Budget*

Savings	100	Homeowners Insurance	28
Retirement Savings/401(k)		Health Insurance	80
		Life Insurance	
Mortgage	162	Disability	
Electric Utilities	114		
Gas Utility		Doctors	40
Telephone	35	Dentists	
Water		Eyeglasses	
Cable	44	Drugs	
Home Maintenance		Household Help	
Lawn Maintenance		Dry Cleaning	
Real Estate Taxes		Beauty Salon/Barber	
Personal Property Taxes		Pets/Vets	
		Subscriptions	
Car Payment	200	Florists	
Car Insurance	77	Gifts	167
Gasoline	50		
Car Maintenance		Church Donations	200
		Community Donations	5
Food	40	Art and Dance	
Toiletries			
Clothing	40	CPA	
Eating Out	35	Professional Dues	
Visa/Amex/MasterCard/Loans		Extra Payment on Home	100
Vacations		Other—Club Dues/Car Phone	68
Childcare/Dependent Care		Other	8
Tuition			
		Monthly Total	**1,593**

Step 3: Written Goals

Goal 1.   Develop a written plan of action.

Goal 2.   Continue to save $100 a month and continue to pay the extra $100 a month to pay off my mortgage.

Goal 3.   When able, increase the systematic investment deposits from $100 a month to $200 a month.

Goal 4.   Increase my emergency funds to $4,500.

Steps 4 and 5: Evaluate the Information and Develop a Plan

Lauren evaluates the information using the following process:

(a) Using a current pretax figure of $30,000, she has inflated that number at a 3 percent inflation rate for 29 years to realize she could need $70,697.10 to have the same standard of living in her first year of retirement.

Current income	$30,000
Anticipated rate of inflation	3%
29-year factor per $1,000	$2,356.57
Times 30 (because she has $30,000 today) =	$70,697.10

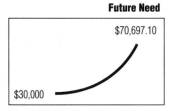

Future Need

$70,697.10

$30,000

Current Income

(b) Therefore:

Future value of income needed:	$70,697
Minus projected pension:	None
Minus projected Social Security:	$20,000
Minus other income:	None
Total supplemental income needed from investments:	$50,697

(c) Now that we have determined Lauren's needed income, the third step is determining how much principal she will need to accumulate to provide her with future income. This is accomplished by dividing the amount of future income she expects to need ($50,697) by the systematic withdrawal rate (the rate at which she expects to withdrawal the money on a regular basis). In this example we are using a 6 percent systematic withdrawal rate (see the explanation of how to arrive at the systematic withdrawal rate on page 235). So:

$50,697	Future income needed
Divided by 6%	Systematic withdrawal plan
$844,950	Future principal needed

This means Lauren needs to accumulate a total of $844,950 to reach her future goals.

(d) Assuming her current assets of $20,036 are able to grow at an average after-tax annual growth rate of 10 percent over the next 29 years, her current assets should grow to $317,832.93.

Current assets	$20,036
Anticipated rate of return	10%
29-year factor per $1,000	$15,863.09
Times 20 (because she has $20,000 today) =	$317,261

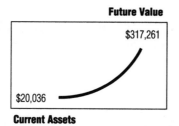

Future Value

$317,261

$20,036

Current Assets

(e) We know she has an estimated future need of $844,950
Minus the estimated future value of $317,261
Which leaves a future shortfall of $527,689

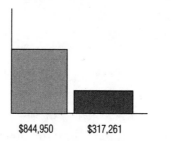

$844,950 $317,261

(f) If Lauren can earn an average annual rate of return of 10 percent per year for 29 years, she will need to save and invest roughly $256.65 per month to fill in that shortfall.

Anticipated return   10%
For 29 years
She would need to save $0.487 per month for every $1,000 needed
Multiply $0.487 by 527 = $256.65 per month

(Her contingency plan assumes an 8 percent return on current investments and an 8 percent return on additional investment contributions. With these assumptions, Lauren would need to save $479.02 a month to reach the same goal.)

Step 6: Implement the Plan

Lauren has been an avid saver for the last five years. She has constructed a well-defined budget that allows her to save $100 for her retirement and $100 a month to make additional payments on her home. Paying off her home is one of Lauren's favorite goals. It gives her a sense of permanence and accomplishment. As a single woman, she realizes she may not have anyone else to depend on for her retirement income. Therefore, she is committed to planning for a secure retirement future. She is a conscientious spender and plans carefully for extras. She credits her ability to budget to her family and hopes that if she ever has children, she will teach them the value of a dollar as well.

Step 7: Monitor the Plan

Review progress in 12 months.

CASE STUDY 2   L. J. and Lee Brooks

Assumptions and policy statement for L.J. and Lee Brooks

- L.J. is 66 and Lee is 62.
- He is retired as Director of Missions for a local church in the state of Colorado. Both work part-time for pleasure.
- Current income is $54,000 per year.
- Consider themselves ultraconservative investors
- Would like to anticipate an average total return of 4 percent
- Are currently saving $800 a month from current income
- Consider themselves knowledgeable about savings accounts and CDs

Step 1: Money Mission Statement

"We have worked all of our lives to help other people. Money has been a by-product of that work. We will continue to use our financial resources to take care of ourselves and to help others."

Step 2: Gather Data

Total debts	None
Total cash	$143,500
Total CDs	$131,152
Total stocks	$9,100
Total	$283,752

Current Allocation

Stocks $9,100
Cash $143,500
CDs $131,152

FIGURE 12.2 *L.J. and Lee Brooks's Budget*

Savings	800	Homeowners Insurance	54
Retirement Savings/401(k)		Health Insurance	379
		Life Insurance	
Mortgage		Disability	
Electric Utilities	100		
Gas Utility		Doctors	200
Telephone	30	Dentists	50
Water		Eyeglasses	20
Cable	32	Drugs	80
Home Maintenance	100	Household Help	
Lawn Maintenance	15	Dry Cleaning	10
Real Estate Taxes	100	Beauty Salon/Barber	15
Personal Property Taxes	10	Pets/Vets	10
		Subscriptions	10
Car Payment		Florists	
Car Insurance	80	Gifts	220
Gasoline	40		
Car Maintenance	10	Church Donations	450
		Community Donations	
Food	200	Art and Dance	
Toiletries			
Clothing		CPA	8
Eating Out	180	Professional Dues	
Visa/Amex/MasterCard/Loans		Miscellaneous/Termite Control	8
Vacations	100	Other—Club Dues/Car Phone	3
Childcare/Dependent Care		Other	
Tuition			
		Monthly Total	**3,314**

Their budget (shown in Figure 12.2) totals $3,314 per month. This figure includes $800 going into their savings accounts and $450 a month that is given away.

The best thing this couple has done is to remain totally debt free. If they couldn't afford to buy it, they waited. They have entered their retirement years with a home that is completely paid for and absolutely no consumer debt.

Step 3: Set Written Goals

Goal 1. Safety of principal

Goal 2. Continue reinvestment of interest income

Goal 3. Continue saving $800 a month while working part-time

Steps 4 and 5: Evaluate the Information and Develop a Plan

After reviewing their budget and income, we can see that L.J. and Lee have invested their nest egg in an appropriate manner. They could add a few more growth items to their overall portfolio, but with an ultraconservative level of risk tolerance, there's no real reason to take on any additional risk. This couple decides to continue down their current path.

This couple's current monthly budget includes an $800 monthly deposit into savings. In order to more accurately run their financial plan, we will reduce their monthly budget of $3,314 by $800 to reflect their actual spending of $2,514 per month. This is, of course, a post-tax number, so we will adjust to $43,000 for pretax income needed.

(a) Using a current pretax figure of $43,000, I have inflated that number at a 3 percent inflation rate for one year to realize they need $44,290 to have the same standard of living in their first year of retirement.

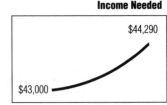

Income Needed

Current income need	$43,000
Anticipated rate of inflation	3%
1-year factor per $1,000	$1,030
Times 43 (because they have almost $43,000 today) =	$44,290

Current Pretax Income

(b) Therefore:

Future value of income needed:	$44,290
Minus projected pension:	$36,432

Minus projected Social Security: None
(not covered because of their service in the church)
Minus other income: $17,600
(part-time work)
Total supplemental income needed from investments: –$9,742

Because this couple currently has more income than they require to live today, they decide to test their financial plan using a "what-if" assumption of stopping part-time work and not receiving the additional $17,600 of income.

Under this assumption:

Future value of income needed: $44,290
Minus projected pension: $36,432
Minus projected Social Security: None
Minus other income: None
Total supplemental income needed from investments: $7,858

(c) Now that we have determined the income they need, the third step is determining how much principal they will need to provide them with their future income. This is accomplished by dividing the amount of future income they expect to need ($7,858) by the systematic withdrawal rate. In this example we are using a 3 percent systematic withdrawal rate because of the couple's ultraconservative risk tolerance. So:

$7,858   Additional supplemental income needed
Divided by 3%   Systematic withdrawal rate
$261,933   Total future value needed to reach their goals

This means L.J. and Lee might need to accumulate a total of $261,933 to reach their future goals.

(d) In one year, using an average after-tax return of 4 percent, their current assets would grow from $283,752 to $294,320.

Current assets $283,752
Anticipated rate of return   4%
1-year factor per $1,000 $1,040
Times 283 (because they have
   over $283,000 today) = $294,320

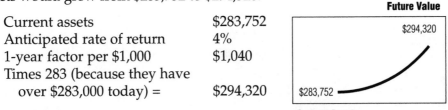

Future Value

$294,320

$283,752

Current Assets

(e) This is the ideal situation, referred to as a *negative shortfall* or surplus. This couple has accumulated more money than they require to fund their supplemental retirement income needs.

They have a future need of: $261,933
They have an estimated future value of: $294,320
This leaves a surplus of: $ 32,387

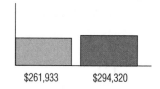

$261,933 $294,320

(f) This couple has a surplus and thus don't require any additional payments.

Step 6: Implement the Plan

This retired couple has already implemented a terrific investment strategy that they plan to stick with.

Step 7: Monitor the Plan

Review progress in 12 months.

The best part of this success story is the fact that even though they have entered their retirement years, they are still saving an average of $800 per month.

NOTE:
There are many ways to accomplish financial independence. One is to work in a profession or for a company that provides a pension income, as this couple has done. Another is to keep your expenses well within your budget, as this couple has done. And, finally, save on a monthly system-atic basis to accumulate additional financial assets, which they have been able to do over the last five to ten years.

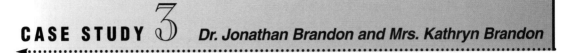

CASE STUDY 3   *Dr. Jonathan Brandon and Mrs. Kathryn Brandon*

Assumptions and policy statement for Dr. Jonathan Brandon and Mrs. Kathryn Brandon

- Jonathan is 35 years old; Kathryn is 33.
- He is a physician; she is a homemaker.
- Current income is $156,000 per year; annual bonuses vary from $12,000 to $25,000.
- He plans to retire at 62.
- Fairly aggressive investor
- Would like to anticipate an average total return of 10 percent but will run a contingency plan at 8 percent
- Is currently saving whenever a surplus becomes available
- Both cooperate to make investment decisions.

Step 1: Money Mission Statement

"We want to change from our current investment approach to a proactive written investment plan. We want a consistent plan that will allow us to become debt free, plan for our children's education, and accumulate an adequate net worth to feel financially secure throughout our retirement years."

Step 2: Gather Data

Current Allocation

Cash $14,357

Stocks $ 116,410

Total debts	Home—$110,000
Total cash	$14,357
Total CDs	$0
Total stocks	$116,410
Total	$130,767

Based on their $156,000 annual income, the Brandons have a regular monthly pretax income of $13,000 ($156,000 divided by 12 equals $13,000 per month). Their quarterly bonuses vary.

Before they created their written financial plan, the only systematic savings were Mrs. Brandon's $166 monthly IRA deposit and the $100 deposits for their children's college education funds.

FIGURE 12.3   *Budget for Dr. and Mrs. Brandon*

Savings			Homeowners Insurance	115
Retirement Savings/401(k)	166		Health Insurance	
			Life Insurance	85
Mortgage	1660		Disability	
Electric Utilities	160			
Gas Utility	75		Doctors	316
Telephone	95		Dentists	
Water			Eyeglasses	
Cable	50		Drugs	
Home Maintenance	200		Household Help	440
Lawn Maintenance	110		Dry Cleaning	
Real Estate Taxes			Beauty Salon/Barber	25
Personal Property Taxes	125		Pets/Vets	
			Subscriptions	
Car Payment			Florists	25
Car Insurance	89		Gifts	300
Gasoline	70			
Car Maintenance	100		Church Donations	1020
			Community Donations	42
Food	850		Art and Dance	
Toiletries				
Clothing	400		CPA	25
Eating Out	250		Cell Phone	60
Visa/Amex/MasterCard/Loans			Home Security	28
Vacations	400		Other—Club Dues	197
Childcare/Dependent Care	220		Other—Internet	15
Tuition				
			Monthly Total	**7,713**

Step 3: Written Goals

Goal 1. Develop a written financial plan that outlines specific future financial goals.

Goal 2. Set aside specific amounts of money each month to fund each of these goals.

Goal 3. Become more knowledgeable and confident so the daily fluctuations in the markets don't influence our investment decisions.

Goal 4. Become totally debt free within five years.

Steps 4 and 5: Evaluate the Information and Develop a Plan

The gathered information was run through several future value calculations and the following plan was developed. After reviewing their budget, income, and current investment approach, it was determined that the Brandon's would like to retire with a monthly income equivalent to $10,000 in today's money.

(a) Using a current pretax figure of $120,000 (12 months times $10,000), I've inflated that number at a 3 percent inflation rate for 27 years to realize they need $266,554.80 to have the same standard of living in their first year of retirement.

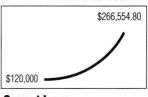

Income Needed

$266,554.80

$120,000

Current Income

Current income needed	$120,000
Anticipated rate of inflation	3%
27-year factor per $1,000	$2,221.29
Times 120 (because they have $120,000 today) =	$266,554.80

(b) This couple has decided not to include any future Social Security income into these projections. Therefore:

Future value of income needed:	$266,554
Minus projected pension:	None
Minus projected Social Security:	None
Minus other income:	None
Total supplemental income needed from investments:	$266,554

(c) Now that we have determined the income needed, the third step is determining how much principal they will need to accumulate to provide them with their future income. This is accomplished by dividing the amount of future income they expect to need ($273,630.94) by the systematic withdrawal rate. In this example we are using a 6 percent systematic withdrawal rate. So:

$266,554	Future supplemental income needed
Divided by 6%	Systematic withdrawal rate
$4,442,556	Future value of assets needed to reach their future goals

This means Dr. and Mrs. Brandon might need to accumulate a total of $4,442,556 to reach their future goals.

(d) Assuming their current assets of $130,767 are able to grow at an average after-tax annual growth rate of 10 percent over the next 27 years, their current assets should grow to $1,704,298:

Current assets	$130,767
Anticipated rate of return	10%
27-year multiplier per $1,000	$13,109.99
Times 130 (because they have over $130,000 today) = $1,704,298	

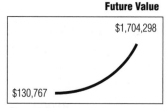

Future Value

$1,704,298

$130,767

Current Assets

(e) We know they have an estimated future need of $4,442,556
Minus the estimated future value of $1,704,298
Which leaves a future shortfall of $2,738,258

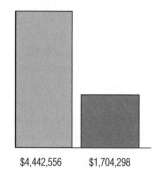

$4,442,556 $1,704,298

(f) If they can earn an average annual rate of return of 10 percent per year for 27 years, they will need to save and invest $19,812 a year, or roughly $1,651 a month, to fill in that shortfall.

Anticipated return	10.00%
For 27 years	
They would need to save	$0.603
Multiply $0.603 by 2,738	$1,651 per month

NOTE:

When we first met, Dr. Brandon wanted to retire at 55. In order to retire in 20 years rather than 27 years, the couple would have had to save $42,894 a year. By waiting until age 62, that number dropped to the more reasonable $19,812; and if they decided to wait until he was 65, that number would drop to $13,623! Having a realistic outlook for the number of years you will need to work to reach your future retirement goals is a very important part of your financial plan.

This couple is a clear example of how many affluent Americans work hard for years to begin to accumulate a nest egg. The problem is that the Brandons had no written plan of action. They were saving money, but they considered themselves to be "reactive" investors. They reacted to the markets and made investments based on the latest investment tip that was swirling through the news media at the time. They felt that they were always one step behind everyone else, and more than anything else, they wanted to organize their finances and take some positive steps toward becoming "proactive" investors.

Once they had this plan in hand and realized that all it should take was a $2,000 systematic deposit each month, Mrs. Brandon looked straight at me and with a gleam in her eye said, "I can do that!" I heard the confidence in her voice, but I felt the sense of relief coming from her heart. These are the moments I enjoy most about creating financial plans.

Step 6: Implement the Plan

By taking the time to create a money mission statement and moving through the additional steps necessary to create a written financial plan, the Brandons believe they have taken a gigantic leap toward financial independence. They have already taken specific actions to implement four specific systematic investment plans that will allow them to fully fund their investment goals. In addition, they have very strong feelings about paying off their home. Mrs. Brandon is very good with numbers and had determined that if they make one additional payment of $1,600 per quarter, they can pay off their mortgage within five years.

In addition to the retirement plan, they are also regularly funding college education accounts for their children.

We have also discussed working to increase their emergency funds/cash holdings from the current $14,357 to $30,000, which would give them almost four months of their monthly expenses.

Step 7: Monitor the Plan

Review progress in 12 months.

CASE STUDY 4   *Ted and Rita Rowell*

Assumptions and policy statement for Ted and Rita Rowell.

- Ted is 60; Rita is 55
- He is a dentist; she is a personal trainer.
- Current income is $120,000 per year.
- He plans to retire at age 65.
- Moderate risk tolerance
- Would like to anticipate an average total return of 8 percent but will run a contingency plan at 6 percent
- Currently saving $1,100 per month
- Both work together to make investment decisions.

Step 1: Money Mission Statement

"Our money should only be viewed as the vehicle for planning for our future. We want to take as much emotion out of the planning process as possible and use our written plan as our guide."

Step 2: Gather Data

Total debts	Home—$0, Other—$0
Total cash	$9,117
Total bonds	$309,930
Total stocks	$452,206
Total	$771,254

Current Allocation

Cash $9,117
Stocks $452,206
Bonds $309,930

The Rowells have estimated they will need a monthly pretax income equivalent to $6,560.

Step 3: Set Written Goals

Goal 1. Develop a written financial plan, which outlines specific future financial goals.

Goal 2. Keep our current asset allocation in line with our risk tolerance.

FIGURE 12.4   *Budget for Ted and Rita Rowell*

Savings		Homeowners Insurance	160
Retirement Savings/401(k)		Health Insurance	125
		Life Insurance	282
Mortgage		Disability	
Electric Utilities	175		
Gas Utility	75	Doctors	100
Telephone	30	Dentists	
Water		Eyeglasses	10
Cable	37	Drugs	75
Home Maintenance	100	Household Help	200
Lawn Maintenance	175	Dry Cleaning	100
Real Estate Taxes	115	Beauty Salon/Barber	100
Personal Property Taxes	60	Pets/Vets	
		Subscriptions	10
Car Payment		Florists	30
Car Insurance	125	Gifts	250
Gasoline	200		
Car Maintenance	20	Church Donations	
		Community Donations	
Food	800	Recreation	150
Toiletries			
Clothing		CPA	30
Eating Out	300	Cell Phone	100
Visa/Amex/MasterCard/Loans		Home Security	22
Vacations	250	Other—Club Dues	
Childcare/Dependent Care		Other—Internet	20
Tuition			
		Monthly Total	**4,226**

Goal 3.   Continue to use the regular systematic investment plans that we started in 1993.

Goal 4.   Allow Ted to be able to retire fully within five years.

Steps 4 and 5: Evaluate the Information and Develop a Plan

The gathered information was run through several future value calculations and a plan was developed.

After reviewing their budget, income, and current investment approach, they would like to retire with a monthly income equivalent to $6,560 in today's money.

(a) Using a current pretax figure of $78,720 per year, I have inflated that number at a 3 percent inflation rate for five years to realize they might need $91,582 to have the same standard of living in their first year of retirement.

Income Needed

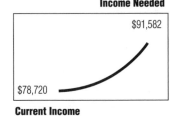

Current income needed	$78,720
Anticipated rate of inflation	3%
5-year multiplier per $1,000	$1,159.27
Times 79 (because they need almost $79,000 today) =	$91,582

(b) This couple has estimated they will qualify for $13,500 of Social Security income when he is ready to retire. She will still be too young to collect Social Security income in five years.

Therefore:

Future value of income needed:	$91,582
Minus projected pension:	None
Minus projected Social Security:	$13,500
Minus other income:	$27,000 (from her work)
Total supplemental income needed from investments:	$51,082

(c) Now that we have determined the income needed, the third step is determining how much principal they will need to accumulate to provide them with their future income. This is accomplished by dividing the amount of future income they expect to need ($51,082) by the systematic withdrawal rate. In this example we are using a 6 percent systematic withdrawal rate. So:

$51,082	Supplemental income needed from investments
Divided by 6%	Systematic withdrawal rate
$851,366	Future value of financial assets needed to reach their goals

This means Ted and Rita might need to accumulate a total of $851,366 to reach their future goals.

(d) Assuming their current assets of $771,254.13 are able to grow at an average after-tax annual growth rate of 6 percent over the next five years, their current assets should grow to $1,031,775.

Current assets $771,254

Anticipated rate of return   6%

5-year multiplier per $1,000 $1,338.23

Times 771 (because they have over
$771,000 today) = $1,031,775

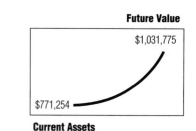

Future Value

$1,031,775

$771,254

Current Assets

(e) We know they have an estimated
      future need of $851,366

Minus the estimated future value of $1,031,775

Which leaves a future surplus of $180,409

$851,366 $1,031,775

(f) Even though their financial plan reflects that they don't require additional contributions, they are so used to the systematic withdrawals that they plan to continue making the
monthly deposits until they are ready to retire. They are currently adding $525 every month to bond investments and $575
every month to a blue chip stock mutual fund.

Step 6: Implement the Plan

This plan was originally designed on October 12, 1993. Some changes oc-
curred in the couple's life, and they realized that Ted's retirement was
quickly approaching. They decided it was time to prepare for a more secure financial future, so they agreed that they would do whatever it took
to come up with the $1,100 a month that was estimated it would take to
fund their retirement goal.

    They also sold a lake house property that they had inherited, which
generated an additional $200,000 deposit into their plan.

Step 7: Monitor the Plan

Review progress in 12 months.

NOTE:
The Rowells were committed to their financial plan, which was implemented in October 1993. The
year 1994 was a difficult one for both stocks and bonds. While it was not easy to keep a long-term
perspective as the value of their investments were declining, their patience has paid off. This is a
wonderful example of mapping out a strategy and sticking to it.

CASE STUDY 5   *Steve and Jill McKinney*

Assumptions and policy statement for Steve and Jill McKinney

- They are both 65.
- He is retiring as the chief financial officer (CFO) of a well-known public company. His wife is a consultant for a major advertising agency.
- Their last year's income was $250,000, including salary and bonuses.
- Moderate risk tolerance
- They would like to anticipate an average total return of 8 percent but will run a contingency plan at 6 percent
- While he is knowledgeable about the various markets, his wife has had more interest in managing their money and is therefore the primary decision maker.
- Steve has accumulated $1.5 million in his company's 401(k) plan primarily as the result of the performance of the company's stock. A large portion of his 401(k) is held in company stock. Both Steve and Jill are concerned about their lack of diversification.
- Jill has recently received a lump sum cash inheritance of $750,000 from her family.
- The McKinneys have no will and no estate plan.
- Until now they have never had a written financial plan. They have accumulated a large sum of assets and with the addition of the inheritance, they are beginning to feel out of control.
- They recently cashed in company stock options and as a result have received an additional $250,000 in cash. At the same time, Steve is still holding $500,000 of highly appreciated company stock in his lockbox.

This is a wonderful example of being in the right place at the right time. But now that they are retiring, Steve and Jill want to take the assets they have accumulated and invest that money in a manner that will allow them to spend the rest of their retirement years worrying less and enjoying life more. In fact, they have set that as their money mission statement.

Step 1: Money Mission Statement

"Worry less. Enjoy life more!"

Step 2: Gather Data

Current Allocation

CDs $425,000

Cash $1,100,000

Stocks $2,000,000

Total debts	Lake house mortgage $275,000
Total cash	$1,100,000
Total CDs	$425,000
Total stocks	$2,000,000
Total	$3,525,000

The McKinneys are used to a $250,000 pretax income and in the last few years have been able to save a portion of that income.

While Steve and Jill had some idea of how much money they were spending on a monthly basis, they had never actually created a written monthly budget. But after reviewing their expenses and placing them into the proper budget categories, they decided they could live comfortably on a pretax monthly income of $15,000, or $180,000 a year.

Taking the time to create a simple budget has made both Steve and Jill that much more excited about leaving nine-hour workdays behind. Because they have a realistic understanding of how much income they want and need, they were able to review their current assets and determine that $3,525,000 should be more than enough principal to provide them with their retirement income.

Step 3: Written Goals

Goal 1.   Develop a written financial plan that will allow us to gain control over our large financial asset base.

Goal 2.   Create a new asset allocation model that will allow us to feel more comfortable with our investment holdings.

Goal 3.   Roll over Steve's 401(k) plan to an IRA so we can have increased flexibility in managing our assets.

Goal 4.   Hire a tax attorney to write a will and then develop our estate plan.

Goal 5.   Consider buying life insurance to defray some of the expected costs of estate taxes.

FIGURE 12.5　*Budget for the McKinneys*

Savings			Homeowners Insurance	295
Retirement Savings/401(k)			Health Insurance	
			Life Insurance	
Mortgage			Disability	
Lake House Mortgage and Fees	1875			
Electric Utilities	450		Doctors	50
Gas Utility	125		Dentists	20
Telephone	225		Eyeglasses	20
Water			Drugs	50
Cable	100		Household Help	400
Home Maintenance	250		Dry Cleaning	100
Lawn Maintenance	125		Beauty Salon/Barber	50
Real Estate Taxes	400		Pets/Vets	25
Personal Property Taxes	50		Subscriptions	25
			Florists	50
Car Payment	500		Gifts	400
Car Insurance	150			
Gasoline	110		Church Donations	250
Car Maintenance	100		Community Donations	150
			Art and Dance	
Food	650			
Toiletries			CPA	50
Clothing	400		Cell Phone	100
Eating Out	650		Home Security	45
Visa/Amex/MasterCard/Loans			Other–Club Dues	125
Vacations	400		Other–Internet	25
Childcare/Dependent Care				
Tuition				
			Monthly Total	**8,790**

Steps 4 and 5: Evaluate the Information and Develop a Plan

The McKinneys are in a situation that allows them freedom from a strict budget. But the first step was to review their current spending habits and be assured that their retirement income (while definitely lower than the $250,000 they had earned while both were employed) would be more than acceptable. They determined that they could easily work within a $15,000 per month amount, which will give them an estimated pretax income of $180,000 a year.

(a) Because this couple is retiring in the next few weeks, there is no need to inflate their pretax income of $180,000 a year.

Estimated Income Needed

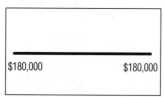

(b) This couple has decided to include any future Social Security income into their projections, assuming the 1998 monthly benefit of $2,013 for a couple. They are also able to include Steve's anticipated $75,000 pension income. Therefore:

Future value of income needed: $180,000
Minus projected pension: $75,000
Minus projected Social Security: $24,156
Minus other income: None
Total supplemental income needed from investments: $80,844

(c) Now that we have determined their needed income, the third step is determining how much principal they will need to accumulate to provide them with their future income. This is accomplished by dividing the amount of future income they expect to need ($80,844) by the systematic withdrawal rate. In this example we are using a 6 percent systematic withdrawal rate. So:

$80,844   Supplemental income needed from investments
Divided by 6%   Systematic withdrawal rate
$1,347,400   Future value of financial assets needed to reach their goals

This means Steve and Jill McKinney might need to accumulate a total of $1,347,400 to reach their future goals.

Current Value and Future Value

(d) Remember they have already accumulated financial assets of $3,525,000.

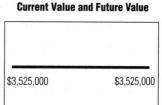

(e) We know they have an estimated future need of $1,347,000

    Minus the estimated future value of $3,525,000

    Which leaves a future surplus of $2,178,000

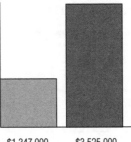

$1,347,000 $3,525,000

(f) There is no shortfall to fill. This couple has done an excellent job of saving and investing for their retirement years.

Step 6: Implement the Plan

Even though by the world's standards the McKinneys would be considered wealthy, they had never had a sense of exactly how much money it would take for them to live before they created this plan. By reviewing their plan in writing, the McKinneys are much more confident about beginning their retirement.

Now it's time to implement their plan and invest the money it has taken them a lifetime to accumulate. This is no easy task. The McKinneys have almost always invested in the stock market, but they agree with their financial adviser that it's time to move a large portion into bonds to generate an ongoing income stream and reduce the overall risk of their portfolio. They have chosen to invest in a combination of short-term certificates of deposit and intermediate tax-free municipal bonds. Because they agree that no one can be certain of the direction of interest rates, they have chosen to use a laddered approach and stagger their maturity dates as follows:

Income Investments—$1,762,500

- $102,500 in a money market
- $100,000 in a CD maturing in one year
- $100,000 in a CD maturing in two years
- $100,000 in a CD maturing in three years
- $100,000 in a CD maturing in four years
- $100,000 in a CD maturing in five years

This leaves $1,160,000 for bonds. They will put $660,000 in municipal bonds for tax-free income. These bonds will be held in their personal account.

- $260,000 in municipals maturing in six years
- $100,000 in municipals maturing in seven years
- $100,000 in municipals maturing in eight years
- $100,000 in municipals maturing in nine years
- $100,000 in municipals maturing in ten years

The remaining $500,000 of their bond allocation will be held in Steve's IRA rollover.

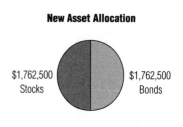

New Asset Allocation

$1,762,500 Stocks

$1,762,500 Bonds

- $100,000 in a CD maturing in one year
- $100,000 in a CD maturing in two years
- $100,000 in a CD maturing in three years
- $100,000 in a CD maturing in four years
- $100,000 in a CD maturing in five years

The McKinneys have implemented a laddered bond strategy for their bond investments.

Growth Investments—$1,762,500

As for stocks and growth investments, the McKinneys decide to keep the $500,000 in company stock—partly for sentimental reasons and because they have such a low cost basis and partly because they believe it will continue to be a premier growth company.

In order to reach the recommended asset allocation of 50 percent in cash and bonds and 50 percent in stocks, the remaining $1,762,500 is left for stocks and other growth investments. Remember that they plan to keep $512,500 of company stock, so that will leave $1,250,000. Because of tax benefits (they can buy and sell stocks within the IRA without having to pay any capital gains taxes), they plan to hold most of the growth assets in the IRA rollover.

For illustration purposes, Jill *could* put one-fifth of their holdings into each of the different types of securities we discussed in Chapter 10:

- *$250,000 of individual securities.* Jill has always had an interest in investing in individual stocks, so she chooses some of the companies she has always wanted to own. These are not shares she intends to trade but are shares she intends to hold for the long term. She reads, researches, diversifies, and then buys.

- *$250,000 in mutual funds.* Jill uses mutual funds to fill in some specific growth categories such as aggressive growth, midcap growth, small cap growth, and global stocks. She looks for well-known funds with long-term track records.

- *$250,000 with individual professional money managers.* Here Jill chooses two money managers for large cap stocks. One specializes in managing large cap growth stocks and the other in managing large cap value stocks. This approach will help her reduce the volatility of the cycles between growth and value stocks.

- *$250,000 in a unit trust.* This structure offers several unique investment strategies. Jill may choose from the "Dogs of the Dow" strategy—the ten highest-yielding stocks in the Dow Jones Industrial Average—or she may choose the "Low Five"—the five lowest-priced of the ten highest-yielding stocks—or she may choose from several other sector-specific trusts such as technology, Internet, bank, or utility trust.

- *$250,000 in variable annuities.* In this last structure for growth, Jill uses annuities to give her many of the same benefits that regular mutual funds have along with their other benefits discussed in Chapter 10. The primary benefit is that the initial investment

FIGURE 12.6   *Large Cap Value versus Large Cap Growth*
Rolling 12-Month Quarterly Excess Returns, January 1, 1975–March 31, 1999

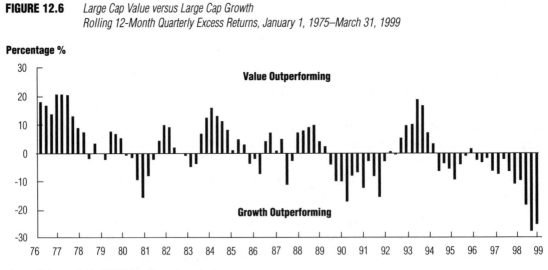

Source: Data supplied by BARRA, Inc./Standard and Poor's.

FIGURE 12.7   *The McKinneys' Investment Plan*

Income $1,762,500   Growth $1,762,500

Personal holdings

$102,500	Money market
$100,000	One-year CD
$100,000	Two-year CD
$100,000	Three-year CD
$100,000	Four-year CD
$100,000	Five-year CD
$260,000	Six-year municipal bond
$100,000	Seven-year municipal bond
$100,000	Eight-year municipal bond
$100,000	Nine-year municipal bond
$100,000	Ten-year municipal bond

$512,500	Company stock

IRA holdings

$100,000	One-year CD
$100,000	Two-year CD
$100,000	Three-year CD
$100,000	Four-year CD
$100,000	Five-year CD

$250,000	Individual stocks
$250,000	Mutual funds
$250,000	Individual professional money managers
$250,000	Unit trusts
$250,000	Variable annuities

amount carries a mortality benefit that guarantees you never receive less than you initially invested in the event of your death.

While it is likely you may find one or two other structures that best suit your investment needs, this short illustration gives you some idea of how the various structures might benefit an individual investor.

Finally, the McKinneys are encouraged to seek legal counsel for establishing their will and implementing an entire estate plan to help protect the assets they have accumulated. They have indicated that at some point in the future they may want to give away some or all of the highly appreciated company stock they are holding in their personal account.

They have said they would enjoy making a large charitable gift to their local university, and they also plan to discuss the idea of implementing a charitable remainder trust (CRT), whereby they could donate the highly appreciated stock to the school. They would receive an immediate tax deduction for a portion of the value of the gift, and they would establish an annuity structure whereby they would receive an income of between 5 and 8 percent for the rest of both of their lives.

Step 7: Monitor the Plan

Theirs would be a wonderful nest egg to accumulate. But don't be fooled: managing a sum of money this large carries a large responsibility. By taking the time to develop a budget and create a written financial plan, the McKinneys have found a new sense of freedom. What was once confusion and chaos is now order.

The McKinneys have requested a meeting with their financial adviser once every three months for the first year. They want to make sure they understand how to ready their statements and get their feet on the ground. After the first year, they plan to meet once every six months.

CONCLUSION

Five case studies, five very different situations. All of these people had different goals and objectives, but they all hoped for one final destination: financial security. They wanted to arrive at the place where they no longer had to watch every penny, where they did not worry so much about next month's bills, where they had structured their investment portfolio in a manner that allowed them to sleep peacefully.

The hardest question of all to answer may be: How much money is enough money? A well-designed financial plan should help you answer that question. But it all goes back to being willing to walk through the seven steps of the financial planning process:

Step 1: Create your mission statement

Step 2: Gather data

Step 3: Create your written goals

Step 4: Evaluate the information

Step 5: Develop a plan

Step 6: Implement the plan

Step 7: Monitor the plan

Now the question becomes: Are you willing to start the journey to finding your financial independence? The journey begins with the action steps outlined throughout the book. Each step will take you closer to your destination. While each of these steps will take some effort to complete, it is my hope that you will enjoy the trip.

Try not to view these action steps as drudgery or as some sort of mathematical torture, but rather view them as the path to your financial future. Of all the people I meet with, the most common comment is, "I wish I would have started saving earlier." Please don't delay the process of creating your personal financial plan. I believe you will find this to be a wonderful and fulfilling experience.

College Planning, Gift-Giving Strategies, and Estate Planning

> "When I was 17 years old, I wanted a $500 stereo system (a Pioneer stereo with big speakers, a turntable, tuner, and cassette player). I just had to have it. That was in 1980. My father, not a music lover, said he would buy me either the stereo or $500 worth of Wal-Mart stock. I had never thought about stock before. . . . I took the stock, which is now worth almost $10,000!"
>
> **Bridgette Arnold,** 35
> *Jonesboro, Arkansas*

> "Money in our society is a very powerful symbol. It represents life. Money, like all powerful symbols, communicates more than we imagine. For example, in our work we trade a portion of our life for money and think that the more money we make, the more valuable our life. Even though most of us wish it weren't true, money talks."
>
> **Larry and Ann Dodgen,** 64 and 62
> *Paragould, Arkansas*

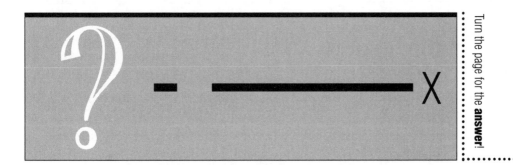

Turn the page for the **answer!**

Close your right eye, hold out this drawing between 6 and 12 inches, and stare at the *X*. At some point the broken space will mysteriously disappear and the line will look whole. Now you are about to complete this entire book and I hope many of the questions you had regarding your personal financial plan have now been addressed. However, I felt three issues had not been covered: college planning, strategies for giving, and estate planning.

"Investing in a 401(k) plan was the best advice my husband and I ever received as newlyweds. In 1988 I invested at the lowest percentage level. If my annual raise was 4 percent, I would increase my contribution by 2 percent and still have a 2 percent raise in payroll. We won't miss money that comes out before it reaches our bank account. Over only 11 years, I maxed out at the 16 percent level in my 401(k) and never stressed our budget. We now have a bright retirement future."

Sherry S. Gray, 43
Jonesboro, Arkansas

COLLEGE PLANNING

In a survey published by Fidelity Distributors Corporation and based on a 1996 survey conducted by Richard Day Research, college planning was listed as the number one financial planning concern for 44 percent of the people surveyed. Surprisingly, college planning was ranked ahead of retirement planning, which received 39 percent of the vote.

The very best time to begin saving for your children's college education is *before* they are born. By implementing prudent budgeting techniques before your children are born, you should be able to accrue the necessary money to help you reach your financial goals. This is another example of how the five-step process of quantifying your goals can be put to use.

The Five-Step Process

1. Find out the cost of a college education in today's dollars.
2. Multiply that figure by the number of years you need to fund the goal.
3. Inflate that cost to see what it will be in the year you need the money.

4. Determine an assumed annual rate of return.

5. Use the tables in the appendix to determine exactly how much money you will need to save on an annual or monthly basis to fund that goal within the designated time frame.

Choose the first specific financial goal you need to quantify. Then apply the five-step process:

1. Cost in today's dollars _____

2. Number of years _____

3. Inflate _____

4. Annual rate of return _____

5. Tables_____

To help you quantify your goals, you'll find listed on the following pages actual costs for a number of colleges and universities. This information was made available through the College Planner Module in Wiesenberger's Investment View Hypothetical Software program, which lists costs for over 6,000 schools.

The annual cost figure includes estimated tuition; fees; room and board; books and supplies; miscellaneous on-campus expenses; and estimated travel expenses. The annual average rate of inflation for tuition and fees nationally from 1981 to 1999 was 8.12 percent. Costs for state universities assume you are a state resident.

Just for fun (and as a point of comparison), I am also listing some well-known colleges and universities as well as my alma mater, William Woods University in Fulton, Missouri.

GIFT-GIVING STRATEGIES

At some point in the financial planning process you may ask, "How much is enough?" Of course, there is no single answer. But if your planning is successful, you may have the opportunity to give some of your money away. The following information is provided for educational purposes only. You should always check with your qualified tax adviser and/or attorney before implementing any type of gift-giving strategy.

1. Deductible gifts of cash to charities.   It's a simple process to pull out your checkbook and give away a potion of your annual income or any amount of your accumulated wealth to the charity of your choice. The ben-

State	Description	Annual Costs
Alaska	University of Alaska/Anchorage	$ 9,281
Alabama	University of Alabama/Birmingham	11,511
Arkansas	Arkansas State University	7,934
	University of Arkansas	10,600
Arizona	University of Arizona	11,486
California	University of California/Berkeley	13,676
Colorado	University of Colorado	10,590
Connecticut	University of Connecticut	13,268
Delaware	University of Delaware	11,673
Florida	University of Florida	8,945
Georgia	University of Georgia	10,078
Hawaii	University of Hawaii/Manoa	10,574
Iowa	University of Iowa	10,536
Idaho	University of Idaho	8,127
Illinois	University of Illinois/Chicago	11,210
Indiana	Indiana University/Purdue University	11,945
Kansas	University of Kansas	8,631
Kentucky	University of Kentucky	9,404
Louisiana	University of New Orleans	8,299
Massachusetts	University of Massachusetts/Dartmouth	12,011
Maryland	University of Maryland/Baltimore	13,023
Maine	University of Maine/Farmington	10,551
Michigan	University of Michigan/Ann Arbor	14,670
Minnesota	University of Minnesota/Twin Cities	11,833
Missouri	University of Missouri/Columbia	10,056
Mississippi	University of Mississippi	8,742
Montana	University of Montana	9,476
North Carolina	University of North Carolina/Charlotte	8,569
North Dakota	University of North Dakota/Grand Forks	8,491
Nebraska	University of Nebraska/Lincoln	9,296
New Hampshire	University of New Hampshire	13,520
New Jersey	Rutgers College	13,317
New Mexico	University of New Mexico	8,769
Nevada	University of Nevada/Las Vegas	10,139
New York*	New York University	33,329

Ohio	Ohio University/Columbus	11,643
Oklahoma	University of Oklahoma/Norman	9,789
Oregon	University of Oregon/Eugene	11,500
Pennsylvania*	University of Pennsylvania	32,959
South Carolina	University of South Carolina/Spartanburg	11,658
South Dakota	University of South Dakota	8,398
Tennessee	University of Tennessee/Knoxville	9,443
Texas	University of Texas/San Antonio	10,454
Utah	University of Utah	14,736
Virginia	University of Virginia	11,230
Vermont	University of Vermont	15,017
Washington	University of Washington	11,477
Wisconsin	University of Wisconsin/Madison	14,010
West Virginia	West Virginia University/Morgantown	9,573
Wyoming	University of Wyoming	8,937

State	Description	Annual Costs
Alabama	Auburn University	$14,780
California*	Pepperdine University	31,289
Colorado	U.S. Air Force Academy	2,329
Connecticut*	Yale University	34,000
Illinois	Lake Forest College	27,129
Massachusetts*	Boston College	30,619
Massachusetts*	Harvard University	33,434
Missouri	William Woods University	19,500
North Carolina*	Duke University	32,591
New York*	Cornell University	34,924
Tennessee*	Vanderbilt University	31,944
Indiana	Notre Dame	10,574
Texas	Baylor University	17,841

*Most of these costs are for in-state residents attending their local university. The costs listed for schools marked with an asterisk may apply to out-of-state costs; they may be private schools and/or Ivy League schools.

Source: Copyright © 1999 Wiesenberger, a Thomson Financial Company. Reprinted by permission.

efits are many. Most important, you can help a cause that you believe in. Second, you remove the gifted money from your estate so that it will not be subject to estate taxes. And if you itemize deductions on your annual income tax return, you can deduct gifts from your income for federal (and usually state) income tax purposes. If you contribute large gifts or have a high gross income, certain limitations and restrictions may apply to the amount you can deduct in any one year. Amounts not deductible in a given year may, in some circumstances, be carried forward to future years. Be sure to check with your tax adviser.

2. Nondeductible gifts of cash to individuals.   You can also use your checkbook to make gifts to anyone you choose. You can give any individual up to $10,000 a year without triggering gift taxes. In fact, every year you can give as many people as you want up to $10,000 each without triggering gift taxes. This is a very popular way to reduce your estate and help children and grandchildren achieve their goals. In addition to the $10,000 a person each year, you can contribute, on behalf of anyone, an unlimited amount to a medical or educational facility to avoid being included in the $10,000 limit. For example, a grandparent could pay a grandchild's college tuition in a check made out directly to the university and give that same grandchild a $10,000 check to invest for their future!

3. Using appreciated assets as charitable gifts.   This strategy is based on the assumption that you have an asset that has appreciated in value and that you are charitably inclined. For example, assume you bought XYZ stock for $2,500 and its value has now increased to $5,000; you have doubled your money. You also want to use this money to make a donation to your favorite charity. You have two choices. (1) You can sell the stock and give the proceeds to the charity. After taxes, you would net approximately $4,500 (the $5,000 value of the stock minus the 20 percent tax on the $2,500 gain). You can write a check to the charity for the $4,500 cash and then take an income tax deduction for that $4,500. (2) Or you can give the stock to the charity. The charity gets $5,000 instead of $4,500 because you don't have to pay the capital gains tax. (Don't worry—the charity doesn't pay this tax either because qualified charities don't pay income or capital gains taxes!) And you get to take a $5,000 income tax deduction.

Usually, donating an appreciated asset works out better for both you and the charity! And this doesn't apply only to stocks. Appreciated assets may include mutual funds, bonds, real estate, art—virtually any asset that a appreciated and that a charity can liquidate to raise cash.

4. Charitable remainder trusts (CRTs).   This is another way to give away highly appreciated assets. However, in addition to funding charitable interest, removing assets from your estate, and providing you with a current income tax deduction, charitable remainder trusts (CRT) allow you to retain an income flow from the asset during your (and potentially your spouse and/or children's') lifetime. It is a strategy that works especially well when you have highly appreciated assets that currently generate little or no cash flow (like small cap growth stocks that pay no dividends).

Here's how it works. You start by having an attorney write an irrevocable CRT document in which you are named as the income beneficiary and a charity of your choosing is the remainder beneficiary. Once the CRT is established, you "gift" a highly appreciated asset to the trust. With this one gift, you have removed the asset from your estate, generated a current income tax deduction (for the present value of the gift that the charity will ultimately receive at your death), avoided the capital gains tax on that asset, and made your favorite charity very happy. Now that this highly appreciated asset is owned by the CRT, the asset can be sold (without creating tax consequences) and the proceeds can be reinvested in something that is likely to provide annual income in addition to growth of the principal. You (and, if you'd like, your spouse and/or children) get a portion of the income that the trust investment generates each year. (The portion that you get depends on the specific type of CRT and the target income that you specified in the trust document.) After the death of the last income beneficiary (you, your spouse, and/or your children), the named charity gets what's accumulated in the trust.

DESIGNING YOUR ESTATE PLAN

Although I cannot give you any tax or legal advice, I can provide some statistics. Less than 70 percent of Americans have a will or any type of document that will aid them in the disposal of their assets after they die.

Some famous people:

Name	Gross Estate	Total Settlement Costs	Net Estate	Percent Shrinkage
Stan Laurel	$ 91,562	$ 8,381	$ 83,181	9%
Marilyn Monroe	819,176	448,750	370,426	55
W. C. Fields	884,680	329,793	554,887	37
Humphrey Bogart	910,146	272,234	635,912	30
Franklin D. Roosevelt	1,940,999	574,867	1,366,132	30
Clark Gable	2,806,526	1,101,038	1,705,488	31
Gary Cooper	4,984,985	1,530,454	3,454,531	31
Elvis Presley	10,165,434	7,374,635	2,790,799	73
John D. Rockefeller, Sr.	26,905,182	17,124,194	9,780,194	64

Don't Allow Your Estate to Be Caught Off Guard

Estate planning is a process, not a product. It involves seeking advice, reviewing options, and creating a plan for ensuring that

- your assets are sufficient to meet your objectives for your heirs;
- your heirs receive those assets in the proportion, manner, and time frame you choose;
- income taxes, estate taxes, gift taxes, inheritance taxes, and transfer costs are minimized and then paid as cheaply as possible; and
- liquidity exists to pay taxes and transfer costs when they are due.

Like many other processes discussed in this book, estate planning is not a one-shot deal. You need to review and update your estate plan at many different stages during your lifetime. Your plan will be affected by changes in your family, your wealth, your health, your charitable interests, and the laws and regulations that govern wealth transfer and taxation.

The consequences of not planning for your estate transfer can be severe.

- If you die without a will, the state creates one for you. It may or may not be what you would have wanted. In some states, dying without a will results in most of your assets going to your children, with only a small remainder left for your surviving spouse.
- If you have not appointed a guardian and a trustee for your minor children, at your death the state will appoint them for you. It may, or may not, be the persons you would have chosen to raise your children and oversee their assets.

- If your estate is illiquid and you have not planned for estate tax payment, valuable assets may have to be sold to pay estate taxes. This could mean having to sell the family farm or business that you wanted to give, intact, to your children. It could mean having to sell securities or real estate when the market is down. And it might even mean selling your surviving spouse's home.
- Estate tax, inheritance tax, and transfer costs can take more than 60 percent of your hard-earned estate away—before it goes to your heirs. Planning in advance can significantly increase the amount going to the people and charities you care about.

Review the following list periodically and discuss any shortcomings you find with your professional financial, tax, and legal advisers.

1. Do you have a written estate plan?
   - Do you understand it?
   - Has it been reviewed within the past three years?
   - Does it include an analysis of all potential strategies?
   - Did you fully implement the selected strategies?
2. Do you have a will?
   - Has it been reviewed within the past three years?
   - Was it updated when you moved to a new state, got married or divorced, had a baby, lost a parent, or experienced any other significant family change?
   - Does your will name a guardian for your children if both you and your spouse are gone?
   - Does your will create a trust (and name a trustee) to control assets for minor children if both you and your spouse are gone?
   - Have you made appropriate provisions for any special-needs children?
   - Are you comfortable with the executor(s) and trustee(s) you selected?
3. Have you considered a living trust to avoid probate?
   - If you have a living trust, have you retitled your assets in the name of that trust?

4. Have you delegated appropriate powers of attorney so that, in the event of your mental or physical incompetence, your affairs can be managed by people you choose?

5. Are you taking full advantage of the marital deduction?
   - Have you considered establishing a credit shelter (A/B or marital) trust?
   - Have you retitled assets in the name of this trust?

6. Have you set up irrevocable life insurance trusts to ensure your life insurance proceeds are not taxed as part of your estate?
   - Did you retitle existing life insurance policies into the trust?
   - Is the amount of insurance in the trust sufficient to pay estimated taxes and transfer costs due at your death? Have you reviewed this estimate within the last three years?
   - If you need to add more insurance to the trust, have you done so?
   - Are you routinely sending out any required "Crummey" letters for these trusts?
     A Crummey notice/letter is sent to the beneficiary of an irrevocable life insurance trust containing Crummey powers. It provides clear notice that the beneficiary has a right to withdraw assets from the trust within a specific time period, generally 30 days, which qualifies the gifted assets (usually equal to the annual exclusion amount, $10,000/person/donor) to the trust as a present-interest gift.

7. Are you taking maximum advantage of the $10,000 annual gift tax exclusions?
   - Have you considered annual gifts to your children and grandchildren?
   - If so, do you make them outright gifts or gifts to a trust for their benefit?

8. Are you taking maximum advantage of medical and education gift tax exclusions?
   - Do you have grandchildren in college (or private/parochial elementary or high schools) who could use help with their tuition?
   - Do you have parents or grandparents in hospitals or nursing homes who could use help with their medical bills?

9. If you have highly appreciated assets that don't generate current income, have you considered using them to fund a charitable remainder trust?

10. If you are a sole proprietor, a partner, or an owner of a closely held corporation:
    - Do you have a buy-sell agreement for the business?
    - Have you considered key person life and disability coverage?
    - Is there a written business continuation plan?

The bottom line: If you have taken the time to create a net worth, you need to complete the process by careful and skillful transition planning. Make sure your money goes to the people and causes you care about—in a time and manner you choose!

A discussion of estate planning would not be complete without a quick review of life insurance. Life insurance, in the investment context, can be used to protect your family, your business, or your other assets. This information is provided for educational purposes only. It is always recommended that you consult qualified advisers before implementing these or any other type of life insurance strategy.

LIFE INSURANCE

Protecting Your Family

Perhaps you know someone who missed out on going to college, who had to move out of the family home, or who had to go back to work when the children were small (or after he or she had retired)—all because the family breadwinner died without enough life insurance. This is the first and foremost reason to buy life insurance. Insurance cannot replace you when you die—but it can replace the income you would have provided for your family. Your financial adviser can help you estimate how much insurance you need for this purpose. In most cases, you'll want the insurance amount to be enough

- to replace the income your family needs;
- to complete your plan for funding your childrens' college education;
- to pay any expenses that result from your death (typically, probate costs, medical expenses of the final illness, funeral expenses, and estate/inheritance taxes); and
- to pay off any outstanding debts (like the mortgage or car loan).

Even if you aren't the family breadwinner, you should think about life insurance. If you are, for example, the parent who stays home to care for your children while your spouse works at the office, your death places a significant financial burden on your surviving spouse. He or she will have the additional expenses of child care in order to continue working—or will have to quit working to stay home with the children. In either case, life insurance could be set up to provide needed funds.

There are many different types of life insurance that can appropriately provide income replacement for your family.

Term insurance pays your family a stated amount (the insurance policy "face" amount) if your death occurs during a specified period of time (for example, the next 10 years). Typically, the premiums you pay for term insurance increase annually, although some companies now sell term insurance with premiums that are level for 10 or 20 years. Term insurance is useful when the insurance need is short lived.

For example, you only need to protect your childrens' college funding plans until the last of your children is about 22. If you live longer than that, this need for insurance will disappear. Likewise, your mortgage will be paid off at some point and your need to provide for child care eventually ceases to exist.

Permanent insurance (also known as whole life insurance or universal life insurance) pays your family the face amount no matter when your death occurs. Typically, the premiums you pay for permanent insurance stay the same for your entire life. These premiums are higher in the early years than term insurance premiums would be, but in the later years, they are substantially lower. Permanent insurance policies also build up something known as a "cash value"—essentially, your premiums are invested by the life insurance company and earn interest. You can access this cash value in an emergency by taking a loan against the insurance policy or, in some cases, by withdrawing amounts from the policy. Of course, if you borrow or spend down the cash value, there is a face amount available to your family in the event of your death.

Permanent insurance can be either fixed or variable. If it is fixed, the underlying investments are chosen by the insurance company and the growth of your cash value is guaranteed at some stated interest rate. If the insurance is variable, the underlying investments are mutual-fund-like subaccounts. You choose which subaccounts to invest in and your cash value fluctuates up and down with the value of the investments in the chosen subaccounts.

Permanent insurance is best used for those insurance needs that never go away. For example, permanent insurance should be used as funding to support your spouse through a lifetime.

From a purely investment perspective, life insurance is unique. The expected "return" on a life insurance policy is impossible to calculate. If you die prematurely, the return to your family is immeasurable. However, if, as I hope, you live a long and happy life, the numeric return may be minimal—but the peace of mind from always knowing your family could live as you wanted them to is huge.

A few other life insurance facts you should be aware of: Life insurance is tax deferred during your lifetime (that is, you don't pay taxes on any earnings that are left to accumulate inside the policy) and the face amount passes income tax free to your heirs at your death. If you name a beneficiary other than your estate, the face amount of your life insurance policy passes directly to that beneficiary—avoiding the cost, delays, and potential publicity of the probate process.

The other form of insurance that you should consider to protect your family is *disability insurance.* Nearly one in three Americans between the ages of 35 and 65 will experience a disability that takes the worker out of the workforce for 90 days or more (U.S. Congress, House Committee on Ways and Means, 1991). Disability insurance can be used to provide income for your family during these times.

Protecting Your Business

A complete discussion of business insurance is beyond the scope of this book. However, if you run a business, there are several reasons to consider insurance.

- Insurance can protect a business from economic loss when the business loses key knowledge, skills, experience, funding, or contacts as the result of an important employee's death or disability. This is referred to as "key person" insurance.

- In a sole proprietorship, partnership, or closely held corporation, business continuation following the death or disability of an owner is critical to the surviving owners and employees. In many cases, the business has to be liquidated to settle the estate of the deceased owner. Buy-and-sell agreements, funded by life and disability insurance on the life of the owners, allow the surviving owners (or employees) to buy out the deceased owners' interest without liquidating the company and to maintain the business as an ongoing concern.

- Life and disability insurance can be used for credit enhancement. Generally, banks will be willing to loan more, at better terms, if they know the business is indemnified for the loss of a key person and are assured that the business can continue in the event of the death of the owner.

- Life insurance can also be used in a business situation to fund special employee benefits, such as nonqualified deferred compensation and split-dollar plans.

Protecting Your Assets

Now, let's assume you have read this book carefully. You have created a financial plan and successfully stuck to it for years. You have accomplished your goals and are comfortably retired. You have accumulated quite a sum and are happy that someday your children will thank you for a sizable inheritance. Guess what? Your children will not get it all—the government may take more than one-half of your assets in estate taxes after your death!

Current federal estate and gift tax rates start at 37 percent and can be as high as 60 percent. And some states also have inheritance taxes.

Once you have accumulated assets, your next step should be creating a plan to pass those assets to the people you care about—in the most tax-efficient manner possible. This is part of a process called *estate planning*. (The estate planning process is discussed in Action Step 21.) While life insurance is only a piece of the estate planning process (trusts and gifting strategies also play a huge role), it is an important piece.

Life insurance can be used to fund estate and inheritance taxes. Because life insurance provides cash at exactly the time when estate and inheritance taxes need to be paid, having life insurance designated for this purpose can mean that your family doesn't have to sell off other assets (like the family home or business) to pay the taxes. Typically, life insurance purchased for this need is permanent insurance and is held in an irrevocable life insurance trust.

The other key use for life insurance in your estate plan is to substantially increase gifts to loved ones or charities. Life insurance leverages your bequest assets. A relatively small premium can fund a large life insurance face amount that can be used to provide gifts, at your death, to anyone you want—including favorite charities, your spouse and children, other relatives, key employees, and special friends.

So many people look at the expense of life insurance and think, "This could never happen to me." What follows is the story of someone whose life was dramatically changed by the sudden death of her husband.

We'd always struggled with finances, making every dollar count, as most young couples do with an 18-month old. But when I turned 29, I became a widow in the blink of an eye. Almost just as fast, I became responsible for the largest sum of money that I ever imagined would cross my path.

There was plenty of money to set aside a trust for our son and plenty of time for it to grow. I felt proud and relieved knowing that there would be college money and enough to provide a nest egg for him to start his adult life. But I had worked in a bank and had seen customers go through large amounts of money quickly and then wonder where it went.

I felt immense pressure to be wise with the money left to me but careful not to let it consume me. At times I was overwhelmed and maybe even naive about my finances. I suppose after working with my husband for so long to make ends meet, I felt guilty because now my ends met, but he wasn't here to enjoy this easier life-style. I decided to be as thankful and humble as I could, remembering to watch out for opportunities to help others, just as we had been helped when we struggled.

I felt it was also important not to give up the "sale racks" in my life. It's a way to stay grounded and to assure discipline so that my days and nights don't leave me wondering, "Where did it all go?" Don't misunderstand; there are times when I still buy something new "just because,"; I just don't do it often. After all, it's best to be careful with your spending and investing regardless of the bottom line.

—P.A.N., Arkansas

It's Your Turn

> "Just before the market dropped precipitously in July 1997, I sold some stocks to reduce my exposure to the market. Sure enough, the market took a drop from 9,338 to around 7,400 on the Dow Jones Industrial Average. That move looked good at the time, but I never did feel good about getting back in the market, and now with the Dow Jones over 11,000 I still have not gotten back in the market."

Robert Anthony, 57
Little Rock, Arkansas

> "The most important thing we've found in sticking with a budget is that both the husband and the wife must be committed to it."

Jason and Julie Wilkie, 29
Mobile, Alabama

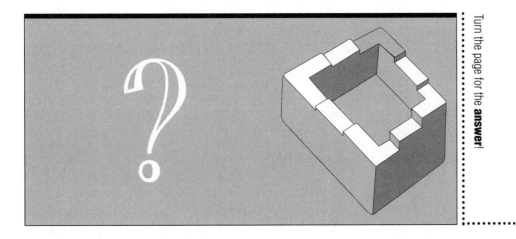

Turn the page for the **answer!**

Developing your personal written financial plan can feel like trying to climb this never-ending set of stairs. No matter how much you understand, there is more to learn. No matter how many things you do right, there are always unexpected circumstances. Yet the victory is in the effort. If you commit to completing these final few steps, you may always have to climb but may find newer and more entertaining paths to explore. Proper planning opens up your opportunities.

"Find out about your company's 401(k) plan and invest as much as you possibly can, as soon as you can."

Sam Brown, 41
Switzerland (U.S. citizen working abroad)

"Having lost my husband six years ago, I was thrust into the role of financial manager and investor for my family. My greatest asset has been my trusted financial adviser."

Jeanne Henry
Jonesboro, Arkansas

These final action steps will complete the process of creating your written financial plan. You will be able to compile in one format all the data necessary to finish the seven steps in the financial planning process.

It's your turn.

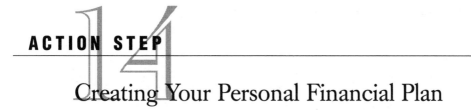

ACTION STEP 14

Creating Your Personal Financial Plan

You have finished reading about other people's financial plans. Now it's time to complete the retirement section of your personal financial plan. The following worksheet will take you through the process. This action step can revolutionize the way you manage your money.

Assumptions

Age _____

Occupation _____

Current income _____

Age you plan to retire _____

Risk tolerance level _____

Anticipated inflation rate _____ Anticipated average total return _____

How much are you currently saving per month/year? _____

How do you categorize your investment knowledge and skill level? _____

_____

Step 1: Restate Your Money Mission Statement

_____

_____

_____

_____

_____

Step 2

Gather data

Total debts $\quad$ \$_____

Total cash $\quad$ \$_____ $\quad$ _____%

Total bonds $\quad$ \$_____ $\quad$ _____%

Total stocks $\quad$ \$_____ $\quad$ _____%

Grand Total $\quad$ \$_____ $\quad$ 100%

My budget is as follows:

Year _____	Past Annual Sub Totals
Personal Savings/Investments	
Retirement Investments	
Mortgage/Rent	
Electric Utility	
Gas Utility	
Telephone/Other Phone Costs	
Cell Phone	
Pager	
Water	
Cable TV	
Home Maintenance	
Lawn Maintenance	
Real Estate Taxes	
Car Payment	
Car Insurance	
Gasoline	
Car Maintenance	
Food/Groceries	
Toiletries	
Eating Out	
Entertainment	

Clothing	
Vacations	
Childcare/Dependent Care	
Tuition	
Visa	
MasterCard	
Discover	
Other Consumer Debt	
Student Loans	
Homeowners Insurance	
Health Insurance	
Life Insurance	
Disability Insurance	
Doctors—Copay	
Dentists	
Eyeglasses	
Prescription Drugs	
Household Help	
Dry Cleaning	
Beauty Salon/Barber	
Pets/Vets	
Subscriptions	
Florists	
Gifts	
Church Donations	
Community Donations	
Art /Dance/Misc. Personal	
CPA	
Professional Dues	
Club Dues	
Miscellaneous	
Other	
Annual Total	

Step 3: Set Your Written Goals

Goal #1 _____

Goal #2 _____

Goal #3 _____

Goal #4 _____

Goal #5 _____

Steps 4 and 5: Evaluate the Information and Develop a Plan

1. (a) List your current income $_____

    (b) List your anticipated inflation rate   _____%

    (c) List the number of years until retirement   _____

    (d) Locate the multiplier in Appendix A   _____

    (e) Multiply by your current income divided
           by 1,000

This is the anticipated future value amount of income you could require during the first year of your retirement.

2. Therefore:

    (a) Future value of income needed: Insert from A   _____

    (b) Minus projected pension: _____

    (c) Minus projected Social Security: _____

    (d) Minus other income: _____

    (e) Leaves total supplemental income
           needed from investments:

3. Determine how much principal you will need to accumulate to reach your future financial goal for retirement.

    (a) Future value of income needed: Insert from step B _____

    (b) Divided by the systematic withdrawal rate: _____

    (c) Future value of principal needed:

4. Determine the future value of your current assets.

    (a) Value of your current assets: Insert from Step 2 _____

    (b) Anticipated rate of return: _____

    (c) List the number of years until retirement: _____

    (d) Locate the multiplier in Appendix A: _____

    (e) Multiply by your current assets divided
         by 1,000 _____

5. Determine your future shortfall or surplus.

    (a) Future value of principal needed:
         Insert from step C _____

    (b) Minus future value of current assets:
         Insert from step D _____

    (c) Equals your shortfall or surplus:

6. If you have a shortfall, this step will determine how much money you need to save and invest to fill that shortfall within a specific period of time.

    (a) Anticipated rate of return: _____

    (b) List the number of years until retirement: _____

    (c) Locate the multiplier in Appendix B: _____

    (d) Multiply by your shortfall divided
         by 1,000

This is the amount of money you will need to invest every month to reach your future goals. This is point B!

Step 6: Implement the Plan

Describe how you anticipate implementing your financial plan.

1. _____

2. _____

3. _____

4. _____

5. _____

Step 7: Monitor the Plan

Set up the schedule that you expect to use to monitor your new financial plan.

Month 1 _____

Month 2 _____

Month 3 _____

Month 4 _____

Month 5 _____

Month 6 _____

Month 7 _____

Month 8 _____

Month 9 _____

Month 10 _____

Month 11 _____

Month 12 _____

Your Financial Overview Checklist

My three top financial goals are:

1. _____

2. _____

3. _____

I have quantified those goals to realize that I must save and invest the following amounts on a monthly basis to reach my top three goals:

Goal	Monthly Savings Needed
1. _____	_____
2. _____	_____
3. _____	_____

_____ My timeline is completed.

_____ I have created a realistic annual forward-projecting budget.

_____ I have developed a monthly systematic investment strategy that will allow me to save and invest _____ (amount) each month and I plan to invest as follows:

Investment Strategy	Amount
1. _____	_____
2. _____	_____
3. _____	_____
4. _____	_____
5. _____	_____

My risk tolerance level can be categorized as:

_____ Ultraconservative   _____ Fairly aggressive

_____ Fairly conservative   _____ Ultra-aggressive

_____ Moderate

My current ssset allocation is: Dollar Amount   Percentage

Cash $_____   _____%

Fixed income $_____   _____%

Stocks $_____   _____%

_____ My asset allocation matches my risk tolerance and will help me achieve my stated goals and objectives.

_____ My asset allocation does not currently match my risk tolerance and will not necessarily help me meet my stated goals and objectives. Therefore, I plan to take the following steps to correct the situation.

_____

_____

_____

_____

I do/do not wish to include the following charitable strategies into my financial plan:

1. Charitable/deductible gifts of cash

2. Nondeductible gifts of cash

3. $10,000 gifts

4. Using appreciated assets as charitable gifts

5. Charitable remainder trusts

I have _____children.

CHILD #1

Age:

Will attend college in _____ years

We will plan for him/her to attend _____ (name of college).

The total cost of a four-year education is _____.

Assuming a _____ percent annual average rate of return, we will need to save $_____ each month to reach that goal.

CHILD #2

Age:

Will attend college in _____ years

We will plan for him/her to attend _____ (name of college).

The total cost of a four-year education is _____.

Assuming a _____ percent annual average rate of return, we will need to save $_____ each month to reach that goal.

CHILD #3

Age:

Will attend college in _____ years

We will plan for him/her to attend _____ (name of college).

The total cost of a four-year education is _____.

Assuming a _____ percent annual average rate of return, we will need to save $_____ each month to reach that goal.

_____ I have reviewed my disability insurance, life insurance, and annuity policies to make sure they are current and appropriate for my family.

_____ I have reviewed the current beneficiary status on all life insurance, annuity policies, my 401(k) plan, and IRAs.

_____ I have contacted an attorney regarding a review of my current estate plan, and I am committed to implementing all of the necessary steps to protect the assets I have accumulated and to distribute them appropriately after I am gone.

_____ I have completed Action Steps 14 and 15. These two steps allow me to have a financial plan.

Signed: _____ Date: _____

Signed: _____ Date: _____

16 Your One-Year Strategy

The first-year strategy is to design your financial plan and begin to implement your strategies. One outline might be:

Month 1

1. Read this book.
2. Complete all of the Action Steps.

Month 2

1. Monitor your newly designed budget.
2. If you have decided to work with a financial adviser, contact him or her and begin to review each portion of your financial plan.
   - Review budget
   - Review current goals and objectives
   - Review current risk tolerance
   - Review current asset allocation
   - Review monthly investment strategy
3. Implement your plan

Month 3

1. Continue to monitor your budget.
2. Learn how to read your monthly investment statements.
3. Learn how to follow your investments in the newspaper or on the Internet.

Months 4 through 12

1. Continue to monitor your budget.
2. Monitor your new investment strategy.
3. Commit yourself to learning more about planning for your financial future.

ACTION STEP

Your Five-Year Strategy

Year One

This plan is described in Action Step 16. Review page 294.

Year Two

1. Review your budget.
2. Monitor the performance of your investments.
3. Review your asset allocation.

Year Three

1. Review your budget.
2. Monitor the performance of your investments.
3. Review your asset allocation.
4. Check your progress versus your timeline.
5. Review your mission statement.

Year Four

1. Review your budget.
2. Monitor the performance of your investments.
3. Review your asset allocation.
4. Check your progress versus your timeline.
5. Review your mission statements.

Year Five

1. Review your budget.
2. Monitor the performance of your investments.
3. Review your asset allocation.
4. Check your progress versus your timeline.

5. Review your mission statements.

6. Compare your investment choices versus the appropriate benchmarks. If they compare favorably, leave the plan alone. If they are underperforming, consider looking for alternatives within the appropriate asset classes.

18

Your Lifetime Strategy

During each phase of the long-term planning process, your financial plan is a constantly changing and evolving process. What might have been prudent five years ago may not be appropriate for you today. Your financial circumstances can change because of one or more of the following:

- Death
- Buying or selling a business
- College
- Unexpected expenses
- Windfalls
- New job
- Marriage
- Children
- New home
- New car
- Divorce

Any one of these occurrences can affect your financial plan. So how do you plan for the unexpected? You create contingency plans. You look at the above list and ask yourself a series of difficult questions:

1. What would happen to my family if I:

- Died?
- Lost my job?
- Retired?
- Bought a new car?

2. How much of my portfolio would need to be available in short-term/liquid investments for me to:

- Take care of emergencies?
- Invest?
- Buy a business?

3. Is my insurance coverage adequate to cover:

- Health problems?
- Short-term/long-term disability?
- Long-term care?
- Death?

4. At the end of my life, will I feel that my financial plan helped me attain a better quality of life?

- Was I satisfied?
- Would I make any changes?
- Did my money make a difference?
- Did I work too hard? Not hard enough?
- Was my family happy?
- Did I have enough money?

I promise that I will continue to let all of my financial decisions flow out of the basic values established by my mission statements.

Staying
Motivated

> **❝**To me, investing is a means of making your money work for you. Everyone works hard to earn a living and tries to save money for the future. Why not put that money in a vehicle that allows your savings to be maximized? Through prudent investing, money saved on a routine basis can lead to financial security. It's the power of compounding!**❞**
>
> **Lisa Pals,** 36
> *New York, New York*

> **❝**Before his death ten years ago, my husband had always managed our investments and I had never given it much thought. After his death I was frightened to realize that my financial future was dependent on the decisions I made. But if you take a balanced approach and take the time to learn more about investing, you may enjoy managing your money.**❞**
>
> **Linda Thompson,** 57
> *Little Rock, Arkansas*

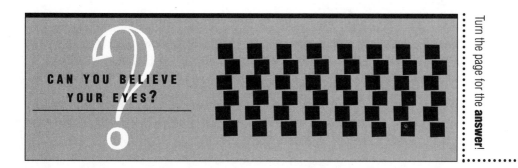

CAN YOU BELIEVE YOUR EYES?

Turn the page for the **answer!**

These apparently wedge-shaped blocks create an illusion called the "café wall." It is an ideal example of how most people feel about the current structure of their financial plan—slightly out of balance and disorganized. The intent of this book was to motivate you to pull together all the information you have learned about various investment alternatives and your personal financial plan and help you create your own plan.

The "café wall" is a perfect illustration for many of you. If you turn the page and look at the illusion from the side, you'll see that confusion and chaos were actually never there. In fact, all of the blocks are completely rectangular and the lines are already parallel. It is your perspective that you must change. You must begin to have confidence in your ability to make prudent financial decisions by, it is hoped, increasing your understanding of the basic building blocks you have now created for your plan. But that written document is just the beginning. You have only started the process of creating and managing a net worth that will sustain you and your family throughout your life. This last brief section attempts to answer the question: "How do you stay motivated?"

> **"**It is amazing to me that I have built such a phenomenal account balance from doing nothing more remarkable than saving and investing on a regular basis.**"**
> **Kristy Maher,** 35
> *Cincinnati, Ohio*

HOW TO STAY MOTIVATED

For many people a job done well is all the motivation they need, but the rest of us are looking for something a little more substantial. Personally, my motivation stems from the belief that tending to the net worth of and for my family is part of being a good steward of the money we have accumulated.

Life is short. Money is just money. While it can at times make life easier, it can't make you happy.

As I stated in my family's money mission statement:

"We will purposefully work to plan with and enjoy the money we have been given, knowing that money is not our true security. Our true joy is found in faith, family, good health, and our friends."

To stay motivated, set very specific short-term goals, and reward yourself as you hit each target.

You may want to use this checklist:

- Have you created your money mission statement?

- Have you gathered the data that tells you where you are financially today?

- Have you taken your budget through the Checkbook Test?

- Have you set written financial goals?

- Have you evaluated the financial information you gathered?

- Do you have a plan of action?

- Have you implemented your plan?

- Do you have a schedule set to monitor the performance of your plan?

- Do you have a better knowledge of the investment world?

- Do you have a better understanding of your investment alternatives?

- Do you believe you could choose a financial adviser who will match your needs?

- Have you completed the written action steps?

CONGRATULATIONS!!!

If you have accomplished these tasks, you have undoubtedly increased your potential for financial success significantly. By now you should feel that you are in control. You have taken the necessary steps to put your personal financial house in order. My hope for you is that financial prudence and responsibility will become a part of your everyday life. Managing money is an important part of everyone's life, and by completing this book you have proven that you care about your financial future.

I said in the introduction that this was the time to begin the journey. You are now on your way. Like any journey, your investment experiences will be filled with many adventures and plenty of periods of uncertainty. Your job is not to time the stock market or make the perfect asset allocations. Your job is to trust your intuition and make wise choices. Don't be swayed by the latest investment craze. Try not to let your emotions influence your decisions. You are more likely to stay on the right track by using the best tool of all—your heart.

Remember that money isn't nearly so important as most people try to make it. Look for the real treasures in life and spend the best years pursuing *them*. Those treasures will certainly be the best investment you will ever make.

EPILOGUE: *True Confessions!*

I felt that I couldn't end this book without a few true confessions. Until December 1998, I was the owner of *two* "million-dollar cars." My husband drives a 1996 Ford Explorer that required a payment of roughly $367 a month. I drive a 1997 Toyota Avalon, and through December 1998 we were paying $500 every month on my car—a total of $867 in car payments every month. In December 1998 we paid off the balances on both cars in full.

The same is true for eating pizza. We love pizza—in fact, we had pizza for supper the night I wrote this page, but that expense has been placed into our monthly budget.

New cars and pizza are not the issue. The purpose of this book is to encourage you to follow the seven steps for creating your financial plan. For those of you who have taken the time to write out your budget and map out your financial plan, you now know exactly which financial decisions will be best for you.

Remember, life is short. Your future financial success is really a simple matter of choices. My hope is that the tough choices have been made a little easier.

Appendix A
The Inflation and
Future Value Calculator

You will use this page to calculate the five-step process found on page 67 and to compose your personal financial plan beginning on page 285. Full explanations are found in those sections of the text. The following chart shows the future value of $1,000 based on the number of years it's invested and the anticipated rate of inflation or return.

For example, assume you wanted to calculate how much $1,000 would be worth in ten years if it has an average annual rate of return of 8 percent. You would locate the ten-year column and follow that over to the 8 percent return column to reveal that your $1,000 would grow to $2,158.92.

	3%	4%	5%	6%	7%
1	$1,030.00	$1,040.00	$1,050.00	$ 1,060.00	$ 1,070.00
2	1,060.90	1,081.60	1,102.50	1,123.60	1,144.90
3	1,092.73	1,124.86	1,157.63	1,191.02	1,225.04
4	1,125.51	1,169.86	1,215.51	1,262.48	1,310.80
5	1,159.27	1,216.65	1,276.28	1,338.23	1,402.55
6	1,194.05	1,265.32	1,340.10	1,418.52	1,500.73
7	1,229.87	1,315.93	1,407.10	1,503.63	1,605.78
8	1,266.77	1,368.57	1,477.46	1,593.85	1,718.19
9	1,304.77	1,423.31	1,551.33	1,689.48	1,838.46
10	1,343.92	1,480.24	1,628.89	1,790.85	1,967.15
11	1,384.23	1,539.45	1,710.34	1,898.30	2,104.85
12	1,425.76	1,601.03	1,795.86	2,012.20	2,252.19
13	1,468.53	1,665.07	1,885.65	2,132.93	2,409.85
14	1,512.59	1,731.68	1,979.93	2,260.90	2,578.53
15	1,557.97	1,800.94	2,078.93	2,396.56	2,759.03
16	1,604.71	1,872.98	2,182.87	2,540.35	2,952.16
17	1,652.85	1,947.90	2,292.02	2,692.77	3,158.82
18	1,702.43	2,025.82	2,406.62	2,854.34	3,379.93
19	1,753.51	2,106.85	2,526.95	3,025.60	3,616.53
20	1,806.11	2,191.12	2,653.30	3,207.14	3,869.68
21	1,860.29	2,278.77	2,785.96	3,399.56	4,140.56
22	1,916.10	2,369.92	2,925.26	3,603.54	4,430.40
23	1,973.59	2,464.72	3,071.52	3,819.75	4,740.53
24	2,032.79	2,563.30	3,225.10	4,048.93	5,072.37
25	2,093.78	2,665.84	3,386.35	4,291.87	5,427.43
26	2,156.59	2,772.47	3,555.67	4,549.38	5,807.35
27	2,221.29	2,883.37	3,733.46	4,822.35	6,213.87
28	2,287.93	2,998.70	3,920.13	5,111.69	6,648.84
29	2,356.57	3,118.65	4,116.14	5,418.39	7,114.26
30	2,427.26	3,243.40	4,321.94	5,743.49	7,612.26
31	2,500.08	3,373.13	4,538.04	6,088.10	8,145.11
32	2,575.08	3,508.06	4,764.94	6,453.39	8,715.27
33	2,652.34	3,648.38	5,003.19	6,840.59	9,325.34
34	2,731.91	3,794.32	5,253.35	7,251.03	9,978.11
35	2,813.86	3,946.09	5,516.02	7,686.09	10,676.58
36	2,898.28	4,103.93	5,791.82	8,147.25	11,423.94
37	2,985.23	4,268.09	6,081.41	8,636.09	12,223.62
38	3,074.78	4,438.81	6,385.48	9,154.25	13,079.27
39	3,167.03	4,616.37	6,704.75	9,703.51	13,994.82
40	3,262.04	4,801.02	7,039.99	10,285.72	14,974.46

	8%	9%	10%	11%	12%
1	$ 1,080.00	$ 1,090.00	$ 1,100.00	$ 1,110.00	$ 1,120.00
2	1,166.40	1,188.10	1,210.00	1,232.10	1,254.40
3	1,259.71	1,295.03	1,331.00	1,367.63	1,404.93
4	1,360.49	1,411.58	1,464.10	1,518.07	1,573.52
5	1,469.33	1,538.62	1,610.51	1,685.06	1,762.34
6	1,586.87	1,677.10	1,771.56	1,870.41	1,973.82
7	1,713.82	1,828.04	1,948.72	2,076.16	2,210.68
8	1,850.93	1,992.56	2,143.59	2,304.54	2,475.96
9	1,999.00	2,171.89	2,357.95	2,558.04	2,773.08
10	2,158.92	2,367.36	2,593.74	2,839.42	3,105.85
11	2,331.64	2,580.43	2,853.12	3,151.76	3,478.55
12	2,518.17	2,812.66	3,138.43	3,498.45	3,895.98
13	2,719.62	3,065.80	3,452.27	3,883.28	4,363.49
14	2,937.19	3,341.73	3,797.50	4,310.44	4,887.11
15	3,172.17	3,642.48	4,177.25	4,784.59	5,473.57
16	3,425.94	3,970.31	4,594.97	5,310.89	6,130.39
17	3,700.02	4,327.63	5,054.47	5,895.09	6,866.04
18	3,996.02	4,717.12	5,559.92	6,543.55	7,689.97
19	4,315.70	5,141.66	6,115.91	7,263.34	8,612.76
20	4,660.96	5,604.41	6,727.50	8,062.31	9,646.29
21	5,033.83	6,108.81	7,400.25	8,949.17	10,803.85
22	5,436.54	6,658.60	8,140.27	9,933.57	12,100.31
23	5,871.46	7,257.87	8,954.30	11,026.27	13,552.35
24	6,341.18	7,911.08	9,849.73	12,239.16	15,178.63
25	6,848.48	8,623.08	10,834.71	13,585.46	17,000.06
26	7,396.35	9,399.16	11,918.18	15,079.86	19,040.07
27	7,988.06	10,245.08	13,109.99	16,738.65	21,324.88
28	8,627.11	11,167.14	14,420.99	18,579.90	23,883.87
29	9,317.27	12,172.18	15,863.09	20,623.69	26,749.93
30	10,062.66	13,267.68	17,449.40	22,892.30	29,959.92
31	10,867.67	14,461.77	19,194.34	25,410.45	33,555.11
32	11,737.08	15,763.33	21,113.78	28,205.60	37,581.73
33	12,676.05	17,182.03	23,225.15	31,308.21	42,091.53
34	13,690.13	18,728.41	25,547.67	34,752.12	47,142.52
35	14,785.34	20,413.97	28,102.44	38,574.85	52,799.62
36	15,968.17	22,251.23	30,912.68	42,818.08	59,135.57
37	17,245.63	24,253.84	34,003.95	47,528.07	66,231.84
38	18,625.28	26,436.68	37,404.34	52,756.16	74,179.66
39	20,115.30	28,815.98	41,144.78	58,559.34	83,081.22
40	21,724.52	31,409.42	45,259.26	65,000.87	93,050.97

Appendix B
Monthly Savings Calculator

How much money do you need to save on a monthly basis to reach your future financial goals?

For every $1,000 that you want to accumulate within a specific period of time, find the appropriate number of years and the anticipated average annual rate of return and use that multiplier to calculate the amount of money you'll need to save on a monthly basis to achieve your specific goal.

For example, assume you wanted to calculate how much money you would need to save every month to accumulate $1,000 in ten years if the average annual rate of return is 8 percent. You would locate the ten-year column and follow that over to the 8 percent return column to reveal that you would need to save $5.430 each month to reach that goal.

	4%	5%	6%	7%	8%	9%	10%	11%	12%
1	$81.545	$81.103	$80.663	$80.225	$79.790	$79.356	$78.925	$78.495	$78.068
2	39.958	39.540	39.125	38.713	38.305	37.900	37.499	37.101	36.706
3	26.104	25.697	25.295	24.899	24.506	24.119	23.736	23.358	22.984
4	19.182	18.784	18.393	18.008	17.629	17.256	16.889	16.527	16.172
5	15.033	14.644	14.261	13.887	13.520	13.160	12.807	12.462	12.123
6	12.271	11.889	11.515	11.151	10.795	10.447	10.108	9.778	9.456
7	10.301	9.926	9.561	9.206	8.860	8.525	8.200	7.884	7.577
8	8.827	8.458	8.101	7.755	7.421	7.097	6.784	6.482	6.191
9	7.682	7.320	6.971	6.634	6.310	5.998	5.698	5.410	5.133
10	6.769	6.413	6.072	5.744	5.430	5.129	4.841	4.566	4.304
11	6.023	5.674	5.340	5.021	4.717	4.428	4.152	3.890	3.641
12	5.404	5.061	4.735	4.425	4.130	3.851	3.588	3.338	3.103
13	4.882	4.545	4.226	3.925	3.640	3.372	3.119	2.882	2.660
14	4.435	4.105	3.793	3.500	3.225	2.967	2.726	2.501	2.291
15	4.050	3.726	3.421	3.137	2.871	2.623	2.393	2.179	1.982
16	3.714	3.396	3.099	2.822	2.565	2.328	2.108	1.906	1.720
17	3.419	3.107	2.817	2.548	2.301	2.072	1.863	1.672	1.497
18	3.158	2.852	2.569	2.308	2.069	1.851	1.651	1.470	1.306
19	2.926	2.625	2.349	2.096	1.866	1.657	1.467	1.296	1.142
20	2.717	2.423	2.154	1.909	1.686	1.486	1.306	1.145	1.001
21	2.530	2.241	1.979	1.741	1.527	1.336	1.165	1.013	0.878
22	2.361	2.077	1.822	1.592	1.386	1.203	1.040	0.897	0.772
23	2.207	1.929	1.680	1.457	1.259	1.085	0.931	0.796	0.679
24	2.067	1.795	1.552	1.336	1.146	0.979	0.834	0.707	0.598
25	1.939	1.672	1.436	1.227	1.045	0.885	0.747	0.629	0.527
26	1.821	1.560	1.330	1.128	0.953	0.801	0.671	0.559	0.465
27	1.713	1.458	1.234	1.039	0.870	0.726	0.603	0.498	0.410
28	1.613	1.363	1.146	0.957	0.796	0.658	0.542	0.444	0.363
29	1.521	1.277	1.065	0.883	0.728	0.597	0.487	0.396	0.320
30	1.436	1.197	0.991	0.815	0.667	0.542	0.439	0.353	0.283
31	1.357	1.123	0.922	0.753	0.611	0.493	0.395	0.315	0.251
32	1.283	1.054	0.859	0.696	0.560	0.448	0.356	0.282	0.222
33	1.215	0.991	0.802	0.644	0.514	0.407	0.321	0.252	0.196
34	1.151	0.931	0.748	0.596	0.472	0.371	0.290	0.225	0.174
35	1.091	0.877	0.698	0.552	0.433	0.337	0.261	0.201	0.154
36	1.035	0.825	0.653	0.512	0.398	0.307	0.236	0.180	0.136
37	0.982	0.778	0.610	0.474	0.366	0.280	0.213	0.161	0.121
38	0.933	0.733	0.570	0.440	0.336	0.255	0.192	0.144	0.107
39	0.887	0.692	0.534	0.408	0.309	0.233	0.174	0.129	0.095
40	0.843	0.653	0.500	0.379	0.285	0.212	0.157	0.115	0.084

Appendix C

How Many Years Will $100,000 Last?*

Yearly Withdrawals	Rate of Return				
	4%	5%	6%	8%	10%
$ 5,000	20	22	25	26	Should be perpetual
7,500	13	14	15	18	24
10,000	10	10	11	12	14
12,500	8	8	8.5	9	10
15,000	6.5	6.5	7	7.5	8

*Assumes a single withdrawal at the start of every year beginning the first year and increasing that amount by 4 percent in subsequent years to account for inflation.

This information assumes you are willing to deplete your accumulated savings. It is offered only as an example of how long your money would last under various scenarios.

Appendix D
IRS Life Expectancy Tables

Your age	# of yrs the IRS expects you to live	Your age	# of yrs the IRS expects you to live	Your age	# of yrs the IRS expects you to live	Your age	# of yrs the IRS expects you to live
35	47.3	52	31.3	69	16.8	86	6.5
36	46.4	53	30.4	70	16.0	87	6.1
37	45.4	54	29.5	71	15.3	88	5.7
38	44.4	55	28.6	72	14.6	89	5.3
39	43.5	56	27.7	73	13.9	90	5.0
40	42.5	57	26.8	74	13.2	91	4.7
41	41.5	58	25.9	75	12.5	92	4.4
42	40.6	59	25.0	76	11.9	93	4.1
43	39.6	60	24.2	77	11.2	94	3.9
44	38.7	61	23.3	78	10.6	95	3.7
45	37.7	62	22.5	79	10.0	96	3.4
46	36.8	63	21.6	80	9.5	97	3.2
47	35.9	64	20.8	81	8.9	98	3.0
48	34.9	65	20.0	82	8.4	99	2.8
49	34.0	66	19.2	83	7.9	100	2.7
50	33.1	67	18.4	84	7.4		
51	32.2	68	17.6	85	6.5		

Appendix E

Social Security Benefits Information

Approximate Monthly Benefits If You Retired
at Full Retirement Age and Had Steady Lifetime Earnings

Your age in 1998	Your Family	$20,000	$30,000	$40,000	$50,000	$65,400 or more[1]
45	You	$ 809	$1,076	$1,265	$1,390	$1,592
	You and your spouse[2]	1,213	1,614	1,897	2,085	2,388
55	You	809	1,076	1,265	1,377	1,525
	You and your spouse[2]	1,213	1,614	1,897	2,065	2,287
65	You	784	1,043	1,197	1,269	1,342
	You and your spouse[2]	1,176	1,564	1,795	1,903	2,013

[1]Earnings equal to or greater than the Social Security Old-Age, Survivors, and Disability Insurance (OASDI) wage base from age 22 through the year before retirement.

[2]Your spouse is assumed to be the same age as you. Your spouse may qualify for a higher retirement benefit based on his or her own work record.

Note: The accuracy of these estimates depends on the pattern of your actual past earnings and on your earnings in the future.

Appendix F

How a $10,000 Investment Would Have Performed from December 31, 1988, through December 31, 1998

Name	10 Year Total Return	Average Annual Total Return
Microsoft	$937,606	57.47%
Intel	405,802	44.82
Coca-Cola	138,980	30.11
General Electric	117,457	27.93
Wal-Mart	110,239	27.13
Proctor & Gamble	103,950	26.38
General Dynamics	97,666	25.60
Merck	96,740	25.48
Phillip Morris	93,517	25.05
Allied Signal	71,367	21.72
United Technologies	70,110	21.50
McDonald's	69,311	21.36
Walt Disney	58,045	19.23
American Express	57,174	19.05
Ford Motor Company	55,390	18.67
Union Carbide	54,983	18.58
Chevron	54,237	18.42
Exxon	50,461	17.57
AT&T	50,153	17.50
DuPont	49,908	17.44

Name	10 Year Total Return	Average Annual Total Return
Amoco	$47,307	16.81%
J.P. Morgan	44,658	16.14
IBM	39,809	14.81
Sears	38,829	14.53
Texaco	37,510	14.13
Caterpillar	34,542	13.20
Aluminum Company of America	34,454	13.17
MMM	32,501	12.51
Boeing	29,272	11.34
Eastman Kodak	28,450	11.02
General Motors	26,254	10.13
Goodyear Tire	25,272	9.71
International Paper	24,946	9.57
Dow Chemical	23,597	8.96
Westinghouse	16,175	4.93
Apple Computer	11,012	0.97
Tenneco	10,493	0.48
Bethlehem Steel	3,845	(9.11)

Source: Hypo®, TowersData Systems, Bethesda, MD.

Index

A

Aley, James, 5
American savings statistics, 5–6
American Stock Exchange, 141, 210
Annual rate of return, 183
    determining assumed, 67–68
Annual reports, 143
Annuities, 215–18
Anthony, Robert, 283
Arnold, Bridgette, 267
Ask price, 142–43
Asset(s)
    appreciated, as charitable gifts, 272–73
    documents, 23–24
    protection of, 280–81
Asset allocation, 102, 148, 149–50, 157–60
    diversification, 168
    risk tolerance and, 154–56, 164
Asset classes
    cash/short-term investments, 131–34, 148
    bonds/fixed-income investments, 134–38.
        See also Bond(s)
    stocks, 139–48, 149. *See also* Stock(s)
Asset management account, 229–30
AT&T, 119–20
Australia, stocks, 205
Austria, stocks, 204

B

Balanced investments, 63, 201
Barling, Aaron F., 62
Baruch, Bernard Mannes, 161
Basic materials sector, 175
Belgium, stocks, 204
Berkshire Hathaway, 101
Bid price, 142–43
Bland, Glen (*Success*), 70
Blue chip stocks, 146, 194. *See also* Stock(s)
Bond(s), 132, 134–38, 144–45, 210–11
    basics, 135–36
    benefits, 134
    corporate, 135, 191

    interest paid on, 136, 139, 171
    municipal, 135, 184, 190
    ratings, 135–36, 191
    and stocks compared, 140
    strategies, 136–38
    zero-coupon, 136, 138, 149
Borrowing, on margin, 229
Bowman, Beverly, 91
Brandon, Jonathan and Kathryn, 247–51
Brooks, L.J. and Lee, 242–46
Brown, Sam, 284
Budget, 24–25, 109
    budgeting process, 26–29, 32
    personal spending review, 25–26
    worksheets, 30–31, 52–55, 58
Buffett, Warren, 101, 164
Burkett, Larry, 25, 35
Business risk, 169
Buy-and-sell agreements, 279

C

Capital gains/losses, 230
Capital goods sector, 174
Capitalization, measuring, 194
Capital Research Associates, 6
Case studies, 234–65
    Brandon, Jonathan and Kathryn, 247–51
    Brooks, L.J. and Lee, 242–46
    McKinney, Steve and Jill, 256–64
    Rowell, Ted and Rita, 252–55
    Skyler, Lauren, 238–42
Cash/short-term investments, 131–34, 148, 171
CDA Technologies, 167
CDs, 132
    90-Day, 184, 186
    safety and risk, 93–96
    6-month return, 94
Certificates of deposit. *See* CDs
Certified financial planner, 81, 82
Certified public accountant, 82
Charitable gifts, 269, 272–73
Charitable Remainder Trusts, 273, 277

Checkbook budget method, 26–29
Checking accounts/checking privileges, 132, 229
Cheesman, Bea, 61
Children, guardian/trustee for, 274
Citigroup, 169
Clark, Madelene, 107
Closely held corporations, 279
Coca-Cola, 123–24, 166, 169, 192, 193
Colgate-Palmolive, 122
College Planner Module, 269
College planning, 68–69, 267–68
    education gift tax exclusion, 272, 276
Commodities, 168, 206–7
Company stock purchase plan, 117
Compound interest, 21, 170–73
Computer analysis, 82
Consumer cyclical/durables, 175–76
Consumer cyclical/nondurables, 176, 194
Consumer debt, 32–37
Core holdings, 169
Corporate bonds, 135, 191
Covey, Stephen (*Seven Habits of Highly Effective People*), 10
CPA, 82
Credit, 32–37
    life/disability insurance and, 280
Cummings, Wallace, 91

D

Dalbar, 113–14, 85
Death expenses, 277
Debit card, 229
Debt, 32–37
    documentation, 24, 32–37, 43–44, 59
    reduction strategy, 35–37, 59
Deductions
    cash gifts to charities, 269, 272–73
    marital, 276
Dell, Michael, 5
Dell Computer Corporation, 5
Dellionaires, 5
Denmark, stocks, 204
Disability insurance, 279–80
Disney, Walt, 4
Diversification, 168–69
    building blocks for, 184
    business risk, 169
    market risk, 168–69
    unit trusts and, 214
Dividends, 112, 124, 139
Documents. *See* Financial data, gathering

Dodgen, Larry and Ann, 179, 267
Dollar cost averaging, 115–16
Domestic equities, 192–202
Dow Jones Industrial Average, 193

E

Earnings per share (EPS), 140–41
East, Mary S., 91
Eastman Kodak, 193
Education gift tax exclusion, 272, 276
Education IRA, 230
Einstein, Albert, 21
Electronic bill payment services, 230
Emergency fund, 133, 148
Energy sector, 175
Equity income, 202
Erstine, Jon Mark, 130
Estate planning, 273–77, 280
    charitable gifts, 276
    variable annuities, 202
European stocks, 204
Expenses, 32. *See also* Budget; College planning; Debt
    death, 277
    personal, 24–26
Exxon, 120, 166–67, 169, 192, 193

F

Fear, 86–87, 110
Federal Deposit Insurance Corporation, 93
Federal Reserve Board, 94
Fidelity Distributors Corporation, 268
Financial adviser, 80–83, 96, 221–32
    certified financial planner, 81, 82
    choosing, 222–24
    cost of, 227
    defined, 224
    initial meeting with, 227–31
    interviewing prospective, 226–27
    matching to your needs, 226
    services of, 225–26
    stockbroker, 81, 82
    tax adviser/CPA, 82
Financial data, gathering, 22–58
    assets, 23–24, 43
    budget, 24, 26–32, 52–58
    debt, 24, 32–37, 43–44, 59
    income, 24, 43
    investment profile worksheet, 44–51
    personal expenses, 24–26
Financial futures contracts, 168

Financial industry/financial sector, 175, 194
Financial goals. *See also* Financial plan
    action steps, 71–77
    determining parameters, 64–65
    establishing time span, 65–66, 72–74
    financial overview checklist, 291–93
    mental vs. written goals, 70
    monthly investing strategy, 77
    quantifying specific, 66–69, 75–76
    setting objectives, 63–65, 71
    systematic plan for reaching, 115–17
Financial Peace (Dave Ramsay), 171
Financial plan. *See also* Financial goals
    creating/developing, 83–84, 285–90
    financial advisers and, 82–83, 223–25
    five-year strategy, 295–96
    gathering data for. *See* Financial data,
      gathering
    implementing, 85–87
    lifetime strategy, 297–98
    mission statement, 10–19
    monitoring, 87–88
    one-year strategy, 294
    sample case studies, 234–65
    working from, 149–50
    written, 83–85
Financial planner. *See* Financial adviser
Finland, stocks, 204
Fixed annuity, 215–17
401(k) plan, 117, 268, 284
    rollover, 231
France, stocks, 204
Franklin, Benjamin, 56
Futures Pooled Index, 184, 206
Future value calculator, 303–5

G
General Electric, 166–67, 169, 192, 193
General Motors, 193
Generic Money Market Index, 181–85
Gift-giving strategies, 269, 272–73, 276
    appreciated assets, as charitable gifts, 272
    charitable gifts, deductible, 269, 272
    Charitable Remainder Trusts, 273
    individual gifts, nondeductible, 272
Gillespie, Dr. Tharp and Miriam, 127–28
Goals
    financial, written. *See* Financial goals;
      Financial plan
    quantifying, 66–68
    retirement, 7–8

Gold, 184, 207
Government bonds, 135
Gray, Bequita, 162
Gray, Sherry S., 268
Growth and income funds, 200
Growth stocks/industries, 146–47, 194
Guardian, for minor children, 274

H
Harral, Stacey, 22
Happiness, 127–28
Health care, 176, 194
Henry, Jeanne, 284
Historical performance. *See* Investment data,
    historical performance
Hong Kong, stocks, 205
Housing, U.S., 144–45
Howard, Thelma Pearl, 4
Hudson, Don and Karen, 233

I
Ibbotson, 181
IBM, 166–67, 192, 193
Immediate annuity, 217
Income
    annuities and, 216–17
    CDs and, 95
    documentation, 24
    equity income, 202
    financial plan considerations and, 235–37
    retirement, 6–7
    shelters, 121
    tax-free, 190
Index, 181
Individual retirement accounts (IRAs), 230–31
Individual securities, 210–11. *See also* Bond(s);
    Stock(s)
Inflation, 67, 133, 144–45
    calculator, 303–5
    core holdings and, 170
    gold, as hedge against, 207
    purchasing power and, 95–96
Inheritance taxes, 280
Insurance
    annuities and, 215
    disability, 279–80
    life, 277–81
Intel, 166–67, 169, 192
Interest, compound, 21, 170–73
Interest rates
    bonds and, 135–38, 148
    short-term investments and, 148

International equities, 203–5
International Equities Index, 184, 203
    (Europe) Index, 204
    (Pacific) Index, 205
Internet services, 229
Internet stocks, 147, 164–65
Investment(s). *See also specific investment*
    balanced, 63, 201
    benefits. *See* Investment data, historical
      performance
    diversified. *See* Diversification
    fear and, 110
    laws, 162–77
    male vs. female approach to, 117–18
    myths, 91–105
    parameters, determining, 64–65
    procrastination and, 112
    profile worksheet, 44–51
    quality, 169
    risk, 162–67
    strategy, monthly, 77
    and trading compared, 113–15
    truths, 107–28
Investment clubs, 124–27
Investment data, historical performance
    reading the research, 181–83
    sources, 181
Investment grade bonds, 136. *See also* Bond(s)
Investment Performance Digest, 203
Investment vehicle rankings, 1994–1998, 102
IRAs, 230–31
Irrevocable life insurance trust, 276
IRS life expectancy tables, 311
Ireland, stocks, 204
Italy, stocks, 204

J–K

Japan, stocks, 205
Johnston, Jim, 161
Kemp, Mel, 209
Key person life insurance, 277, 279

L

Laddered bond strategy, 137–38. *See also* Bond(s)
Large caps, 194
Lewis, Allyson White, 61
Lewis, Jill, 233
Life expectancy tables, 311
Life insurance, 277–81
    asset protection, 280–81
    business protection, 279–80

    cash value, 278
    permanent (whole/universal), 278
    term, 278
    variable annuities, 202
Limited partnerships, 121
Limit order, 143
Lipper, 181
Living trust, 275

M

McDonald's, 169
McKinney, Steve and Jill, 256–64
Maher, Kristy, 300
Managed futures, 168, 206
Margin borrowing, 229
Market risk, 168–69
Mason, Richard, 3
Medical gift tax exclusion, 272, 276
Men, investment approach of, 117–18
Merck, 166, 169, 192
Merrill Lynch savings study, 6
Microsoft, 166–67, 169, 192
Midcap companies, 196–97
Milam, Geraldine, 108
Miles, Mrs. Donald, 179
Mission statements, 10–19
    money, 10, 13–14, 18–19
    personal, 15, 16–17
    vocational, 10–13, 17–18
Mitchell, Elizabeth S., 3
Modern Portfolio Theory, 163–67
    asset allocation strategies, 164
    efficient markets, 163
    investors and risk, 163
    optimality, 164–67
Money
    magnets, 27
    understanding your own, 108–10
Money managers, individual professional, 213–14
Money market accounts, 117, 132
Money mission statement, 10, 13–14, 18–19, 109
Monthly investing strategy, 77
Monthly Rates, 183
Monthly savings calculator, 68, 307–8
Moody's ratings, 135
Morningstar, 103, 167, 181
Motivation, 299–302
Municipal bonds, 135, 184, 190
Mutual fund(s), 102–3, 104, 211–13
    diversification and, 169, 212
    growth and income, 200

investment objectives, 211
of midcap growth companies, 196
stock funds, 212
trading and investment compared, 113–14
Myths, 91–105

N

Nasdaq (National Association of Security Dealers
Automated Quotes), 141, 210
index, 101–2
National Association of Investment Clubs, 127
Netherlands, stocks, 204
New York Stock Exchange, 141, 210
New Zealand, stocks, 205
Nordlund, Dennis, 3
Norway, stocks, 204

O–P

$100,000, calculating longevity of, 309
Optimality, 164–67
Optimization, 183
Pacific region stocks, 205
Pals, Lisa, 299
Partnerships, life insurance and, 279
Permanent insurance, 278
Personal mission statement, 15, 16–17
Pfizer, 166, 192
Phillip Morris, 166, 192
Portugal, stocks, 204
Powell, Bryan and Melissa, 129
Powers of attorney, 276
Precious metals, 168
Press reports, 98
Price swings, 165
Professional money managers, 213–14
Purchasing power, CDs and, 95–96. *See also* Inflation

Q–R

Quality, of investments, 169
Quarterly reports, 143
Ramsay, Dave *(Financial Peace)*, 35, 171
Randle, Charles and Emma, 222
Rates of return, 98–101, 182
1990 through 1998, 99
Ratliff, Gene and Clois, 129
Real estate, 168
Recommendation review, 208
ReliaStar Financial Corp., 21
Retirement
401(k) plans, 117, 268, 284
goals, 7–8

income, 6–7
IRAs, 230–31
-planning investments, 202
Roth IRA, 230
Richard Day Research, 268
Risk, 64–65, 112, 162–67
asset allocation strategies and, 164
business risk, 169
investors and, 163
market efficiency and, 163
market risk, 168–69
measurement of, 180, 182
optimality and, 164–67
tolerance, 103, 105, 151–56, 223
Roberts, Frankie, 80
Roth IRA, 230
Round lots, 143
Rowell, Martha, 118
Rowell, Ted and Rita, 252–55
Rule of 72, 171

S

Salomon Brothers
Corporate Bonds 10+ Years Index, 184, 191
Treasury Bonds 10+ Years Index, 184, 189
Treasury Notes 3–7 Years Index, 184, 188
Savings/money market accounts, 132
American statistics, 5–6
Secondary stock issue, 140. *See also* Stock(s)
Sector analysis/rotation, 168, 174–76
Securities and Exchange Commission, 140
Settlement date, 143
Seven Habits of Highly Effective People (Stephen
Covey), 10
Short-term investments (cash), 131–34, 148
Singapore, stocks, 205
"Skimpy Savings," 6
Skyler, Lauren, 238–42
Small cap growth companies, 198
Small company value stocks, 199
Snowball effect, 35–36
Social Security Administration, 6
benefits information, 313
Sole proprietorship, 277, 279
Spain, stocks, 204
Speculators, 114–15
Spread, 142
Standard deviation, 165–67, 180, 182
Standard and Poor's 500 Stock Index, 167, 181–83,
192
Standard and Poor's ratings, 135

Steed, Sunny, 79, 125
Stock(s), 139–48, 149, 171, 210–11
    bid/ask price, 142–43
    blue-chip, 146, 194
    and bonds compared, 140
    buying, 101–2, 141–44
    classes of, 146–48
    creation of new, 139–40
    dividends, 112, 124, 139
    Dow Jones Industrial Average, 193
    earnings per share (EPS), 140–41
    European, 204
    exchanges, 141
    growth stocks, 147, 194
    Internet, 147, 164–65
    issues, 140–41
    large cap, 146–48, 195
    losses, 115
    management of company and, 141
    midcap, 146–48, 196
    Pacific region, 205
    performance of, 113, 144–46
    round lots, 143
    shareholder rights, 139
    small cap, 146, 199
    S&P 500 Stock Index, 192
    trading and investment compared, 113–14
    value stock, 146–47
Stockbroker, 81–82
Stock market
    drops in, 110, 111, 115
    investment not for everyone, 112–13
    sectors, 168, 174–78
    time/timing and, 96–97, 110–12, 163
    unforeseen surprises, 141
Stovall, Mike, 108
Success (Glen Bland), 70
Sweden, stocks, 204
Switzerland, stocks, 204
Systematic withdrawal plans, 115–17

T
Tax adviser/attorney, 82
Tax-deferred
    annuities, 216
    contracts, 202
    life insurance, 279
    unit trusts, 215
Taxes, estate, 275, 280
Tax-free income, municipal bonds, 135, 138, 184, 190
Taxpayer Relief Act of 1997, 230
Technology stocks/industry, 147, 174, 194

Teegarden, Bob M., 21
Telecommunications industry, 176, 194
$10,000 investment performance, 315
Term insurance, 278
Thompson, Linda, 299
Ticker symbol, 141–42
Timing, and the stock market, 96–97
Transportation sector, 174
Treasury securities. *See* U.S. Treasury securities
Trustee, for minor children, 274
Trusts
    Charitable Remainder Trusts, 273, 277
    irrevocable life insurance, 276
    unit trusts, 214–15

U
U.S. Census Bureau, 6
U.S. Treasury securities, 144–45
    6-month, 184, 187
    10-year bond yield, historical chart, 137
    zero-coupon, 138, 149
United Kingdom, stocks, 204
Unit trusts, 214–15
Universal life insurance, 278
Utilities, 120–21, 175

V–Z
Value Line, 167
Variable annuities, 202, 215–17
Vocational mission statement, 10–13, 17–18
Volatility, 112, 116, 165–67. *See also* Risk
Wal-Mart, 5, 166, 169, 192
Walton, Sam, 5
White, Ann R., 61
Whole life insurance, 278
Wiesenberger, 144, 181, 203
    Investment View Hypothetical Software, 269
Wilkie, Jason and Julie, 283
Will, 274, 275
William Woods University, 269
Wilshire
    Large Company Growth Index, 184, 194
    Mid-Cap Growth Index, 184, 196
    Mid-Cap Value Index, 184, 197
    Small Company Growth Index, 184, 198
    Small Company Value Index, 184, 199
Wilson, Philip, 164
Wilson Associates International, 167, 181
Women, investment approach of, 117–18
Wortham, Mary Nell, 122–23
Zero-coupon bonds, 136, 138, 149. *See also* Bond(s)
Zick, Bernard, 171